Introducing Psychology

Social Psychology

Grange Books

This edition published in 2005 by Grange Books
an imprint of Grange Books Plc
The Grange
Kingsnorth Industrial Estate
Hoo, Near Rochester
Kent ME3 9ND
www.Grangebooks.co.uk

ISBN: 1-84013-806-8

Printed in China

Editorial and design:
The Brown Reference Group plc
8 Chapel Place
Rivington Street
London
EC2A 3DQ
UK
www.brownreference.com

FOR THE BROWN REFERENCE GROUP PLC
Editors: Windsor Chorlton, Karen Frazer, Leon Gray, Simon Hall, Marcus Hardy, Jim Martin, Shirin Patel, Frank Ritter, Henry Russell, Gillian Sutton, Susan Watt
Indexer: Kay Ollerenshaw
Picture Researcher: Helen Simm
Illustrators: Darren Awuah, Dax Fullbrook, Mark Walker
Designers: Reg Cox, Mike Leaman, Sarah Williams
Design Manager: Lynne Ross
Managing Editor: Bridget Giles
Production Director: Alastair Gourlay
Editorial Director: Lindsey Lowe

PHOTOGRAPHIC CREDITS
Front Cover: Photodisc: National Cancer Institute (tr); Photos.com (br); Mark Walker (l).
AKG London: 61; **Archives of the History of American Psychology:** University of Akron, Ohio 32, 51, 118, 126, 131, 151; **Columbia University:** 43; **Corbis:** 21, 47, Bettmann 22b, 74, 92, 114, Digital Art 158, Kevin Fleming 148, Owen Franken 50, Mitchell Gerber 34tl, 34tr, Hulton Getty 101, Robbie Jack 75, Wolfgang Kaehler 130, Catherine Karnow 62, Lawrence Manning 84t, Wally McNamee 90, Richard T. Nowitz 142, Paul A. Souders 38, David & Peter Turnley 109, David H. Wells 135, K. M. Westermann 39bl; **Corbis Stockmarket:** Don Mason 103, Mug Shots 87; **Hulton Archive:** 11, 23, George Eastman House/Nickolas Muray122; **Hutchison Picture Library:** N. Durrell McKenna 26, Sarah Errington 24, Philip Wolmuth 54, Andrey Zvozni 10; **Image Bank:** Alan Becker 76, Gary Bistram 70, Werner Bokelberg 150, Mike Brinson 115, Peter Cade 58, Color Day Production 69, 105, Larry Gatz 28, Alfred Gescheidt 29, Guang Hui China Tourism Press.Xie 84b, Hussey & Hussey Photographs 138tl, Romilly Lockyer 36, 81, Paul Oven 98, Ali Meyer 13, Miao China Tourism Press.Wang 82b, Tosca Radigonda 104, Terje Rakke 100, Chris M. Rogers 16, Guido Alberto Rossi 113, Dag Sundberg 9, Maria Taglienti 154, Yan Hong China Tourism Press.Huang 42, Yellow Dog Productions 53, 116; **Koball Collection:** Columbia 49, 145, Orion 44; **Mary Evans Picture Library:** 15, 65, 80, 143; **PA Photos:** 144, EPA 63; **Photodisc:** Geostock 110, Doug Menuez 161, Suza Scalora 162; **Pictor:** 41, 60, 79r, 79l, 94, 119, 138tl, 146; **Popperfoto:** 123; **Rex Features:** Steve Hansen/Timepix 72, Nils Jorgensen 88, Photoreporters Inc 82t, Geoff Robinson 35; **Robert Hunt Library:** 14, 30tl, 30tr, 56, 66, 127, 141; **Science Photo Library:** 152, CNRI 145, Sue Ford 156; **Stanford University:** Dept. of Psychology 140; **Stone:** Bruce Ayres 67; **TCL:** Gary Buss 18, Mark Scott 19, Jerome Tisne 6, Anne-Marie Weber 20; **Travel Ink:** Julian Loader 39br; **University of California:** Human Interactive Laboratory/Paul Ekman 83; **U.S. Dept of Defense:** 22t; p. 71 courtesy Leonard Berkowitz, p. 132 courtesy James Flynn, p. 133 courtesy Harvard University Press, p. 139 courtesy Simon & Schuster.

CONTRIBUTORS

Consultant:
Andrew M. Colman, PhD
Professor of Psychology,
University of Leicester, UK

Authors:
Jonathan M. Cheek, PhD
Professor of Psychology,
Wellesley College, Wellesley, MA
Personality

Nicky Hayes, PhD
Lecturer in Social Psychology,
University of Bradford, UK
People as Social Animals

Robert Kurzban, PhD
Postdoctoral Researcher,
Department of Anthropology,
University of California, LA
Nature or Nurture

Shara Lochun, MSc
Lecturer in Forensic Psychology and
Research Methods, Department of Psychology,
London Guildhall University, UK
Relating to Others

Karin Marson, PhD
Lecturer in Social and Occupational
Psychology, Department of Psychology,
London Guildhall University, UK
Relating to Others

Matthew L. Newman, MA
Researcher and Doctoral Candidate,
Department of Psychology,
The University of Texas at Austin
Intelligence

Paul Rose
PhD student, State University
of New York at Buffalo
Relating to Society

Chris Woodford, MA
Science writer
Communication

Patricia L. Waters, PhD
Assistant Professor of
Psychology, Colorado College,
Colorado Springs, CO
Personality

Contents

About This Set

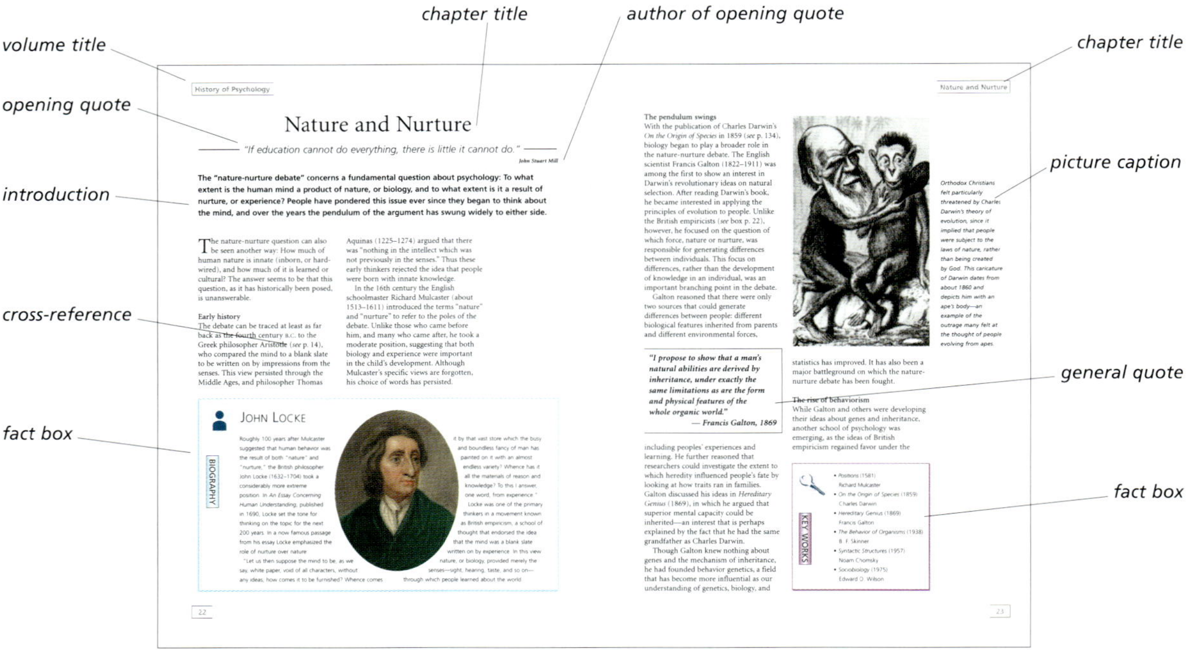

These pages explain how to use the *Psychology* encyclopedia. There are six volumes in the set, each one illustrated with color photographs and specially commissioned artworks. Each volume has its own contents list at the beginning and a glossary at the back explaining important terms. More information, such as websites and related reference works, are listed in the Resources section, also found at the back of each volume.

To find articles on a particular subject, look for it in the set index at the back of each volume. Once you have started to read a relevant chapter, cross-references within that chapter and in the connections box at the end of the chapter will guide you to other related pages and chapters elsewhere in the set.

Every chapter has several color-coded fact boxes featuring information related to the subject discussed. They fall into distinct groups, which are described in more detail in the box opposite (p. 5).

The diagram above shows the typical elements found within a chapter in this set. The various types of fact box are explained more fully in the box shown opposite.

THE SIX VOLUMES

History of psychology (Volume One) takes a look at psychology's development throughout history. It starts in ancient Greece when concepts of "mind" existed only as a topic of philosophical debate, looks at the subject's development into a separate field of scientific research, then follows its division into various schools of thought. It also explores the effects of scientific developments, discusses recent approaches, and considers the effects of new research in nonwestern cultures.

The brain and the mind (Volume Two) analyzes the relationship between the mind and the brain and looks at how the brain works in detail. The history of neuroscience is followed by a study of the physiology of the brain and how this relates to functions such as thinking. Chapters tackle the concept of the mind as an intangible and invisible entity, the nature of consciousness, and how our perceptual systems work to interpret the sensations we feel. In a chapter entitled Artificial Minds the volume explores whether or not machines will ever be able to think as humans do.

Thinking and knowing (Volume Three) looks at how the brain processes, stores, and retrieves information. It covers cognitive processes that we share with animals, such as associative learning, and those that are exclusive to people, such as language processing.

Developmental psychology (Volume Four) focuses on changes in psychological development from birth, throughout childhood, and into old age. It covers theories of social and intellectual development, particularly those of Jean Piaget and Lev Vygotsky. It also covers social and emotional development and how they can be improved and nurtured.

Social psychology (Volume Five) studies people as unique individuals and as social animals. It analyzes the notions of personality and intelligence as well as considering how people relate to and communicate with each other and society, and the social groups that they form.

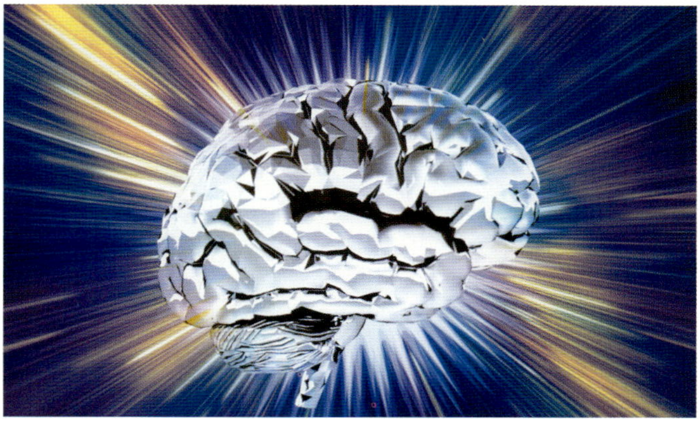

Psychologists using a variety of approaches work in different fields (developmental, social, or abnormal, for example), but all study the brain, trying to figure out how it functions and how it influences people's behavior, thoughts, and emotions.

Abnormal psychology (Volume Six) asks what is abnormality? It shows how the number and types of abnormalities recognized as mental disorders have changed over time and examines specific disorders and their causes. It also looks at diagnosis of disorders and treatments, which can be psychological (talking cures) or physical (drugs and surgery). The social issues associated with abnormality and how society deals with people who have mental disorders are also explored.

KEY DATES
Lists some of the important events in the history of the topic discussed.

KEY POINTS
Summarizes some of the key points made in the chapter.

KEY TERMS
Provides concise definitions of terms that appear in the chapter.

KEY WORKS
Lists key books and papers published by researchers in the field.

FOCUS ON
Takes a closer look at either a related topic or an aspect of the topic discussed

EXPERIMENT
Takes a closer look at experimental work carried out by researchers in the field.

CASE STUDY
Discusses in-depth studies of particular individuals carried out by researchers.

BIOGRAPHY
Provides historical information about key figures mentioned in the chapter.

PSYCHOLOGY & SOCIETY
Takes a look at the interesting effects within society of the psychological theories discussed.

CONNECTIONS
Lists other chapters in the set containing information related to the topic discussed.

People as Social Animals

"People's thoughts, feelings, and behavior are affected by . . . other people."

Gordon W. Allport

Social psychology is about the study of individuals and society. Social psychologists approach this from two directions: the outside in, and the inside out. Meaning, they explore the causes and mechanisms that produce social behavior in individuals (inside out), and they explore the influences of shared social experience on the individual (outside in).

All our lives we are surrounded by other people. We work with other people, study with other people, live with other people, and encounter other people just about everywhere we go. Of course, we know some of these people better than others. Family members, close friends, and partners are the best known to us, and we take their different personalities into account during our encounters with them. Other people, such as those we meet regularly at work or school, are familiar to us, but our relationships with them are a little more formal: Our interactions with these people are shaped more by social expectations than by a knowledge of their individual personalities. Generally, most of the people we encounter each day, though, are strangers, and our interactions with them are shaped almost entirely by structured social rules that prescribe exactly how we ought to behave.

All of these different exchanges or encounters between people are called social interactions. Some of them are simple and superficial, such as waving at a friend you pass in the car or paying a fare when you get onto a bus. Other types of social interaction are more complex, such as working closely with a school friend or work colleague on a project or telephoning a friend to catch up on the latest gossip. And some kinds of social interaction, such as the exchanges between parents and children or between married couples, are so complex that it would take a lifetime's research to unravel all their layers of meaning.

WHAT IS SOCIAL PSYCHOLOGY?

It is such social interactions and behaviors that social psychologists seek to understand. To do so, they study individuals: how and why they think

As they chat on the phone, these two girts are interacting socially. What they say and how they feel is not only determined by each girl's personality, but also by group dynamics (what others say and feel) and the social situation itself. Social psychologists study such cross-links between individuals, their social behavior, and society.

KEY POINTS

WHAT IS SOCIAL PSYCHOLOGY?

- Social psychology is the study of how people think and feel about their social world and about how they interact and influence one another.
- Social psychology involves the study of individual psychology, or personality (*see* pp. 94–117), how we relate to and communicate with others (*see* pp. 28–49; pp. 72–93), how we relate to society (*see* pp. 50–71), and whether our social behavior is learned or preprogrammed from birth (*see* pp. 142–163).
- Exchanges or encounters between people are called social interactions. They have varying levels of complexity and are closely bound up in people's relationships.

HISTORY OF SOCIAL PSYCHOLOGY

- Social psychology began with the work of Wilhelm Wundt and with the concepts of mass hypnotism and suggestion via social influence.
- In the early 20th century social psychologists studied social behavior from the individual's standpoint and the role of social context in structuring individual processes.
- After F. H. Allport published *Social Psychology* in 1924, social psychologists focused on studies of the individual until the 1970s. Key concepts at this time were the ideas of shared attitudes and social influence.
- From the late 1960s psychology began to move toward a more cognitive viewpoint. In the United States this created an interest in "social cognition," or how people's how people's interpretations of a situation influence their social behavior. In Europe social psychologists emphasized the importance of groups and shared social experience.
- Modern social psychology combines both approaches.

THE SOCIAL SELF

- The concept of social identity is central to social psychology. It is a person's own definition of who he or she is, including individual attributes (such as self-concept) as well as shared attributes, such as gender, relationship to others (brother or mother, for example), vocation (for example, student or tax collector), and ethnic group.
- The self-concept is an organized collection of beliefs individuals hold about themselves. These beliefs are based on a person's relations with others and society at large.
- The two main components of a person's self-concept are self-image and self-esteem.
- Self-image includes factual descriptions, such as the subjects people study or the work that they do, where they live, what color their hair is, and so on.
- Self-esteem is all about how people feel about themselves and their particular skills.
- Social comparisons (the ways in which a person compares themselves to others) contribute to self-esteem.
- Social psychologists also study social groups (two or more interacting people with common goals and a stable relationship who are interdependent). The social groups people belong to form the basis of their social life.

and feel about society and others, and how and why they think, feel, and behave in social situations. Social psychologists do not only consider the individual, however.

> ***"The focus, in social psychology* [at the time of quote]*, is on the individual . . .* [but] *individuals do not exist in isolation from social and cultural influences."***
>
> ***—Robert A. Baron & Donn Byrne, 1974***

Culture and society have, in turn, a huge impact on people. So, social psychologists also consider how society and social situations affect the individual.

Sociology and individual psychology

Social psychology is closely related to the disciplines of sociology and individual psychology. Sociology also studies society, but unlike social psychology it is not concerned with the behavior and thoughts of individuals. Practitioners of the two might study similar topics, such as violent crime, but their approaches would differ. A sociologist might, for example, compare the crime rates of different social groups, while a social psychologist would look at what causes particular people to carry out those violent crimes.

Social psychology builds on individual psychology (how people think and feel about themselves; *see* pp. 94–117) by considering these issues from a social standpoint: An important area of study within social psychology is how people

HINDE'S RELATIONSHIP DIMENSIONS

Content	The type of activities participants take part in together.
Diversity	The number and range of activities participants take part in together.
Quality	How the participants go about the interaction—for example, whether a parent is sensitive to an infant's signals.
Patterning/relative frequency	Distinctive patterns in the type of interactions, such as whether they are typically affectionate or aggressive.
Reciprocity/complementarity	How far each participant will share or alternate actions (reciprocity); or whether they characteristically take different roles that contribute toward the same goal (complementarity).
Intimacy	How much the people involved reveal the different aspects of themselves to each other.
Interpersonal perception	How each participant sees and understands the other.
Commitment	Each person's view as to the likely duration of the relationship, and belief in their and the other person's commitment to the relationship.

construct their social identities, concerning how they think and feel about themselves in relation to society, and the impact society and other people have, in turn, on those thoughts and feelings. Such aspects of social identity and the social self are considered later in this chapter (*see* pp. 15–25).

Relationships with others

Predictably, social psychologists are fascinated by the relationships between people, which affect how we interact socially. Even a simple social interaction, like waving at a friend, is made more complex by the relationship between the two people, affecting what each understands the wave to mean.

Relationship dimensions There are various dimensions to every relationship. Relationships vary according to the things that people do together, for example, or how long-lasting the relationship is, or whether the people concerned are relatively similar, or whether they have dissimilar personalities that complement each other. In 1987 British biologist Robert Hinde identified a total of eight dimensions that influence a relationship (*see* table above). Each dimension concerns an aspect of how people in a relationship think about each other and their relationship, or how they behave in the relationship and toward each other. Social psychologists have used Hinde's dimensions during their research in a variety of ways. For example, some have focused on one or two dimensions, such as commitment or quality, and collected data on these from many different relationships for comparison. Other researchers have used several or all of the dimensions to explore one or two relationships in detail.

Thinking about others Important aspects to any relationship, no matter how close, are how people think and feel about each other. We are constantly processing social information, and basing our attitudes to others on assumptions that we make about them (*see* pp. 28–49). Social psychologists such as Solomon Asch (1907–1996) have carried out numerous studies to determine how people form impressions (*see* box p. 31) of others. When we meet someone, we are affected by their appearance, their manner, how others treat them, and their treatment of others. While we often make wrong assumptions based on such subjective material, this processing remains a vital, and some would say commonsense, element of social interaction.

Austrian psychologist Fritz Heider described such processing of interpersonal information as "commonsense psychology" and its practitioners "naive scientists," since like scientists they try to link observable things (such as behavior and appearance) to unobservable traits ("kind," "poor," or "cruel"). He realized that members of a particular culture share certain basic assumptions about behavior, enabling them to be relatively successful in their judgments of others.

> ***"It is important that we do subscribe to a common psychology since doing so provides an orienting context in which we can understand, and be understood, by others. Imagine a world in which your version of everyday psychology was fundamentally at odds with that of your friends."***
>
> ***—Fritz Heider, 1958***

A baby waves as his mother holds him (below left). People are sociable from a very early age, and the ability to interact with others is vital to humans.

FOCUS ON

Sociability as a Useful Adaptation

People begin to form relationships from their earliest days. There is evidence that we are born sociable, or a least with a preference to interact with other members of our species: Even newborns respond more readily to other people than they do to nonhuman aspects of their environment (*see* Vol. 4, pp. 130–149), and babies show a preference for the sound of human voices. The fixed focus of a baby's eyes enables it to look at its mother's face while being held in her arms, and a baby is ready to smile at facelike shapes just a few days after birth, gradually refining this preference until it is real faces, rather than just shapes, being responded to.

This preference for other people continues throughout childhood and has some important functions. One of them is that it makes social interaction with other people more likely. Through the process of evolution by natural selection (*see* Vol 1, pp. 134–143) the ability to interact socially (sociability) has proven to be a successful adaptation. An adaptation is a useful physical feature or a behavior that helps an organism survive. Since the first modern humans evolved 100,000 years ago, they have lived as social animals. For infants, who are dependent on adults, that is a very good thing, and it has maximized their chances of survival. If infants smile when someone comes close or look with interest as people move, adults are more likely to enjoy looking after them and carrying out the caretaking every infant needs.

Sociability also enables people to learn from others. Consequently, humans have become the most adaptable species on the planet—not because they have many advantageous physical adaptations but because they can learn and pass on survival techniques, developing new forms of behavior that help them adapt to their environment. Behavior that helps people survive in a tropical climate will see them perish in cold mountainous country, yet people have lived happily in both for thousands of years. This adaptability is made possible by the large and complex human brain, which gives us the ability to learn, and human sociability.

People may or may not be born social animals, but either way the social world they grow up in greatly affects their social behavior and personality. So, these Russians living in the taiga of Siberia, who lead nomadic lives, will think and feel differently about themselves both as individuals and social beings than people who grew up in Texas.

Relationships with society

Social psychologists are also concerned with the effect of group behavior on individuals. They have made some startling discoveries about the impact on people's behavior of the urge to do what others ask (compliance) and the urge to conform with the social group. The impact of the social world on individuals is covered in more detail in Chapter 3 (*see* pp. 50–71).

Communicating with others

In every social encounter, whether we speak or not, we communicate with other people. Even if another person stands with his or her back to you, something, such as lack of interest or anger, has been communicated. The study of verbal and nonverbal forms of communication is central to social psychology. The acquisition of language and the ability to process language are covered elsewhere in this set (*see* Vol. 1, pp. 118–125, and Vol. 4, pp. 24–39). Communication is covered in more detail in Chapter 4 (*see* pp. 72–93).

Nature or nurture?

A debate that has involved many psychologists, including some social ones, has been how much of our behavior is determined by genes (that is, nature) and how much is a result of the world we grow up in (nurture). This debate has been refueled by recent advances in the field of genetics (the scientific study of biological inheritance). We know that children are sociable from an early age, but does this mean that they are born with a gene for sociability? It is unlikely that there will ever be a simple answer to such questions, but social psychologists continue to investigate how much of our behavior is learned, and how much innate (inborn) and, therefore, in our genes. In most cases, any answers will probably be complex, involving the effects of a multitude of genes as well as the effects of the environment on individuals and genes. The relationship between genes and social behavior is covered in more detail in Chapter 6 (*see* pp. 142–163).

HISTORY OF SOCIAL PSYCHOLOGY

Social psychology has often been thought of as a late developer within the field of psychology, but its origins go back to the founding father of psychology himself: Wilhelm Wundt (*see* Vol. 1, pp. 30–39). Wundt is well known for publishing the first psychology textbook, *Principles of Physiological Psychology* (1873), and for establishing the first experimental psychological laboratory in Leipzig,

Germany. But it is less widely known that between 1900 and 1920 he wrote ten volumes of social psychology, which he referred to as "folk psychology." In these works Wundt covered topics such as the relationship between language and thought, and the ways that social and cultural influences shape cognition (information processing) and mental life.

Wundt saw psychology as concerned with the individual and social psychology as complementary. He believed that knowledge of the individual—in terms of physiological and cognitive processes—is important, but that an understanding of the ways that social influences and social contexts color and shape human experience is equally significant. Wundt believed it was necessary to study the two areas separately, however, since he felt they required different forms of knowledge and different research methods. Wundt's work on social psychology is not widely known today but was extremely influential on the work of social researchers such as U.S. philosopher George Mead (*see* pp. 12–13; 15–16) and Russian psychologist Lev Vygotsky (*see* Vol. 4, pp. 40–57)

Mental contagion

Other influences on the development of social psychology emerged from the practices of suggestion and hypnotism. Although often deemed little more than parlor games, they are closely concerned with how people relate to others—to be hypnotized, a person interacts in a specific way with the hypnotist, for instance. Hypnotism and suggestion first attracted interest partly as a result of Anton Mesmer's work in the 1860s and 1870s (influencing Sigmund Freud in his development of his theory of the unconscious mind; *see* Vol. 1, pp. 52–65).

Since the 1760s and throughout the 1800s, society had been rapidly changing as the effects of industrialization took hold. Cities grew as people moved away from the countryside to find work in the emerging factories, population levels rose, and, at times, social unrest seemed to be increasing also, as people rioted over poor pay, lack of food, or limited rights. Social protests had happened before the industrialized era, but with people concentrated in cities the effects were more noticeable and more likely to spread. Some social theorists tried to explain the apparently irrational violence of mob behavior using concepts of mass hypnotism and social influence. This approach, summarized by Gustave Le Bon in 1908, was based on "mental contagion": the idea that social unrest could spread like an infectious disease and that social suggestion and mass hypnotism were the mechanisms through which it spread.

Two approaches

By the beginning of the 20th century, two main approaches had emerged in social psychology. Social psychologists considered both these perspectives.

Inside out The first looked at social behavior primarily from the individual's standpoint (that is, from the inside out). One of this school's main proponents was W. McDougall, whose *Introduction to Social Psychology* was published in 1908. McDougall emphasized the instinctive roots of social behavior, theorizing that

A crowd attacks German shops in England, 1915, when the two countries were at war. In 1908, Gustave Le Bon described mob behavior as a result of social influence and mass hypnotism. Le Bon, Wilhelm Wundt, and other early theorists on group behavior were the forerunners of modern social psychologists.

people have an inborn tendency to note and respond to particular stimuli for the purpose of attaining goals.

Outside in The second approach in social psychology at that time focused on the role of social context in structuring individual processes (that is, from the outside in), as exemplified by E. A. Ross, whose textbook *Social Psychology* was also published in 1908. His work was among the first to pursue a comprehensive sociological theory, analyzing the links between people and society.

Social psychology in the United States

In 1924, however, the balance between these two perspectives changed when F. H. Allport published his influential text *Social Psychology*, in which he defined social psychology unequivocally as the study of the individual.

This form of social psychology, which in many ways remains current to this day, was concerned with individual behavior. Researchers explored the factors involved in different types of social behavior, often using laboratory methods to tease out causes and other influences, while supplementing these with observations drawn from everyday life. By trying to understand the social forces acting on individuals they hoped to provide the key to understanding social living, since social living was self-evidently the result of individuals interacting with one another.

One of the key concepts in social psychology at this time was attitude. Attitudes are the evaluations people make (often based on "common sense" but not necessarily accurate psychology) about aspects of the social world. It was apparent that people differed in their evaluative approach to others and to the things that happened in society, and that these differences were sometimes consistent across cultures or ethnic groups.

Much of what psychologists study, such as attitudes and emotions, is difficult to quantify (measure). The development of accurate psychological testing was led by psychologists such as Rensis Likert, who devised the Likert scale in 1932. A typical question using a Likert scale might pose a statement (such as, "Politicians are responsible for society's problems") and ask respondents whether they strongly agree, agree, are undecided, disagree, or strongly disagree. This type of attitude scale enables the analysis and averaging of scaled responses. Likert-type scales are still used today.

The work of social psychologists in the United States, in particular, played an important part in a rising tide of xenophobia (dislike of foreigners) and racism. H. H. Goddard, for example, used a culturally biased "IQ" test to judge many U.S. immigrants as genetically inferior, starting a trend for deportation (which increased by 350 percent) and compulsory sterilization of these "mental deficients." Goddard claimed that the "feeble-minded" should not be allowed to reproduce, but he based his theories on misrepresented and incorrect evidence (especially regarding the Kallikak case study) and even altered photographs to illustrate "moronic" features.

> ***"The intelligence of the average 3rd-class immigrant is low, perhaps of moron grade."***
> ***— H. H. Goddard, 1917***

By the 1930s other social psychologists were concerned about this rising tide of prejudice, and they traced its origins to individual but widely shared attitudes. Researchers subsequently developed several techniques for measuring these attitudes, including the Likert scale (*see* left and figure below) and the semantic differential, both still in use today.

Backlash Although much of social psychology was then focused on the individual approach (that is, the inside out approach), sight had not been lost of the effect of social contexts on individuals (that is, the outside in approach). Wundt's influence had been widely felt in the United States as well as in Europe, and one of the most important U.S. researchers, George Mead, was profoundly influenced by Wundt's ideas. Although a philosopher,

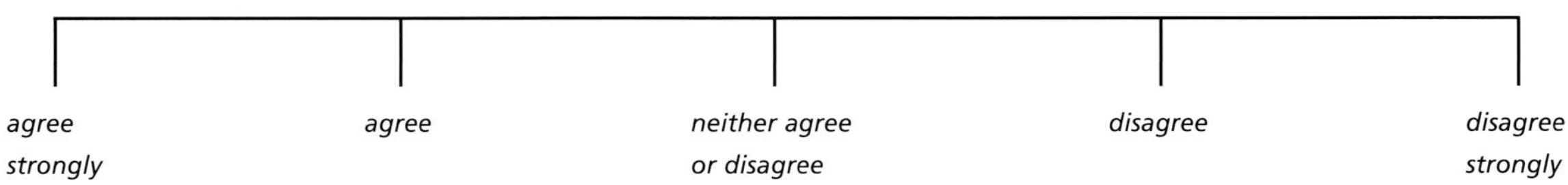

Mead was concerned with the origins of social action, and his book *Mind, Self, and Society* (1934) shaped the discipline of social psychology and elaborated on concepts of the social self (*see* pp. 15–16).

Gestalt psychology There were other influences, too. Several European Gestalt psychologists (*see* Vol. 1, pp. 46–51) emigrated to the United Sates from the 1930s on as a result of the growing Nazi influence in Germany and the persecution of Jews. Gestalt psychologists consider the individual as one part of a whole, which includes the social landscape. Many of them became interested in social psychology, applying insights from Gestalt psychology as they tried to understand the ways that people's membership in or interaction with social groups affected social behavior and social influence.

> ***"In the future history of our psychological era there are two names which, I believe, will stand out above all others . . . Freud will be revered for his first unraveling of the complexities of the individual history, and Lewin for . . . envisioning the laws according to which individuals behave."***
>
> ***— E. C. Tolman, 1948***

One of the most influential of these psychologists was Kurt Lewin, who developed an approach called field theory. His theory emphasized how the networks of relationships in a social situation shaped social groups and behavior.

Lewin had many followers, and his legacy led to research into conformity and the influence of groups and social beliefs. Muzafer and Carolyn Sherif, Leon Festinger, and Fritz Heider were influenced by his approach, and they, in turn, influenced social psychology with their explorations of group dynamics, group beliefs, and how people understand what is going on around them.

FOCUS ON

Collective Unconscious

One of Sigmund Freud's colleagues, Carl Gustav Jung (1875–1961), believed that people were like a group of islands in an ocean, appearing entirely separate and different on the surface, but in reality created from, and linked by, a deeper layer. He referred to this deeper layer as the "collective unconscious," arguing that people all over the world shared a common "race memory." (He used the term to mean the human race as a whole, not individual ethnic groups.) The influence of the collective unconscious could be seen in powerful symbols called archetypes and people's emotional reactions to them, which were stronger than toward nonarchetype symbols. Archetypes such as the "earth mother" (*see* right) or "sun king" held a powerful resonance in the human mind, and this Jung saw as evidence of the collective unconscious.

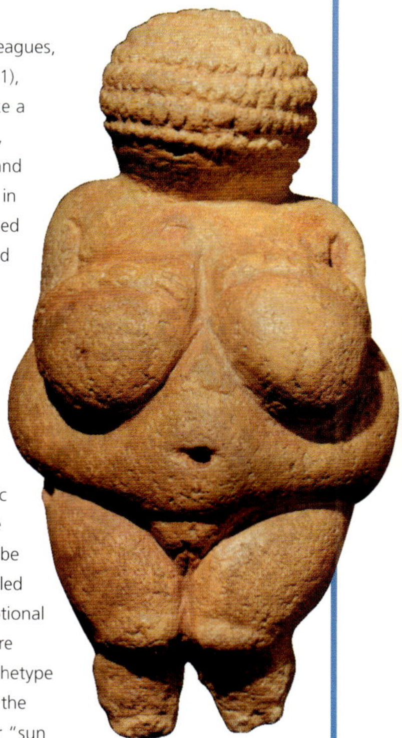

Due to existence of a collective unconscious, archetypes such as the "earth mother" (above), Carl Jung argued, occur throughout the world in legends and folklore and symbolized by artifacts such as this 25,000-year-old statue.

Social cognition

From the 1960s on psychology in general moved away from behaviorism (see Vol. 1, pp. 74–89), with its emphasis on observing how people behaved, toward a cognitive approach (see Vol. 1, pp. 104–117) focusing on how we process information. In social psychology, this shift was reflected by a developing interest in social cognition—or how people's understandings and interpretations of a situation influence their social behavior. This was a new area

European Social Psychology

PSYCHOLOGY & SOCIETY

Londoners take refuge in a subway during World War II (1939–1945). During the 20th century, Europe suffered two world wars and rising persecution of certain ethnic groups, forcing people to dwell on the interactions between people as groups.

The same time that social cognition was taking hold in the United States and elsewhere in the world (*see* p. 13), an alternative approach was emerging in Europe. Based on the work of Henri Tajfel (*see* pp. 21–22) in England and Serge Moscovici in France, so-called European social psychology emphasized the importance of groups and shared social experiences. It described itself as "European" partly to highlight the difference in emphasis between its group-oriented approach and the individualistic approach of U.S. social psychology; and partly because its origins were firmly rooted in Wundt's folk psychology and the research that grew from the Gestalt psychology movement.

European social psychology didn't reject the insights of U.S. social psychology, but built directly on the group-oriented work of Sherif, Festinger, and others in an attempt to understand how the sociocultural aspects of social living shaped people's social processes and social understanding. European social psychology concentrated on the way that social groups influenced human behavior (that is, the outside-in approach). This concern was partly due to historical reasons: Europe had always been a diverse collection of different cultures, languages, and social groups, and the anti-Semitic and other persecutions that occurred in Germany in the 1930s had made it clear how important an understanding of group interactions is. European social psychology also differed from the traditional approach in that it was more theory driven, relying heavily on proposed hypotheses that could be tested in structured experiments. There were two major theories and several minor ones that shaped and structured much of the research carried out by European social psychologists. One of them was social identity theory, which explored the way that people come to see the world in terms of "them-and-us" (*see* p. 22) and the implications this has for social interactions. The other was social representation theory, which explored how shared social beliefs influence and shape social behavior.

for social psychologists, and at first they studied it largely from the individual's viewpoint, investigating how people attribute causes or reasons to things that happen, and how their way of understanding the social world influences their social behavior.

In many ways U.S. researchers had already been studying social cognition during their research into attitudes. Some had explored aspects of social thinking such as stereotyping (*see* pp. 34–35) and prejudice, while others had investigated the factors involved in persuasion, especially in the developing advertising industry. As cognitive psychology became more influential in the 1970s and 1980s, its model of the human mind as similar to a computer began to influence U.S. social psychology, too, and researchers began to explore how social influences on attitudes and other styles of thinking could be used as ways to process social information.

Social psychology today

Modern social psychology incorporates both the U.S. and European traditions (*see* box above). Social psychologists explore the individual causes and mechanisms that produce social behavior (the inside-out approach), and they explore the influences of shared social experience, such as culture and social identity (the outside in approach). And while there are social psychologists who still investigate one approach or the other, in general most combine both approaches, enriching the understandings of social psychology.

THE SOCIAL SELF

Central to any approach within social psychology is the concept of social identity. The social identity is a person's own definition of who he or she is, including individual attributes (such as self-concept) as well as shared attributes, such as gender, relationship to others (brother, sister, mother, for example), vocation (for example, student, builder, tax collector), and ethnic or religious group. A person's self-concept is an organized collection of beliefs people hold about themselves (*see* Vol. 4, pp. 130–149); these beliefs emerge, in part, based on the individual's relations with others.

History of the self-concept

This concept only began to emerge with the work of the 17th-century philosophers who set the foundations for psychology itself. Each of them wrestled with the question of what it was to be a person: French philosopher René Descartes (1596–1650) made a distinction between the human mind and "baser" animal natures, a distinction that we now refer to as Cartesian dualism (*see* Vol. 2, pp. 40–61). English philosopher John Locke (1632–1704) emphasized the importance of learning and experience. He believed that an infant is born a *tabula rasa*, or blank slate, and that his or her mind develops due to our experiences imposed by upbringing and culture.

Significant others Despite these forerunners, in 1890 the founder of U.S. psychology William James (see Vol. 1, pp. 40–45) became the first to argue a clear concept of the self. He recognized that people have the capacity to view themselves objectively and to develop feelings and attitudes about themselves. James felt there were three aspects to the self: the material self, the spiritual self, and the social self, which involves the feelings that people derive about themselves from associations with others. People are continually making social comparisons between themselves and other people whom James called "significant others": those meaningful to a person in some way, including close relations and friends, or even a favorite teacher. James argued that individuals use these comparisons to form an idea of what they are like, developing what he termed the self-concept.

> ***"The development of a healthy self-concept is promoted by a positive self-regard and an unconditional acceptance by the 'significant others.'"***
> ***— Viljo Kohonen, 1992***

Looking-glass self Many psychologists took up James' idea of the self-concept in the early 20th century. In 1902 C. H. Cooley identified feedback (*see* box p. 17) from other people as the crucial factor in social comparison. Cooley described the self-concept as a looking-glass, or mirror, that reflects what individuals believe other people think of them: If others see us as attractive or intelligent, we are more likely to perceive ourselves in those ways.

Internalization U.S. social psychologist George Mead elaborated on Cooley's ideas. Mead accepted Cooley's theory overall, and in 1934 he wrote of

Snow White's queen regards herself in a looking glass. Like most people, although to a greater degree, she is concerned with how others perceive her. Cooley believed that emotions like pride, embarrassment, and self-defensive anger occur as a result of ideas that we have about how other people judge us.

the importance of internalization in the development of a person's self-concept. Instead of simply observing how others react to them and acting accordingly, Mead believed that people use others' behavior as a source of information and then internalize principles and standards from it. They then use these internalized standards to evaluate themselves. Although the self-concept still derived from social experience, for Mead this experience was much broader than just the reactions and judgments of others. It included social norms and cultural patterns, as well as personal values.

> ***"The individual's self-concept is a social product that is shaped gradually through interaction with the environment."***
> ***— Viljo Kohonen, 1992***

According to Goffman, this woman on a first date is role playing. Like an actor, she has dressed for the part and might have even rehearsed some lines.

Role playing In 1959 Erving Goffman defined the self-concept as being essentially a collection of different parts that each person plays in society, or the various social roles that any one person adopts. People have many social roles (brother, student, office worker), and

KEY DATES

1890 William James introduces the concept of "significant others" and argues that it plays an important part in the development of the self-concept.
1902 Cooley identifies feedback from other people as the crucial factor in social comparison.
1900 to **1920** Wilhelm Wundt writes 10 volumes of folk psychology; ideas about mental contagion of mob violence via hypnotism or mass suggestion are popular.
1908 W. McDougall publishes *Introduction to Social Psychology*; E. A. Ross publishes *Social Psychology*.
1924 H. H. Allport publishes *Social Psychology*, defining psychology as the study of the individual.
1930s Attitude studies become popular.
1932 Rensis Likert devises Likert scale for attitude tests.
1934 G. H. Mead publishes *Mind, Self, and Society*.
1938 Guthrie reports on the importance of feedback to self-image.
1959 Goffman defines the self-concept as a collection of the social roles that a person adopts.
1960s Ethics become important in psychological research, shaping new ways of doing research.
1961 Rogers outlines how self-esteem develops from internalized social standards.
1963 Milgram undertakes studies of obedience.
1968 Coopersmith studies self-esteem among U.S. schoolboys, concluding that positive self-esteem is an important aspect of psychological health.
1970 Mbiti describes how African philosophical traditions see the individual self as firmly located within the collective self of the social group.
1972 Orne researches behavior adjustment.
1979 Tajfel and Turner propose that people use social groups as the basic units of their social worlds.
1980s Pilavin and colleagues study helping behavior.
1982 Collins studies mathematical abilities and self-efficacy beliefs in children.
1985 Marsella, DeVos, and Hsu show that a large part of the human world does not share the western concept of the independent self. Bharati describes the Hindu concept of selfhood.
1987 Hinde identifies eight different dimensions that can influence a relationship.
1997 Smith investigates women's experiences of pregnancy using a case study approach.
1997 Bandura argues that self-efficacy beliefs are an important part of how people see themselves.

The Importance of Feedback

CASE STUDY

In 1938 E. Guthrie related an incident that happened among his students that showed how important feedback is for the self-concept. Several of the boys decided to play a joke on a rather plain, unattractive girl in the class, treating her as if she were the most interesting and attractive girl in the whole college and drawing lots to see whose turn it was to ask her for a date. After several dates, however, the girl had changed considerably, and the boys began to look forward to their turn with her. She had become interesting to talk to and lively, even humorous. She even looked more attractive, because she now took more care with her appearance. The feedback she had received from the boys had raised her self-esteem, allowing her to become less self-conscious and more relaxed, and as a result, she became more interesting and attractive.

each role brings with it requirements about how a person in that role should act. These requirements include the expectations of society at large as well as those of the individual in the role. Whenever people take on a new social role, such as a new job or course of study, for example, initially they might feel as if they are acting in the unfamiliar role. But as people become more accustomed to the new role, both the role and its expectations become internalized as just another facet of the self-concept. Goffman saw the self-concept as being the sum of people's various social roles—a bit like many-sided dice that display a different face depending on the situation and the role an individual is playing.

General and role-specific self-concepts More recently, researchers have shown that people have both general and role-specific self-concepts. In 1994 U.S. psychologists B. W. Roberts and E. W. Donahue asked women to describe themselves with respect to the different social roles they held (such as wife, friend, mother, sister, daughter). Donahue and Roberts discovered that how the women described themselves in respect to one role differed from how they described themselves in respect to another role. Donahue and Roberts concluded that people have role-specific self-concepts that differ according to the interpersonal situation. Nevertheless, the women's role-specific self-concepts shared enough similarities to indicate that they also held a general self-concept.

SELF-IMAGE AND SELF-ESTEEM

The self-concept has two parts: self-image and self-esteem. The self-image is the factual part, consisting of descriptions and straightforward information, such as the subjects people study or the work that they do, where they live, what color their hair is, and so on. Self-esteem is all about how worthwhile people judge themselves to be. It involves internalized social judgments and ideas about how good people are at doing things or how positive or negative their character traits are.

> ***"Self-esteem is an experience. It is a particular way of experiencing the self."***
> ***— Nathaniel Branden, 1997***

Self-esteem

An important part of the self-concept, self-esteem is intricately linked with positive social experience and mental health. Who people relate to, and how they relate to others is influenced by a person's self-esteem (*see* p. 43). For example, people who view themselves negatively (that is, who have low self-esteem) often behave in ways that perpetuate this negative assessment: by seeking out partners who also treat them negatively, behaving in ways that will elicit negative reactions, and by perceiving the reactions of others to them as more negative than they in fact are.

Social comparisons

A person's self-esteem is related to social comparisons they make between themselves and others. This is especially true of people with low self-esteem. As already explained, people make self-evaluations by comparing themselves to others. So, if you feel that someone is better than you in some respect, that can lower your self-esteem. And if you feel that you are better than others in certain ways, that can raise your self-esteem. However, it is not quite so simple. The effect of social comparisons on self-esteem depends very much on who you are comparing yourself to. Imagine that you meet someone who is not as clever / attractive / witty as you are (a downward comparison). If this person is a stranger, meeting them makes you feel better about your own attributes, so the effect on your self-esteem is likely to be positive. If that person is someone very close to you, however, like your best friend or mother, then the effect on your self-esteem can be negative: you associate yourself with the same negative qualities.

Upward comparisons are equally complex. If you are watching athletics on TV, you might think "that sprinter runs much faster than I can." But, since the person is a complete stranger this has little effect on your self-esteem. If, however, you compare yourself unfavorably with people closer to you, such as classmates, then the experience has a negative effect—you might think "I can't run as fast as my friends; I'm useless at sports." This can have a negative effect on your self-esteem. If, however, you "upwardly compare" yourself with someone even closer again, such as a brother or your best friend, you might feel that their skills make you look good, too, and so your self-esteem improves—an effect that could be described as "basking in another's glory."

In summary social comparisons (whether upward or downward) that create a positive mood raise self-esteem, while experiences that create a negative mood lower self-esteem. And whether or not a comparison creates a positive or a negative mood depends on who you are comparing yourself to.

Our self-esteem is linked to how we feel about others and their relationship to us. This mother feels pride in her daughter's first prize. The effect on the mother's self-esteem is positive since mother and daughter have a close relationship.

Parenting styles and self-esteem

Stanley Coopersmith discovered that levels of self-esteem correlated with (are linked to) the parental styles people had experienced. Those with high self-esteem had fairly strict parents who set clear limits and high standards for their children, but were also interested in them and talked things over with them. Boys with low self-esteem tended to have

College students relax on the lawn. Researchers have found that in grades above the tenth, self-esteem is higher among African American students than white students. This has been explained as due to the different groups that white and black students compare themselves to. For complex reasons, there are generally more white than black students in higher education. For the black students, the comparison groups that determine self-esteem are no longer other African American classmates but nonclassmates engaged in different activities—many will have finished their schooling to start work, for example. Being able to continue education for longer than others in their social group can raise people's self-esteem.

parents who were much less interested and had low expectations for their children. Often, they did not even know the names of their sons' friends.

In 1961 Carl Rogers (*see* Vol. 1, pp. 66–73) outlined how self-esteem develops from the way that people internalize social standards, or conditions of worth, during their childhood. They are established as a result of parental expectations and everyday interaction. For most people parental expectations are realistic, and these people have a normal self-esteem. But for some the conditions of worth communicated by their parents are not realistic, which means the children can never live up to them. Rogers believed that most children have parents who love them regardless of what they do or how they act, which he called unconditional positive regard. But some children have parents who only show affection if they behave well, which he called conditional positive regard. These children grow up feeling that only ideal people are liked, leading to constant feelings of failure that result in chronically low levels of self-esteem.

Rogers believed that the damage could be repaired later in life if people were shown unconditional positive regard and encouraged to explore their potential for psychological growth, and he developed a successful system of client-centered therapy based on these principles.

Self-efficacy beliefs

People can be good at something, and know that they are, but still suffer from a low sense of self-esteem in other areas of their lives. In 1997 the eminent

CASE STUDY

The Importance of Self-Esteem

Self-esteem is important for psychological and physical health as well as for social interactions. In 1968, during a major study of self-esteem among U.S. schoolboys aged between 12 and 14 years old, Stanley Coopersmith discovered that those with high self-esteem were active, expressive, and successful at school, while those with low self-esteem had low ambitions and were less physically fit. The boys with low self-esteem were also far more likely to suffer from insomnia, headaches, and stomach upsets than those with high or normal levels of self-esteem. Coopersmith concluded that positive self-esteem is an important aspect of psychological and physical health, and his conclusions have been supported by many other researchers.

The Importance of Self-Belief

CASE STUDY

Having positive self-efficacy beliefs can sometimes be much more important than having an ability. In 1982 J. L. Collins looked at math skills and beliefs in children. Some of the children had high self-efficacy beliefs, and some low. The children also varied according to their ability at math. During tests Collins found that the children with high self-efficacy beliefs performed far better than those with low self-efficacy beliefs, even if those with low self-efficacy beliefs had higher levels of mathematical ability.

The reason for these results lay in the amount of effort the children put in to their tasks. Those with high self-efficacy beliefs were more prepared to go back over problems that they had done incorrectly and were more likely to correct themselves a second time since they believed they could be competent if they tried. But the children with low self-efficacy beliefs tended to give up quickly and did not bother making any more effort because they thought it would be useless.

psychologist Albert Bandura argued that self-efficacy beliefs are one of the most important features affecting the way that people see themselves. They are beliefs about competencies, or what people are capable of achieving if they try. These beliefs are partly, though not entirely, based on what people have done in the past. Such beliefs play a vital role when people decide which challenges to tackle.

> ***"Motivation is increasingly seen as being as important as so-called ability."***
> ***— Peter Mortimore, 2001***

Bandura identified four psychological processes affected by self-efficacy beliefs. These beliefs affect cognitive (thinking) processes because they influence what people think they are capable of doing. They affect motivation because the time that people spend trying to achieve something and how hard they work directly depends on whether they believe they are capable of achieving their goal. Self-efficacy beliefs can generate feelings of stress or anxiety if people feel they have become involved in situations they are not competent to deal with. And they affect selection processes and determine choices for action because people generally take on tasks or activities that they feel capable

Self-efficacy beliefs are an important factor in whether or not a person would even attempt such a feat as this. This man must believe that he is able to climb the rock face, no matter how challenging the task, to be able to start and complete the climb.

of managing. Bandura thinks it can be a good thing if people's self-efficacy beliefs are slightly higher than their previous achievements merited, because they would be more likely to put in extra effort and take on new challenges. This would then mean that their abilities would develop even further—so overconfidence can be a good thing in some situations.

SOCIAL GROUPS

A social group is not the same thing as a collection of friends at a party, although that could be an example. According to social psychologists, a social group is formed by two or more interacting people who share common goals, have a stable relationship, and are interdependent in some way—that is, what one does affects the others. Most importantly, members of a social group must also perceive that they are part of a group. Social groups meet these requirements to various degrees. Some social groups are more temporary than others (summer camp, for example), but in all cases the most critical feature is that members perceive themselves as belonging to a group. Examples of social groups include sports teams, drama clubs, workmates, classmates, and Sunday school. Today, social groups can even be virtual and involve no physical contact, as in the case of Internet newsgroups. People may have several social identities, depending on the social group they are currently interacting with.

In 1979 Henri Tajfel and John Turner proposed a different way of looking at how people see themselves with their social identity theory. They argued that people use social groups as the basic units for making sense out of their social worlds, and it is people's membership in

These women form a social group since they interact and share the same goal (to quilt). Most importantly, they also see themselves as members of a group.

KEY TERMS

collective unconscious—Jung's concept of a common race memory shared by people all over the world.
field theory—an approach developed by Kurt Lewin that emphasizes the networks of social relationships in shaping social groups and behavior
self-concept—the set (or sets) of organized beliefs a person holds about who they are and what their attributes are. Self-concepts can be role specific.
self-efficacy beliefs—people's beliefs about their own competences, or the things they believe they are capable of achieving.
self-esteem—the self-evaluations people make about themselves. It is based on how we feel about and relate to others.
social cognition—the way that people's understandings and interpretations of situations and themselves influence their social behavior.
social comparisons—comparisons people make about themselves with reference to other members of society.
social groups—interdependent, interacting people with shared goals who see themselves as part of a group.
social interactions—exchanges or encounters between two or more people.
social roles—the roles that people play in different social contexts.
social identity—people's own definitions of who they are, including individual attributes (such as self-concept) as well as shared attributes such as cultural, gender, and faith, make up their social identity.
social identity theory—an approach exploring the way that people see the world in terms of "us and them."
social representation theory—an approach exploring how shared social beliefs influence and shape social behavior.

these groups that affects how they see themselves. Society is largely composed of different groups of people, and these groups differ in terms of their relative power, status, and influence, and in terms of their functions and areas of relevance.

According to Tajfel, social groups form an important part of human thinking because people have a powerful tendency to categorize and classify their experiences. People categorize themselves as well as other people; so not only do social groups affect the way that individuals relate to other people, but the social groups to which people feel they belong also form a part of their self-concept.

Belonging to a social group that is difficult to get into, such as the Marines, can boost a person's self-esteem.

Why join a social group?

People join social groups for many reasons: to satisfy the need to receive attention and affection from others, to achieve a sense of belonging, to gain access to knowledge or specialized information (as in an evening class, for example), and sometimes for security, since there is safety in numbers.

People also join groups because membership in a social group contributes to a person's social identity. As Tajfel pointed out, the social groups someone belongs to affect both that person's self-esteem and self-concept.

In the 1960s and 1970s people such as Angela Davis redefined what it meant for Americans to be black, enhancing feelings about their social group.

Us-versus-them

People have a tendency to see the world in terms of "us" and "them." What constitutes "us" can vary considerably depending on the situation people are in. Most people have several ingroups ("us"), which are basically any social groups to which the individual belongs.

Yet sometimes, people do not identify with the social group that they belong to. Instead, they try to distance themselves from the other members, believing that they are "not like the others." Or they may try to leave one group and join some other social group instead. According to Tajfel and Turner, people only identify with their group if it provides them with a source of positive self-esteem. Otherwise, they are likely to try to leave the group, or to distance themselves from it.

Sometimes people don't have a choice about whether they belong to a social group or not. For example, changing your gender is not easy, and changing ethnic group is almost impossible. In these instances making sure that their group membership reflects positively on their self-image requires a rather different approach. Sometimes people deal with this by comparing their group only with others that are similar or lower in status, ignoring groups that have a higher social status. Another option is to change the perceived status of the group. A major breakthrough in combating U.S. racism was the 1960s "black is beautiful" movement. It made a great difference to many people's lives because it redefined being black as a positive experience, replacing the negative image that white-dominated, mainstream U.S. culture had previously depicted. Highly visible role models, such as Angela Davis and Malcolm X, spread the message, enabling people to identify with the movement and to feel proud of their social category.

Cultural concepts of self

In recent years some social psychologists have challenged views about the nature of the self. The traditional view of the self-concept assumed that the "self" is an independent entity separate from social context. But many social psychologists now argue that the idea of an independent self is a myth, and that people are more firmly embedded in society and social groups than researchers had realized. This development has been fed by knowledge western psychologists have acquired about different cultures from around the world.

EXPERIMENT

Ultimate Attribution Errors

Some researchers, such as Tajfel, think that merely being in one social group and being aware of the existence of another group is enough for prejudice and even racism to develop. One function of the "us-and-them effect," as explained by Tajfel's social identity theory, is that members of an ingroup ("us") enhance their self-esteem by comparing themselves to other groups ("them")—in the same way that individuals make social comparisons with other people that contribute to their self-esteem (*see* p. 18). Since one reason that people seek to join social groups is to enhance their self-esteem, it follows that the social group, in turn, seeks to enhance group self-esteem. Each group tries to see itself as not only different from other groups but better in some way. Since social groups occur on many levels and can be based on color, gender, faith, even age, people sometimes make negative comparisons between very broad groups, leading to prejudice.

But how exactly can being in a social group lead to prejudice? The blame for this has been laid at the door of an "ultimate attribution error." Attributions are ways in which we explain the actions of people, in this case members of social groups. When we make comparisons between social groups, researchers have found that we judge those in our group more favorably than those not in the group. So, for example, you might think that your friend got an A grade on her paper because she worked hard but that someone you aren't close to got a good grade through luck. Outgroup members ("them") are more likely to be disliked and seen as having undesirable traits (if you're not on the athletics team, you must be unfit). Those not in the group are viewed as being similar to each other and are often subject to generalizations ("Men!" a woman might say if one man annoys her). The tendency to make unfavorable comparisons about members of outgroups and favorable comparisons about members of ingroups have been termed ultimate attribution errors, and racism has been given as an extreme example of such an error.

Racism—a result of the social comparisons we make between "us" and "them"? These members of the Ku Klux Klan might not agree.

FOCUS ON

African Philosophical Traditions

In 1970 John S. Mbiti described how African philosophical traditions see the individual self as being firmly located within the collective self of the "tribe" or ethnic group, which provides the whole context for "being." Trying to separate the self from this context is seen as nonsensical because people are all part of the whole. Of course, people have their own thoughts and ideas, and every person is unique; but each is embedded in the social context. Thus people can only be understood in the context of their families, social groups, friends, and culture. Individualism is seen as irresponsible and virtually uncivilized, since individuals are not simply responsible to themselves, but are interdependent members of the community.

These Dinka women (southern Sudan) are working together to thatch a house. The person who owns the house is obliged to return the favor. In such ways, members of Dinka society are interlinked by responsibilities and obligations.

In 1985 Anthony Marsella, George DeVos, and Francis Hsu showed how a large proportion of the human world simply did not share the distinctively western concept of the independent self, a finding borne out by other researchers. In 1985, for example, Agehananda Bharati described how Hindu culture emphasizes selfhood, rather than society, but how its concept of selfhood is different from the western notion of self. One of the most central Hindu concepts is the idea of the inner, or "true," self—the *atman*—which is closely linked with the oneness of God and can only be reached through meditation and self-discipline. Everyone contains an innermost self, but people have to learn how to reach it. There are also other Hindu aspects of the self, such as the conscious parts that people use when they are interacting with others, and the thoughts and ideas that people find difficult to put into words, which Hindus call the "unexpressible consciousness."

> ***"What then is the individual and his place in the community [in Africa]? . . . . The individual does not exist alone . . . he is simply part of the whole. The community must therefore make, create, or produce the individual, for the individual depends on the corporate group."***
>
> ***— John S. Mbiti, 1969***

The Japanese perception of self, according to DeVos, is particularly concerned with the effect that the individual has on other people. Japanese people are brought up to be extremely sensitive to interpersonal guilt and social shame, and belonging to a group and sharing that group's identity help people avoid the painful self-awareness that is associated with existing as a separate individual. Consequently, personal thoughts are kept private lest they disturb the social balance, and the sense of identity is rooted much more strongly in social relationships and appropriate social behavior than it is in western culture.

Westerners are much more embedded in their social contexts than they realize, however: Families, religious groups, friendship groups, and other aspects of their social networks are crucially important in how people see themselves. And despite the assumption that people are independent entities, much of the psychological research into the self-concept has emphasized how important other people are.

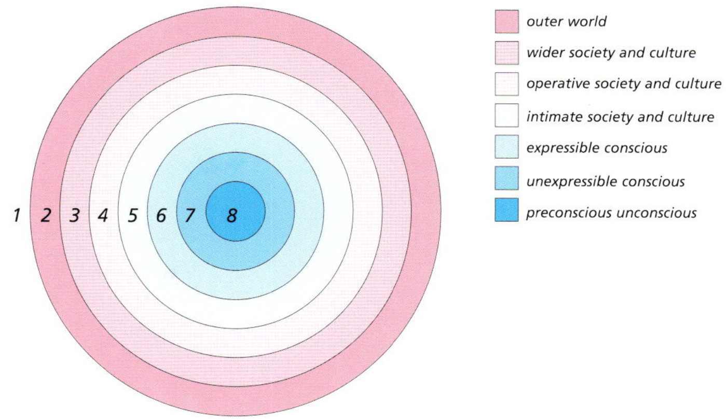

Hsu's multilayered model locates individuals in their social context. From the outside in, the layers move from society at large to layers of the personality.

A multilayered approach

The different ways that the self-concept is regarded around the world show just why and how people have come to challenge the idea of the independent self. Hsu proposed a model for the way that people are located in their social context, taking a multilayered approach that passes from the external world through different layers of the social world to different layers of the individual self.

Hsu believed the third layer in his model—people's intimate society and culture—is quite powerful. It represents the part of the external world to which people feel the strongest degree of attachment, and they often resist any changes to this layer particularly strongly. Nationalism, family loyalties, and other such powerful motivations all stem from this particular layer. Hsu's model provides a way of making sense of the different ways in which the self is perceived and challenges the traditional western view of the independent self being affected by social influences.

RESEARCH METHODS

People's behavior is complex, and how they make sense of what they are doing can be even more complicated. Like other psychologists, social psychologists have to carry out research in a systematic and scientific way, using techniques adapted to the complexity of the material.

A brief history of research

In the earliest days, Wundt's folk psychologies included studies of cultural stories and myths, symbolism, ritual, and many other aspects of social living, including social interactions between individuals and groups. They formed the subject matter of early social psychology, studied through documents, direct observations, and accounts.

As the 20th century went on, cultural approaches to understanding social living were absorbed into the new disciplines of anthropology, sociology, and linguistics, while social psychologists focused on individuals. Research depended primarily on methods that analyzed individuals' experiences. Systematic observations of people's behavior through two-way mirrors or on film were standard practice.

The behaviorist tradition emphasized general trends, laws, and quantification (measurement). Research methods adopted by social psychologists—such as experiments and observations—had to provide numerical data for reasonably large groups of people. These quantitative methods provided data that could be analyzed statistically to identify general trends: an approach called nomothetic research. By collecting information about typicality, or the things that most people did in a given situation, researchers believed they would be able to identify general principles about social behavior.

Ecological validity Social behavior is multilayered and complex, however, and people adjust their behavior to suit a given situation. So, social psychologists attempted to gather data from more realisitic situations, too. Sometimes this meant carrying out experiments in the real world, such as those conducted in the 1980s by J. A. Piliavin and colleagues, who investigated helping behavior by staging a collapse on the New York subway and observing who offered to help. They found that reactions are influenced by the number of other people present. In a large crowd people feel less obliged to help (*see* pp. 65–68). Studying behavior in real-life settings enhances the so-called ecological validity of findings, making them truer to the real world. It is now also recognized that the researcher is an active part of the research process.

Observation Sometimes, social psychologists gathered data by observing people's behavior in a way that provides systematic and consistent statistical information, but this is not simple. Often researchers had to control the situation in some way, for example, by setting up rooms where people's actions could be secretly observed and recorded.

Since the aim was to identify the general principles underlying social behavior, statistical comparisons were all-important—even to the point where some researchers felt that the real meaning of what was being observed was being lost.

In 1997 Jonathon Smith used a case study approach to study four women's experiences of pregnancy, using various methods such as interviews, diaries, and questionnaires. Social psychologists use this approach to gather detailed qualitative data about a few individuals. They cannot use their results to generalize about behavior, but the data help them understand people's cognitive processes. This idiographic approach is widely used by psychology researchers today.

Social cognition This emphasis on general principles dominated social psychological research until the 1980s. Many social psychologists were becoming interested in social meaning and social cognition (the way that understanding and interpretation influence behavior). What people *think* is going on is usually much more important than what *is* going on, because people react to what they think is happening, not to reality.

This led to the use of new forms of qualitative data collection, such as detailed interviews with people about their perceptions and feelings. A subject might be asked to keep a journal or to give a description of an event or person.

Today, social psychologists use both qualitative and quantitative techniques. Quantitative data can be used for number crunching, to figure out, for example, how many social groups people belong to on average, when they join, and how long they remain members of a group. Qualitative methods might reveal *why* people join certain social groups and how the groups affect their lives, and how individuals feel about other members.

Idiographic methods Social psychologists also became interested in what makes individuals distinctive, rather than in typical behavior, leading to the use of idiographic (rather than nomothetic) methods, which focus on individuality and aim to understand individuals in detail. This approach involves case studies and detailed interviews with one or a few individuals.

KEY TERMS

ecological validity—the relevance of research to the real world.

idiographic research—detailed investigative approaches, such as interviews, case studies, or descriptions, that focus on individuality and aim to understand a person in detail.

nomothetic research—experiments, surveys, or observational studies that provide extensive numerical data that can be analyzed statistically to identify general trends.

qualitative analysis—analyzes in-depth data from just a few subjects to reveal hidden meanings and cognitive (information-processing) implications.

quantitative analysis—the statistical analysis of a range of numerical data, which may help support a general theory.

The APA (American Psychological Association) produces ethical guidelines that all research psychologists must abide by. Permission from an Ethics Board is needed to conduct research that goes against guidelines. Previously, social psychologists had routinely engaged in deception, for example, by staging incidents or by giving people false feedback about self-esteem or attitude tests. This is no longer acceptable.

Examples of Ethical Guidelines

Informed consent	Participants should be informed of the objectives of the research, so that they may give informed consent for their participation.
Deception	It is unacceptable to withhold information or give misleading information to research participants. Intentional deception should be avoided.
Debriefing	Participants should be fully debriefed to allow them to complete their understanding of the nature of the research.
Withdrawal	Investigators should emphasize the participant's right to withdraw from the research at any time.
Confidentiality	All data obtained should be treated as confidential unless an agreement to the contrary was made in advance.
Protection from harm	Investigators must protect participants from physical and mental harm, including distress, either during or arising from investigations.
Privacy	Studies based on observation must respect the privacy and psychological well-being of the people studied.

Idiographic research can reveal social cognitive processes—what people think and feel about their social experiences.

Discourse analysis Some social psychologists conduct research in the real world using new methods such as discourse analysis—studies of the way that language is used for social purposes, including analysis of metaphors, imagery, and hidden meanings in conversations. Discourse analysis can reveal meaningful aspects of social situations that are not apparent in the laboratory.

Ethics and responsibility

Until the 1960s researchers assumed their pursuit of knowledge entitled them to engage in any manipulations, strategies, and deceptions that were deemed appropriate. Psychologists were trained to deceive people on the grounds that experimental control required "naïve" subjects who were unaware of what the study was about. This unregulated system produced several extreme experiments. Notable examples were: the Minnesota Starvation Studies of the 1930s, which investigated the effects on adults of several weeks of food deprivation (causing dangerous levels of weight loss); Ian Oswald's studies of army conscripts in the 1960s on the impairments in functioning caused by sleep deprivation (prompting a local DJ to try for a record and sustain irreversible brain damage as a result); and Stanley Milgram's dramatic investigations of obedience (*see* pp. 55) that stimulated a major debate about research ethics in psychology, ultimately leading to ethical guidelines (*see* box above).

CONNECTIONS

- Relating to Others: pp. 28–49
- Relating to Society: pp. 50–71
- Social Development: Volume 4, pp. 130–149
- Cognitive Psychology: Volume 1, pp. 104–117
- Cross-cultural Psychology: Volume 1, pp. 152–161

Relating to Others

"Humans are social animals, created for a communal existence."

Plutarch

Often our responses to other people are more a reflection of our own personalities than an objective assessment of theirs. Many studies of interpersonal relationships suggest that our impressions of new acquaintances and even our judgments of old friends are influenced by previously established attitudes rather than by dispassionate examination of the facts.

Psychologists have always known that people are social animals who spend their lives interacting with others, but it is only recently that they have begun to examine how we process information of a social nature. These researchers study the hidden cognitive processes we use to make sense of our social world—processes that they believe mediate between any incoming social information and our response. These processes determine how we select, interpret, organize, remember, and respond to social information—a research area called social cognition.

In this chapter we will look in detail at how we form our initial impressions of other people, how we try to explain their behavior, and how we attempt to influence their impressions of us. From these early social interactions we then move on to study the more intimate relationships we form with particular people based on our liking or love for them—and to investigate how the formation, maintenance, and breakdown of these relationships are central to all our lives.

FORMING IMPRESSIONS

When we meet people for the first time we immediately form impressions of them—a tendency that was important for survival during our evolutionary history. We form these impressions quickly and easily, and our judgments will guide and influence any future relationship that may develop. Although we may consider information from many diverse sources, we often form these first impressions on the basis of very few facts. There is little about people's overt behavior or appearance that can tell us directly about their personalities, likes, dislikes, and so on; but we still tend to believe there is. For example, if we hear that Julia does voluntary work at the local dog pound, that does not tell us directly any more about her than where she works. However, from this scrap of information we might infer various other things about her such as that she is a dog lover, or that she is a kind and caring person. If we are less charitable, we might suspect her love of animals masks a fear of relationships with other people. Our assumptions may not always be that accurate, but this still becomes our impression of Julia.

We form rapid impressions of other people when we meet them for the first time, making all kinds of judgments about what sort of people they are and whether we will get along. Social psychologists study how we make these judgments and investigate the social clues we use to come to these decisions.

While it is easy to agree with this general account of how we make up our minds about other people, psychologists have set themselves the more difficult task of applying scientific principles to the rich complexity of human social interaction. The first great pioneer in this field was Solomon Asch (1907–1996), who carried out numerous studies to determine how people form impressions (*see* box p. 31). Unlike many researchers, he drew together previously disparate approaches such as experiment and naturalistic observation, nature and nurture, and behaviorism and psychoanalysis to depict people as both complex but researchable and as both independent and socially situated.

Asch decided that when people first meet each other, they do not retain separate pieces of information about their new acquaintances but process the data

KEY POINTS

- People start to form relationships from birth, relating to one another during brief encounters and in close relationships.
- People form impressions of others quickly and easily, and make judgments about the causes of other people's behavior.
- People also try to influence the way others see them.
- Understanding social information requires internal cognitive processes and reliance on personal and causal schemata.
- Biases in people's cognitive processing of social information cause them to make errors in their judgments about others.
- People have a natural need to associate with others that is probably a product of evolutionary adaptation, and this drive is enhanced in frightening or stressful situations.
- Positive relationships and social support are good for people's mental and physical health.
- Proximity and group membership can influence people's choices.
- Developing and maintaining personal relationships requires social skills and competencies that are culturally appropriate, an equitable exchange of rewards, consideration of other people's needs, and an adherence to relationship rules.

People make snap judgments about others based on relatively few facts. If you saw this woman walking dogs, for example, you would immediately make certain assumptions about her. Perhaps you might decide that she likes animals, or that she must have a tolerant personality to cope with so many animals, or even that she is an ambitious person who wants to earn her living in an unconventional way.

Not only do we infer traits from people's known characteristics, but our mental image of them influences our interpretations of the things they say. In experiments a statement about rebellion attributed to ex-president Thomas Jefferson (left) was viewed much more positively than when attributed to the Russian communist leader Vladimir Ilich Lenin (right).

holistically (as a whole). He suggested that in doing this people use implicit theories of personality to interpret and draw inferences from the information they already have. Implicit personality theories are people's expectations about the links between traits—which ones tend to go together, and which ones do not.

> ***"We look at a person and immediately a certain impression of his character forms itself in us."***
> ***—Solomon Asch, 1946***

For example, people who belong to a tennis club might be seen as athletic and sporty, while those who collect for charity might be perceived as kind. Of course, these extrapolations may not be correct—they are just convenient labels that make it easier to pigeonhole people—but they are often necessary for social intercourse.

Most people realize that assumptions such as these run far ahead of the available facts (many sports clubs have purely social members, while some charity workers are acquisitive and mean). But more recent research has suggested that although people are perfectly capable of bearing these qualifications in mind, they usually need an incentive to make them bother. In their everyday dealings, rules of thumb are easier and more convenient than rigorous critical thought.

Social influence

Asch also explored relation-oriented approaches to perception, association, learning, and thinking. One of his areas of study was the extent to which people's judgment of what others say is influenced by the authority of the person who says it—a phenomenon called prestige suggestion. Take the quotation: "I hold it that a little rebellion, now and then, is a good thing, and as necessary in the political world as atoms are in the physical." Asch found that U.S. students were more inclined to agree with this dictum when it was attributed to Thomas Jefferson (who really did say it) than when it was attributed to Vladimir Ilich Lenin, leader of the Russian communist revolution. Behaviorists interpreted this result in terms of simple associations—Jefferson was a founding father of the land of the free and therefore good; Lenin was a Russian communist and therefore bad. Asch, however, showed that the traits people attributed to the author affected the assumed meaning of the quotation. People interpreted Jefferson's statement to mean rebellion for further freedom, while Lenin was thought to be referring to bloodshed and repression. Asch's conclusion supports a central tenet of modern social psychology: Behavior is not a response to the world as it is, but to the world as it is perceived.

Asch's research on conformity also highlighted this difference between physical and social reality. In one famous experiment he asked people to estimate the lengths of various lines—after several other group members (all of whom had been "planted") had given unanimously wrong answers. He found most of the

EXPERIMENT

FORMING IMPRESSIONS OF PERSONALITY

Asch carried out a series of experiments examining the way people combine diverse information to form an overall impression of a person. His most famous experiments in this area were published in 1946 and were a turning point in the literature of impression formation.

In the first experiment Asch split his participants into two groups. He presented the first group with the following list of seven traits describing a fictitious person:

> Intelligent, skillful, industrious, warm, determined, practical, cautious

He presented the second group with the following list:

> Intelligent, skillful, industrious, cold, determined, practical, cautious

The lists were identical apart from the fourth trait. Asch then asked both groups of participants to form an impression of the fictitious person described and to write a few sentences describing him or her. He found that changing the fourth trait from "warm" to "cold" produced noticeable and consistent differences in the answers given. For example, one participant described the "warm" person as: "A person who believes certain things to be right, wants others to see his point, would be sincere in an argument, and would like to see his point won." By contrast, another participant described the "cold" person as: "A very ambitious and talented person who would not let anyone or anything stand in the way of achieving his goal. Wants his own way, he is determined not to give in no matter what happens."

Asch's results provided clear evidence that people go beyond the information they are given (the traits in the list) to form an impression. Instead of using just the facts about a person, they extrapolate much more than they really know for sure.

In the last part of the experiment Asch asked his participants to look at a list of 18 paired adjectives and to decide which adjective in each pair best described the fictitious person. Some examples are:

Generous	Ungenerous
Persistent	Unstable
Good-natured	Irritable
Humorous	Humorless
Sociable	Unsociable
Serious	Frivolous

Asch found that there were wide differences between the adjectives selected to describe the "warm" person and those used to describe the "cold" person. The table below shows the percentage of each group of participants who picked the six traits in the column on the left.

	Warm	Cold
Generous	91%	8%
Persistent	100%	97%
Good-natured	94%	17%
Humorous	77%	13%
Sociable	91%	38%
Serious	100%	99%

As you can see, some traits (generous, good-natured, and humorous) were used to describe the "warm" person more often than the "cold" person; others were thought to be equally applicable. The high percentages showed that most of the participants shared the same beliefs about which traits were associated, suggesting that people infer similar information when forming first impressions.

participants were influenced by the discrepancy between their own perceptions and those of the bogus subjects; only 29 percent of them stuck unwaveringly to their guns and never went along with the views of the majority.

Motivation

Other researchers have suggested that neither Asch nor Anderson (*see* box p. 33) was entirely correct in his explanations for impression formation. Instead, they proposed a theory called the motivated tactician model, which assumes people rely both on implicit assumptions and on specific items of information. The degree to which they use one or the other depends on how motivated they are and whether they have the available cognitive resources. You have probably found from your own experience that there is a limit to the number of things you can do at once. At least part of the reason for this is that, in common with everybody else, you have limited cognitive resources: your mental capacity to process information and act on it. The more different tasks you tackle, the greater the demand on these resources (*see* Vol. 3, pp. 24–43), so you often rely on prior knowledge because you have few resources to spare.

When people are motivated to form a particularly accurate impression of someone else, however, they make more of an effort to use the factual information available to them rather than relying on their preconceived notions of personality. In 1984 Ralph Erber and Susan Fiske demonstrated this principle in a study of 102 undergraduate students. They put the students to work on various tasks with a co-worker whom they described as either "skilled" or "unskilled" and offered prizes for successful completion of some of the tasks. They then gave the students more information about their co-worker that was either consistent (appeared to fit in) with what they had already been told or was inconsistent. Erber and Fiske found that when winning a prize depended on team performance, the students paid more attention to the inconsistent information and sifted it more carefully than when nothing was at stake. Thus the prospect of winning a prize motivated the students to devote more cognitive resources to processing any information that did not fit in with their original impressions.

Solomon Asch was a pioneer in the field of human social interaction, carrying out numerous influential studies to determine how and why people form impressions of others.

Primacy effect

As well as inferring inaccurate traits in people without real reason, there are other potential errors that can bias the way we form impressions. Asch, for example, found that the first information learned about a person tends to have a greater effect on any impression formed than information learned later—a tendency called the primacy effect.

He demonstrated the primacy effect by presenting one group of experimental participants with a trait list starting with the word "intelligent" and ending with the word "envious" and a second group with the same list set out in reverse order. He found that the participants who received the list starting with "intelligent" formed more positive impressions of the person described than those who were given the list starting with "envious." He concluded that the earliest information received colors people's interpretation of all the data that follow. So if the first thing we learn about someone is positive, we tend to interpret all subsequent information in a positive light (and vice versa) to form a consistent overall impression.

Although this may be what people typically do, suspicion remained that they are capable of better judgment. This was confirmed later by Anderson, who found that the primacy effect disappeared if participants were forced to attend equally to all the traits presented.

Distinctive characteristics

Distinctive characteristics also play an important part in influencing our overall impression of a person. A distinctive characteristic or behavior is one that attracts attention in its context, such as the antisocial behavior of a particular person in an otherwise social group. Positive behavior can also be distinctive, such as the actions of a person who stops to put money in a charity collection box when others have passed by without making a donation. Physical characteristics that help us form an impression of a person's age, race, sex, and height can also be distinctive in some contexts.

Although human notions of beauty change over time and across cultures, physical attractiveness is associated with a number of positive traits. Research has shown that we expect good-looking people to be more interesting, warm, outgoing, and socially skilled than ugly people. There is even evidence to suggest that we think beautiful people make good students. In 1975 psychologist Margaret Clifford gave children's photographs and report cards to U. S. primary school teachers and asked them to judge the likely intelligence and academic potential of each child. She discovered the more attractive youngsters were consistently rated as likely to possess greater academic potential and intelligence than the less attractive children—even though her study proved that there was no real relationship between their attractiveness and actual school performance.

> FOCUS ON
>
> ## CRITICISM OF ASCH
>
> Not everyone agreed with Asch's views. One notable critic was psychologist Norman Anderson. On the basis of research starting in the 1960s, he rejected the idea that people's interpretation of personal information is influenced by the information they have previously acquired. Instead, Anderson suggested that people attach some fixed rating of importance to each piece of trait information, forming an overall impression by averaging these ratings across all the things known about an individual. He demonstrated this effect experimentally using a method similar to Asch's and called his theory the cognitive algebra model.

> ***"Physical beauty is the sign of an interior beauty, a spiritual and moral beauty."***
>
> ***—Johann Schiller, 1882***

The expectations associated with physical beauty can also have an effect in the workplace, tending to be advantageous to men but negative for women. In one study four groups of participants were asked to evaluate an imaginary company executive on the basis of a photograph. The researchers showed one group of participants a photograph of an attractive male, the second a photograph of an unattractive male, the third a photograph of an attractive female, and the fourth a photograph of a less attractive female.

Without previous knowledge of these two film stars, what attributes do you think you might associate with them? Research suggests that Brad Pitt's baby-faced features (left) would inspire more positive comments than the rugged features of Gérard Depardieu (right).

They discovered that participants rated the attractive male executive as more able than the less attractive one. For women, however, the opposite was true: Those participants who saw the attractive woman executive seemed to believe she might have been promoted because of her appearance rather than her ability.

Beauty is not the only physical attribute that activates particular expectations or impressions about personality—certain patterns of facial features can also have this effect. Research by Dianne Berry and Leslie McArthur in the mid-1980s found that baby-faced male adults with high eyebrows, big round eyes, and small chins consistently have positive characteristics attributed to them. Specifically, Berry and McArthur found that participants from the United States and Korea viewed baby-faced men as more honest, kind, open, submissive, and warm than those with more mature facial features.

Stereotypes

Both Asch and Anderson discovered that implicit personality theories may be socially shared to some extent. In other words, most members of any particular group make similar extrapolations from known facts about a person. Such theories can be seen as the basis of stereotypes: shared beliefs (or social schemata) about the personality traits of a social group (*see* pp. 50–71 and Vol. 1, pp. 152–161).

When group membership is highly visible (sex or ethnicity) or distinctive (disability or height), we often form impressions based on stereotypes—ignoring or changing information that is inconsistent with the stereotype unless we are sufficiently motivated or have the cognitive resources to do otherwise. Stereotypes can lead us to make incorrect assumptions about others based purely on their group membership (all women are bad drivers, all black men are prone to violence, or all disabled people are stupid). In other words, stereotypes can bias the processes by which we form impressions.

CAUSAL ATTRIBUTIONS

So far we have looked at how we process social information about people we meet, and how we decide what they are like. But there is another part of relating to others: providing explanations for our own and other people's social behavior. For example, you find out that you have done badly on a test while your best friend has done really well. How do you account for this? Explanations for the causes of behavior are known as causal attributions.

Several different theories have been suggested to explain how people make causal attributions. In 1958 Austrian-born U.S. psychologist Fritz Heider produced the first major theory of attribution. Heider saw people as "naïve scientists" who try to link observable behavior to a particular type of cause. He classified potential causes as either internal (due to the person) or external (due to the situation or environment).

In the 1960s two, more complex attribution theories were formulated. Edward Jones and Keith Davis proposed the correspondent inference theory (CIT) in 1965. It differed from Heider's theory by incorporating the concept of intention. CIT suggests that people observe a behavior, infer the intention behind it, and then relate both the behavior and the intention to a trait or characteristic of the person. In this way they explain social behavior in terms of internal traits and supposed intentions. However, this theory is inefficient at explaining unintentional behavior, such as clumsiness.

In 1967 the U.S. psychologist Harold Kelley proposed the covariation model. He suggested that when people have only one example of an individual's behavior, they rely on their learned knowledge (schemata) to explain it. However, when they have more than one example, they look for patterns in the potential causes that occur when the behavior is present and do not occur when the behavior is absent. In other words, they collect covariation information about the behavior and its potential causes. Kelly suggested three categories of cause: the person performing the behavior (the actor), the person or object toward whom or which the behavior is directed (the stimulus), and the situation in which the behavior takes place (the context). People believe a behavior is caused by whichever of these three seems to be present most often when the behavior occurs.

Consistent bias

None of these theories provides a full account of causal attribution, however. Just as in impression formation, research suggests that people make numerous consistent errors and are influenced by

Professor Stephen Hawking celebrates his birthday at Cambridge University in 2002. Despite suffering from motor neuron disease for most of his adult life, he has become a renowned authority in the fields of applied mathematics and theoretical physics. He had a tracheotomy in 1985 and now relies on a speech synthesizer, but he once observed how "if you have a slurred voice, people are likely to treat you as mentally deficient."

consistent biases when explaining the causes of social behavior. One of these biases has been called the fundamental attribution error (FAE) because it is so common. The FAE is people's tendency to underemphasize the role of situation in favor of judgments about the character or disposition of the person displaying the behavior. For example, people tend to think that Joe is claiming unemployment benefits because he is too lazy to get a job (disposition) rather than because he really is unable to find work (situation).

This tendency to underestimate the importance of a situation (as in the FAE) occurs only when we are observing the behavior of others without being involved. This is known as the actor-observer bias. When we are observers, we attribute behavior to disposition; but when we are actors, we attribute our behavior to the situation. For example, if someone drops a glass, we tend to think it is because that person is clumsy; but if we drop a glass ourselves, it is because it was slippery.

Our explanations for social behavior are also determined partly by our motivation or desires. Research on the self-serving attribution bias suggests that we tend to deny responsibility for our failures yet take credit for our successes. Thus we attribute failure to situation and success to disposition.

IMPRESSION MANAGEMENT

So far we have considered how we form impressions of other people—but the people with whom we interact form impressions about us in exactly the same way. Thus social perception is a two-way process in which we are both observing and observed. People are different from other observed stimuli. If you look at the view from your window, it will not be trying to make an impression on you. People, on the other hand, often are. Sociologist Erving Goffman likened social interaction to a theatrical performance in which the actors are "putting on a front." Indeed, it is difficult to think of a social situation in which we are not trying (consciously or otherwise) to influence how people perceive us. Goffman called this impression management: a concept closely related to that of self-presentation.

We actively try to create particular impressions of ourselves to serve different functions depending on the social context

People's interpretation of their own behavior in any social situation is likely to differ significantly from their interpretations of other people's actions. If you spill a drink on someone, you will probably think it is just an unfortunate accident—while the person concerned is more likely to think you are careless, clumsy, or even drunk.

PSYCHOLOGY & SOCIETY

ATTRIBUTION OF BLAME FOR A CRIME

What does casual attribution theory tell us about criminal responsibility? When a crime takes place, do we blame the perpetrator or the victim? Studies by researchers such as Thornton (1992) and Murrell and Jones (1993) suggest we often blame the victims, especially if we see them as dissimilar from ourselves. This self-serving observer bias occurs because we prefer to believe that the world is a just place in which good things happen to good people, and bad things happen only to people who deserve them. We can only maintain this belief if we believe that victims are to blame for the crimes committed against them.

Melvin Lerner, a Canadian psychologist, suggested that we find it comforting to believe in a just world because if we do (and we are generally good people), then we can also believe that we are unlikely to be the victims ourselves. Thus blaming the victim of a crime makes us feel less vulnerable. The disadvantage of this belief is that to support it, we also have to believe that victims get what they deserve. So even if we feel sympathy for crime victims, we tend to think that they are at least partly responsible for their own victimization—usually because they behaved carelessly.

Fundamental attribution error (see p. 36) can also help account for this effect. We explain the victimization of others in terms of their personal attributes or behavior. Thus their victimization is at least partly their own fault.

If we were the victims of a crime, however, we would probably not take this view. Instead, we would be more likely to look for a situational explanation of the crime—for example, it only happened because there were no streetlights in the area (an actor-observer bias). We seldom think that victimization is our own fault.

(circumstances), particularly if we are trying to make a positive impression. Consider your first meeting with someone who can give you something you want, perhaps at a job interview or an audition for a play. In such situations you will try to present yourself as possessing the qualities you think the interviewers will value. For a prospective employer you might emphasize aspects of yourself that reflect reliability and good timekeeping, for example; for the audition panel you would focus on your dramatic skills.

With people we already know, we try to manage the impression we make in order to maintain or challenge the image we believe they already hold of us (that we are a good friend or that we care about the environment, for example). When we are with someone who expects us to behave immaturely and naïvely, we will probably make an extra effort to show our maturity and sophistication. Alternatively, we may be submissive, acquiescently conforming to that person's image of ourselves even though we believe it is inaccurate and perhaps even resent it. Equally, the way we act, our clothing, hairstyles, and the way we talk can all be used to try to tell other people about the social group to which we belong or with which we identify.

Impression management enables us to exert some control over the way other people see us. However, we do not have complete control over the impressions we create. Goffman pointed out that many of our "social performances" are jointly produced. That is, in a social interaction both the impressions we form of others and the impressions we give of ourselves are created partly by the interaction itself—neither party creates an impression entirely on his or her own. The impression others have of us before an interaction or that they make immediately on meeting us affects their subsequent response to us. In 1977 Mark Snyder, Elizabeth Decker Tanke, and Ellen Berscheid studied the

> ***"Behavior is the vehicle through which impressions are usually enacted, and as such, impression management is much like acting."***
> ***—S. Fiske & S. Taylor, 1991***

When people desire a positive outcome from a social interaction, they try to appear as if they possess all the qualities the other person values. In a ballet audition, for example, they might try to demonstrate their precision, grace, and ability to follow complex instructions.

role of social interaction in impression management among a mixed group of students. They found that a male student's impression of a female's attractiveness influenced the way he interacted with her during a conversation and, in turn, how she responded to him. This effect is an example of the self-fulfilling prophecy (*see* box below). It occurs when one person's initial expectations about another cause the second person to behave in ways that confirm or support these expectations.

INTERPERSONAL RELATIONSHIPS

Our interactions with other people form a central part of our everyday lives, and our preoccupation with interpersonal relationships is a timeless phenomenon. Social psychologists distinguish between two types of relating to other people: Social interaction can take place between people who have seldom or never met before, while relationships are continuous associations over time between two or more people. Long-term relationships are based on repeated encounters between people, and the type of relationship that forms depends on the type of interaction that takes place between them.

To interact with other people, we need the appropriate social skills, which change from situation to situation and from culture to culture. For example, most of us use different forms of the same language depending on whom we are addressing—we choose different "registers" to speak to

CASE STUDY

The Self-fulfilling Prophecy

The self-fulfilling prophecy effect can occur in many different contexts and in the 1960s was explored by Robert Rosenthal and colleagues in the United States.

In one study (published in 1968) Rosenthal and Leonore Jacobson showed how the self-fulfilling prophecy could manifest itself in the classroom. They gave teachers a list of some of the students in their classes and told them that based on IQ tests, these students were expected to "bloom" intellectually over the next few months. In all cases the names of the students had been randomly selected. A few months later the researchers returned and measured the performance of these students. They found that the children identified as "bloomers" tended to perform better than their classmates. So it seemed the teachers' high expectations for these children had somehow translated themselves into actual higher scores in just a few months.

How could this have happened? One explanation is that the teachers had given these students more attention and more challenging assignments because they expected them to perform at a higher level, a type of behavior that is known to improve students' performance. By changing their behavior toward these students, the teachers had produced a corresponding change in their performance.

our children from those we would adopt in a conversation with a head of state. Our behavior varies, too. We would usually act quite differently at a friend's birthday party than the way we would behave at a funeral—but even this behavior could depend on context. People at a Catholic funeral in Italy, for example, would behave in a very different manner than those at a Hindu funeral on Bali: Catholics mourn the loss of the deceased, while the Balinese see the funeral as a celebration of the freeing of a soul. People's membership of social groups also has an important effect on their behavior (*see* box p. 40 and p. 48), although this effect may vary according to culture (*see* Vol. 1, pp. 152–161).

Social norms and competence

As children grow up, they learn which social behavior is appropriate in their own culture: a set of rules psychologists call "social norms." This process is known as socialization (*see* pp. 50–71). However, these social skills may not be appropriate when communicating with people from other cultures, and this can be a serious barrier to the formation of cross-cultural relationships. Socialization is therefore an ongoing process that continues into adulthood and is adapted and refined so that people can deal with new and exotic situations. Adults may have to learn new social skills and acquire new information to recognize and understand differences between their own social norms and those of others with whom they wish to relate.

Researchers largely agree that to relate to others, people need social competence. This is defined as the ability to interpret social norms to achieve a desired effect in a social situation—although one person's desired effect may not always be considered positive by other people, since he or she might understand the social norms that apply in a situation but deliberately act against them. Usually, however, people use their social competence to relate positively to others, either maintaining existing relationships or creating new bonds.

Michael Argyle proposed that most people continually modify their behavior in social situations by monitoring how their behavior is received and by changing their actions in response. In other words, social interaction is a process of continual

Behavior that is deemed appropriate in certain social situations, such as at weddings and at funerals, varies greatly between cultures. A Roman Catholic funeral is usually a solemn affair (below left), but in Bali in Indonesia Hindu people celebrate death as a freeing of the soul (right).

PSYCHOLOGY & SOCIETY

INTERPERSONAL VERSUS INTERGROUP BEHAVIOR

Interpersonal relationships refer to two or more people relating to each other as individuals. For example, two students who meet in class and become friends. This type of relationship differs from the kind of interaction that might happen between groups, although the distinction is not always obvious.

Intergroup behavior does not necessarily involve more people—it could still happen between two students. But if both students live in Northern Ireland, and one is a Roman Catholic and the other a Protestant, the social climate and specific context in which they meet can influence whether they treat each other as individuals or interact as members of their respective social groups. Social psychologists distinguish between interpersonal and intergroup behavior to study the different factors that influence the way people relate to others. But it is impossible to draw a distinct line between the two types of interaction. That is because people's perceptual biases and stereotypes about certain groups influence the way they perceive others when they first meet them.

Usually the way people interact on a one-to-one basis depends on the relationship they have with one another. Not only does people's interaction with friends differ from their relationship with strangers, but longstanding friends are more likely to interact as individuals, while strangers often perceive each other (at least initially) in terms of the social groups they do or do not share, such as sex, race, or occupation.

adjustment to and between the people involved. Depending on the variety of their social experiences and observations, these people will have varying collections of stored information about which social behaviors will cause others to respond in certain ways in certain situations—and it is this experience that helps them make sense of another's use of language, facial expression, gaze, body language, and tone of voice. The body language people use depends on the kind of relationship they have with another person, and it can sometimes convey more information than any number of words. Yet as we have seen, despite people's previous experience and knowledge, they are still likely to make unjustified assumptions because they are usually biased in their perceptions and interpretations of others' behavior. It is also important that they understand any cultural differences in communication patterns to minimize the risk of being misinterpreted. For example, while certain facial expressions seem to be universally used and understood (*see* Vol. 2, pp. 86–109), most nonverbal communication is learned within a specific culture.

> ***"The body acts as a medium for communicating things about the interaction itself."***
>
> ***—Alan Radley, 1996***

Other social skills

Social competence also requires various other components, such as assertiveness, empathy, social intelligence, problem-solving behavior, and "rewardingness." The last term refers to some people's tendency to reward others by praising, helping, protecting, or advising them, or by offering encouragement or showing sympathy. Research has shown that people who engage in rewarding behavior are more popular and more successful at influencing others, keeping the rewarders in the situation or the relationship.

Assertive people can control social situations without resorting to aggression, which would damage the relationship. Empathic people take into consideration what others are trying to achieve and show concern for others' feelings. People who show empathy generally avoid disruptions in their relationships and are more successful in cooperating. People with social intelligence are good at interpreting social situations. By understanding the nature and rules of a situation, they are more likely to solve problems through effective negotiation. Michael Argyle called these skills social intelligence because they require people to apply their social knowledge, although he pointed out that they do some of these things automatically as the products of what is sometimes called common sense. Just as skilled drivers do not think about every turn of the wheel, people are not conscious of all the little things they do to relate successfully to others.

> ***"People cannot tell us how they… fall in love or manage other relationships, any more than they can explain how they walk or ride a bicycle."***
> ***—Michael Argyle, 1994***

Natural selection

Evolutionary psychologists contend that people's dominant tendencies and behaviors have become genetically programmed because they were in some way useful to our survival as a species (*see* Vol. 1, pp. 134–143). Relating to others is perhaps one of the most obviously useful of these tendencies: Infants cannot survive without an adult's care, and those who remain close to a caregiver and maintain this relationship until they are able to survive by themselves are more likely to stay alive, become adults, and reproduce. People therefore have a drive to seek nurturing and supportive relationships—an urge known as dependency, which many believe originates in the dependency infants have on their mothers.

Relationships with the opposite sex may also have given people reproductive advantages during their evolutionary history. Even other biological drives such as the need for food and shelter may have contributed to this tendency to relate to others because it was easier (and even essential) to cooperate to accomplish the necessary tasks. Thus it is likely that we have an innate urge to search for safety and cooperation in our close relationships, and to form family units so we can offer security to our children.

AFFILIATION

Psychologists researching motivation have also treated affiliation (relating to others) as an important need in its own right and

Riding a bicycle requires a sense of balance, good muscle coordination, accurate visual processing, and many other mental processes of which we are largely unaware. Managing a successful social interaction is just as complicated—requiring numerous mental tasks that we tackle in a similarly unconscious manner.

Some psychologists believe that people's desire to form close relationships originates in their dependency on their mothers. This desire appears to be stronger in some people than others, however, and some researchers have tried to explain the reasons for this discrepancy.

wondered whether people differ in the extent to which they experience this need. Studies by David McClelland in 1987, for example, demonstrated that people with a strong tendency to seek close relationships were less self-centered and more warm, loving, and cooperative than those in whom this trait was less apparent.

Social comparison

One of the most important contributions to current understanding of the ways in which people relate to each other was made by Stanley Schachter, a professor at Columbia University (*see* box p. 43). In his book *The Psychology of Affiliation* (1959) Schachter discussed how adults are more likely to show dependency and seek affiliation when they find themselves in new situations that make them anxious or afraid. He found that volunteers who believed they would receive electric shocks in an experiment preferred to wait with others for their turn to participate rather than sit alone—but only if the other people in the waiting room were subjects in the same experiment. In other words, the volunteers sought the company of people who were confronting the same difficulty. If such company was not available, they tended to prefer to wait alone. This suggested that the volunteers were not merely looking for distraction from their fear when they sought the company of others. Furthermore, since none of the participants already knew one another, they obviously did not choose their company on the basis of closer relationships. The most likely explanation for this behavior is that when people are unsure about a situation, they tend to look to others faced with the same problem for guidance on their own behavior, opinions, and even emotions. Social psychologists call the process of measuring our behavior against that of others to help us decide how we should react social comparison.

Social support

Schater's findings suggest that we don't just seek the company of those who can provide physical safety and protection (dependency); we also seek instrumental and emotional reassurance. Instrumental support can be given by someone who is familiar with a situation; it provides practical help and advice on how to cope. Emotional support consists of sympathy, listening, understanding, empathy, and encouragement. Although the subjects in Schachter's experiment were looking only for temporary company, they engaged in social comparison with others who shared their experience (and could therefore understand how they felt). That provided them with both emotional support and instrumental social support as they sought to learn from each other how best to cope with the frightening situation.

We particularly tend to value social support in longer-term relationships. If people are experiencing specific problems, they may even get together in support groups to provide each other with mutual instrumental backup and emotional bolstering—for example, the members of Alcoholics Anonymous. This suggests that our affiliation with others who can share our problems and our joys is not only pleasant but good for us. Psychologists interested in relationships and mental health have established that people who have social support available to them are less depressed and suffer less when under stress (*see* box p. 46). They have also highlighted how we seek to compare and share our experiences, our emotions, the meaning of our world, and the meaning of relationships themselves. Steve Duck, professor of interpersonal communication at the University of Iowa, points out that being in a relationship means focusing on trying to understand how another person thinks about life events and experiences.

> ***"A personal relationship . . . is about* sharing *meaning."***
> ***—Steve Duck, 1994***

Self-esteem

Researchers into self-concept and identity have established that our self-esteem is strongly linked to the extent and type of affiliation we have with others. Although we need friends, we also need a sense of our distinctness from other people. This means that in relating to others, we have to find a balance between satisfying our need for affiliation (forming relationships and being part of groups) and being sufficiently different to have an identity of our own. Teenagers who act in ways that are considered antisocial by their parents are often merely attempting to establish their own identities. On the other hand, people often join certain social groups (from street gangs to exclusive clubs) because belonging provides them with a positive social identity. If they feel that a certain group is respected, admired, or considered "cool" by people who matter to them, belonging to that group can make them feel good about themselves (*see* pp. 50–71 and Vol. 1, pp. 152–161).

Loneliness and ostracism

While many researchers now measure the need for affiliation in terms of people's desire for intimacy, the original concept proposed by McClelland consisted mainly of people's need to avoid rejection, criticism, conflict, and isolation. Most people need and appreciate some time and space to themselves, while knowing that close relationships are available when they need them. This balance is important. Loneliness can cause depression; and social exclusion of any kind, even if it is just in a single situation, is an extremely uncomfortable experience.

In 1997 Kipling Williams and Kristin Sommer illustrated the effects of social exclusion in an experiment conducted at the University of New South Wales, Australia. They placed each participant in a waiting room with two confederates, whom the participant believed were other students who had volunteered to take part in an experiment. While they were waiting, all three threw a ball to each other across

FOCUS ON

Stanley Schachter

One of the most influential social psychologists, Stanley Schachter (born 1922) studied many forms of communication and social influence, including group processes, sources of the affiliation motive, the significance of birth order, and the nature of emotional experience. He also looked at people's ability to attribute their behavior correctly to external versus internal causes, studied the causes of obesity and eating behavior disorders, the addictive nature of nicotine, and people's psychological reactions to events that affect stock market prices and their interpretations of "filled" pauses, such as "uh" and "er," in speech. Remarkably, he concluded that just a few powerful theoretical concepts could account for the diverse content of all these studies. In 1983 he was elected to the National Academy of Sciences.

Stanley Schachter studies mass social phenomena and the effects of cognitive, social, and physiological variables on cravings and addictive behaviors.

People often join social groups because belonging provides them with a social identity. Many people, for example, would consider the behavior of street gangs to be violent and antisocial. But for members, belonging to a gang can be a positive experience, earning them the admiration and respect of their peers and improving their self-esteem.

the room. But after a few minutes the two confederates stopped throwing the ball to the participant, thereby excluding this person from the game. This situation was videotaped, and it was obvious from the recordings how uncomfortable this experience of social ostracism was to the naïve participants, despite the fact that it was only about a casual ball game with strangers. They were clearly embarrassed and self-conscious, and showed a strong need to find something else to do. Even people watching the recordings reported feeling extremely uncomfortable, even though the events did not affect them personally. So, avoiding isolation, loneliness, or ostracism is likely to be a major reason for people to seek affiliation.

Duncan Cramer of Loughborough University, England, conducted an extensive review of studies into close relationships. He concluded that people who have supportive relationships are not only less psychologically distressed, but also tend to live longer than those who do not. Although Cramer conceded that not enough longitudinal studies (research conducted by collecting data repeatedly from the same participants over a period of time) have been carried out to be sure how this link is caused, the evidence we have suggests that good relationships have a beneficial effect on health and on longevity. An alternative explanation would be that people who are mentally and physically healthy are more likely to form relationships than those who are not. However, there is no evidence to support this link between well-being and successful relationships. It is possible, of course, that both explanations apply to a certain extent (*see* box p. 46).

Group influence on behavior

This need for affiliation can influence people's behavior in groups. In his famous experiments of 1951 Schachter showed the massive pressures to conform that are brought to bear on deviants from any group norm and the sorts of punishment that are meted out to those who fail to toe the line (*see* pp. 50–71). His studies also showed the incentives or the "carrot" side of group pressure—dissidents who change their opinion to agree with the majority may be fully forgiven for the error of their ways. Schachter also showed how people's interpretations of situations are crucially influenced by the opinions of the people with whom they happen to be at the time. Physical and emotional distance are also vital in determining who communicates with whom—university freshmen are more likely to express the same views as contemporaries sharing the same dorm than to agree with second-year students living on the other side of the campus.

The desire for achievement

Another human attribute that influences people's desire for affiliation and their behavior in social groups is their need for achievement. David C. McClelland and his associates at Harvard University studied this attribute for more than 20 years, reaching the conclusion that the need for achievement is a distinct human motive that is intense in some people and less conspicuous in others (maybe most).

The achievement motive can be isolated and assessed in any group, and McClelland illustrated some of its characteristics in a laboratory experiment.

Participants were asked to throw rings over a peg from any distance they chose. Most people tended to throw at random—now close, now far away—but individuals with a high need for achievement seemed to carefully measure where they were most likely to do best, neither too close to make the task ridiculously easy nor too far away to make it impossible. They set themselves difficult but potentially achievable goals.

McClelland maintains that competitive people engage in an activity only if they know they can influence the outcome. They are not gamblers, preferring to work on a problem rather than leaving the outcome to chance, while people who are less competitive tend to be far more extreme in their attitude to risk, either favoring wild, speculative gambling or minimizing their exposure to losses.

Competitive people also seem to be more concerned with the victory itself rather than with the rewards of success. They derive greater satisfaction from solving a problem or winning a game than from any praise they might receive as a consequence. Even money primarily provides them with a means of assessing their performance and comparing their progress with those of others. Although praise is less important than for many people, highfliers do tend to seek feedback on how well they are doing. They are not interested in comments about personal characteristics, such as how cooperative or helpful they are, but just want to be weighed in the balance and not found wanting. Consequently, they are often found in sales jobs or run their own businesses (*see* box below).

McClelland found that achievement-motivated people are likely to have had parents who expected them to start showing some independence between the ages of six and eight, making choices and doing things without help—such as taking care of themselves around the house and finding their way around the neighborhood. This contrasts with other parents who tend either to expect their children to show independence before they are ready or to smother their children, restricting their personality development. The first extreme seems to foster passive, defeated attitudes by making children feel unwanted in the home and incompetent away from it. The other extreme tends to produce overprotected or overdisciplined children who become dependent on their parents and find it difficult to break away and make their own decisions.

PSYCHOLOGY & SOCIETY

Ambition in the Workplace

Why do achievement-motivated people behave as they do? McClelland claims it is because they habitually spend time thinking about doing things better. He found that whenever people start to think in achievement terms, they seem to make things happen. College students with a high need for achievement, for instance, will generally get better grades than equally bright students with weaker achievement needs, while achievement-motivated employees tend to receive more raises and are promoted faster because they are constantly trying to think of better ways of doing things. McClelland even extended his analysis to countries and related the presence of a large percentage of achievement-motivated individuals to increased national economic growth.

But while achievement-motivated people can be the backbone of a business organization, what can be said about their potential as managers? They get ahead as individuals because they get things done; but once they are promoted, their success starts to depend not only on their own work but on the activities of others. Since they are highly job oriented and work to their capacity, they tend to expect others to do the same. Unfortunately, they may lack the skills and patience to effectively manage people who are competent but have a higher need for affiliation. In this situation a high achiever's preoccupation with success frustrates others and keeps them from maximizing their potential. So high achievers may need to develop their interpersonal skills to be good managers.

The Herzberg link

McClelland's ideas are related to the motivation-hygiene theory proposed by Frederick Herzberg and his colleagues in 1991. They were researching what makes people happy or unhappy in their work and identified two groups of factors that contributed to employee satisfaction. The first set—called intrinsic factors or motivators—included being credited for work, having a manager's trust, being allowed to work without supervision, being given responsibility, and advancing in position. The second set of factors—called extrinsic, maintenance, or hygiene factors—included the workplace, salaries, the management, and general company policies. Herzberg found that although inadequate extrinsic factors (those that related to the working environment) did cause some unhappiness, they did not provide long-term motivation and job satisfaction. They found it was far more important for managers to develop good working relationships with their staff.

EXPERIMENT

Well-being and Belief

Karin Marson, a social psychologist at London Guildhall University, UK, conducted a series of studies in 2001 that provided a link between fear of exclusion and the health benefits of relationships. She found inclusion and relationships were not the only important factors for mental health. The beliefs we hold about our own possibilities for relating to others are also important. Her research showed that people who believe it is easy to become accepted within social groups (work teams, occupational groups, student societies, tutorial groups, and new cultures in the case of refugee resettlement) have significantly better mental health (higher self-esteem and fewer symptoms of depression) than those who expect difficulty in gaining acceptance by others.

Marson was also interested to see whether this link between well-being and beliefs about social acceptance was a universal human phenomenon or specific to western culture, with its many social groups and categories. In 1999 she went on an expedition to the Amazonian jungle and studied indigenous children and teenagers who had no experience of belonging to any social groups other than their tribe and immediate family. She was particularly interested in the beliefs of young people who planned to leave the jungle when they became adults to gain knowledge of the outer world and find work. The results of her study showed that the more these young people believed it would be easy to gain acceptance by the new people with whom they would work, the happier and more positive they were about their future and about growing up. Thus it seems that both relating and belonging are good for us, and that it is important to our well-being to believe that we have the option to relate and belong should we choose to do so.

DEVELOPING RELATIONSHIPS

Psychologists used to believe that newborn infants had no social skills, and that social interaction was initially a one-sided effort from the caregiver. During the 1970s, however, developmental and social psychologists began to study videos of mother-infant communication (*see* Vol. 4, pp. 24–39). They found that even babies as young as a few days old were remarkably good at contributing to social interactions. Thus it seems infants participate actively in forming relationships with their carers a short time after birth.

> ***"The effective attachment between infant and mother can start before birth."***
> ***—Colwyn Trevarthen, 1992***

We now know that babies can start to form their first relationship before they are even born. During pregnancy a fetus learns the specific vocal features of the mother's voice (*see* Vol. 4, pp. 6–23), developing an affinity for this familiar sound in preference to the voice of any other woman—a tendency noticeable just a few hours after birth.

Infants also start forming relationships with other caregivers, including their fathers, grandparents, and older siblings, although caregivers may also be people who are not related to the child. Most contemporary researchers agree that the development of a positive, stable, secure, and close relationship with one or more primary caregivers, whoever they may be, is crucially important to an infant's psychological well-being (*see* box p. 48).

Different types of relationships

In the course of our lives we form many different types of relationships, initially with our parents, siblings, other family members, or caregivers, then with friends and classmates. Later on we have work- and leisure-related acquaintances, close friendships, and intimate sexual and romantic relationships. Dorothy Miell and Rudi Dallos pointed out that each of these relationships fulfill a different need and function, and therefore they are not interchangeable. So it is not the overall amount of social contact that matters, but the quality and variety, so that all our social needs are met.

All relationships depend on a certain degree of attraction between the people involved, and close relationships are based primarily on attraction, liking, and love. But how do these feelings develop? While group membership may influence people's choice of friends to some degree, it seems that proximity, rather than magnetism or social rapport, is an important factor.

The proximity effect

In 1950 Leon Festinger and his colleagues studied friendship trends among students in university accommodation. They found that students in adjacent rooms were more likely to become friends and concluded that proximity led to repeated chance encounters that increased familiarity and finally attraction. Social psychologist Muzafer Sherif developed this idea in the 1960s, conducting a field experiment with groups of teenage boys at a summer camp. He found that even established friendships could be affected by proximity and group membership. Boys who had already formed friendships and were subsequently assigned to different cabins tended to replace their initial relationships with friends from their "own group" (cabin), and by the end of the summer most friendships were between boys staying in the same cabin. Sherif's studies showed that belonging to certain social groups can strongly influence the development and maintenance of friendships no matter how unimportant the basis of a grouping may be. His findings were not conclusive, however, because all the boys came from the same broad social context: If their values, interests, attitudes, and beliefs had varied, it is possible that the results might have been quite different.

A more recent study by Karin Marson (2001) has shown that even the number of friendships people form can be influenced by proximity. She conducted field studies among first-year students on a campus at the University of London, UK, and found that students living in large halls of residence made more acquaintances than those in smaller units. By the end of the first year these students had also formed significantly more close friendships.

How do we form friendships? Are we influenced by shared attitudes and interests, or are more arbitrary factors such as physical proximity a more major cause? Studies of people in shared accommodation, such as these children at summer camp, have suggested that the repeated chance encounters caused by physical closeness are a major factor in friendship formation.

Maintaining relationships

Once attraction and liking have been established, relationships can develop, and the way this happens depends partly on the social competencies of the relationship partners. As we have seen, people with more "rewardingness" tend to be more popular, and the extent to which friends reward each other will influence the development of their relationship.

FOCUS ON

ATTACHMENT

The view that family relationships are particularly important influences in our lives is shared by researchers interested in attachment (*see* pp. 94–117). They argue that people who experience consistency and warmth from their caregivers in infancy and childhood develop an idea of themselves as lovable and of other people as reliable, consistent, and warm. From an attachment perspective problematic relationships in adulthood might be linked to attachment experiences in infancy.

Social psychologists Cindy Hazan and Philip Shaver explored this link in 1987. Using attachment theory as a basis, they studied adult love relationships, discovering that attachment in adult romantic relationships was similar to that in relationships between infants and caregivers. They also found that depending on their attachment style, adults reported different beliefs about the nature and course of romantic love and about the availability and trustworthiness of love partners.

The fact that the same attachment styles can be found among adults and children does not necessarily mean that any one person keeps the same attachment style from childhood into adulthood. Other researchers have investigated this topic since, however, and in line with attachment theory evidence from long-term population surveys suggests that adults who experienced rejection in their relationships with their parents report lower self-esteem than those who did not. Thus it seems people's family relationships not only have a powerful influence on their behavior while they are still part of the family system, but their early experiences of close relationships may have an effect on how they feel about themselves and how they relate to others in adulthood.

Research has also shown that lasting relationships are characterized by concern for the other person's needs—not just the personal rewards. Nevertheless, people are most satisfied when they feel they are receiving their fair share, bearing in mind their own contribution—a tendency called equity theory. The same theory proposes that people are dissatisfied in situations in which they benefit more than they feel they should. In 1987 Karen Rook at the University of California demonstrated how equity and reciprocity (mutual rewarding) are important in friendships. She found that elderly women felt lonely when they believed they either overbenefited or underbenefited in their friendships, although equity was not as important to their satisfaction in their relationships with their adult children. This highlights the point made earlier that different types of relationships fulfill different functions.

> ***"A relationship can, perhaps, be seen like a snowball rolling in the snow: Where it has rolled and what it has incorporated into it affects how it behaves in the future, what more it can absorb and how it can grow."***
>
> ***—Rudi Dallos, 1996***

Another influential factor in friendship maintenance seems to be the extent to which people respect the "relationship rules." Most of these rules are not written down, and many are not even explicitly taught, but they encompass certain basic expectations that people have about their relationships. Different sets of rules apply to different relationships, such as those with friends, lovers, and work colleagues.

Social systems

Some social psychologists offer an alternative perspective on relationships and the ways in which they influence individuals. Building on ideas proposed by psychiatrist Murray Bowen in the 1970s, these researchers emphasize that psychologists should not merely study individuals and their behavior, but should also bear in mind that each person is part of several social systems: groups of people that function as an entity, such as a family, a work group, or a sports team. They argue that membership in these social systems determines the behavior of the individual (*see* box p. 48).

The family as a system is a particularly important influence on its members. Some researchers maintain that the behavior of adolescents cannot really be explained unless it is considered within the broader context of how the entire family functions—a view that highlights how relationships can do more than just add something to people's lives. Family members and people in other close groups are all mutually dependent and constantly influence each other. Changes in one person's life inevitably introduce changes for all other members of the system.

Conflict and relationship breakdown

Numerous psychological studies have shown that relationships break down most commonly when one or more members fail to adhere to the unwritten rules. In friendships, for example, some of the most important reasons for people falling out were discussing with others what was said in confidence, being intolerant of other friends and relationships, and not volunteering to help in time of need.

> ***"The problem is not so much getting married, which is achieved by most people, but staying married."***
>
> ***—Michael Argyle, 1994***

Friendship rules also need to be respected in marriage, along with more specific rules such as being faithful, showing affection and emotional support, and having sex. In 1985 Michael Argyle and Monika Henderson stated that "divorce is the most acute problem in the whole field of social relationships," and this still applies today. Although divorce is one of the most distressing and damaging life events, a large proportion of people still choose to get married, and research shows that marriage provides greater satisfaction and health benefits than any other form of relationship. Argyle and Henderson also suggest that many break-ups could be avoided if people were more aware of the rules and realized that conflict and argument are a normal part of both marriage and other relationships.

Marriage breakups can be devastating for both the adults and the children involved —a subject depicted in the 1979 film Kramer vs. Kramer. *In it Dustin Hoffman portrays a father's struggle to provide a suitably nurturing environment for his son after his wife walks out and leaves them both struggling to come to terms with her rejection.*

CONNECTIONS

- Cross-cultural Psychology: Volume 1, pp. 152–161
- Fetal Development: Volume 4, pp. 6–23
- Infant Cognition: Volume 4, pp. 24–39
- Emotional Development: Volume 4, pp. 112–129
- Social Development: Volume 4, pp. 130–149
- People as Social Animals: pp. 6–27
- Relating to Society: pp. 50–71
- Communication: pp. 94–117

Relating to Society

"Man seeketh society in comfort, use, and protection."

Francis Bacon

Most of us desire the companionship and acceptance of others, and in social situations that can have a powerful effect on our thoughts and behavior, even when we are in the company of strangers. Certain social situations can influence our attitudes and our tendency to help others, while other situations can cause us to come into conflict with other members of society.

Everyone is part of human society and has some kind of relationship with others—even hermits who avoid company and people who are shunned by their peers. Most of us choose to belong to some social groups; but we are also influenced by other people we encounter, be they work associates, traveling companions, authority figures, or strangers on the street.

Agreeing with others

Most of us prefer to be accepted by other people, and we are often willing to change our behavior to fit in with a social group even on a temporary basis. We do so by trying to understand the norms and rules of a group, conforming to avoid rejection. Social psychologists have observed that our strong need to be accepted makes us conform to group norms even in unusual situations. In one of the earliest studies of conformity, published in 1936, Muzafer Sherif (*see* box p. 51) showed how quickly people can "fall in line." In Sherif's experiment participants sat in a darkened room and were asked to say how far a pinpoint of light moved. In fact the light did not move at all: Any movement people thought they saw was an optical illusion. Initially participants were asked to make their estimates while alone in the room. They were then asked to sit in a small

Most of us encounter many different social situations during our lives, and the people around us can greatly influence our behavior. Picture yourself in the beach scene below, for example, and consider how the behavior of others might influence your decision to go swimming, to play loud music, or perhaps to sunbathe topless.

BIOGRAPHY

MUZAFER SHERIF

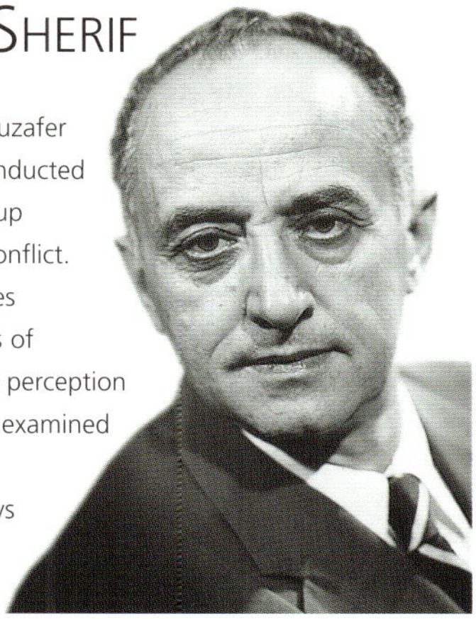

Turkish psychologist Muzafer Sherif (1906–1988) conducted classic research on group processes and group conflict. His most famous studies investigated the effects of conformity on people's perception of optical illusions and examined conflict and resolution between groups of boys staying in Robbers Cave State Park (*see* p. 64). His best-known book, *The Psychology of Social Norms*, was published in 1936.

Sherif obtained his PhD at Columbia University in 1935. He returned to the United States in 1944 after he was jailed in Turkey for criticizing Nazism.

group and to call their previous estimates out loud. Sherif found that participants gave varying answers when they were on their own; but when they had to call out their answers so that others could hear, their estimates of the light's movement became more consistent. Gradually they conformed to what others in the group said, even if these answers were different than those they had given originally.

> ***"We must all hang together, or assuredly we shall all hang separately."***
> ***—Benjamin Franklin, 1776***

But how far will people go to conform to the norms established by other group members? Will they conform even if they know a norm is incorrect or immoral? In the early 1950s Solomon Asch (*see* pp. 29–33) conducted experiments in which participants sat in groups and looked at a series of cards with lines on them (*see* diagram above, right). They were asked to judge which of the lines on one card was the same length as a single line on another card. Although the task was easy, all the group members apart from one were "plants" who had agreed to give the wrong answer. Out of 18 trials in which his accomplices gave a unanimous wrong answer, Asch found that the participants gave the same wrong answer more than 35 percent of the time, with almost 75 percent succumbing to peer pressure at least once, even though it was obvious that the other members of the group were wrong.

Asch's research shows that social situations can have a powerful influence on our behavior and decisions. One of the reasons for this is that we seem to have a natural desire to fit in and to be accepted by others, being willing to conform to a majority opinion (even if it differs from our own) and to modify our behavior to avoid standing out from the crowd.

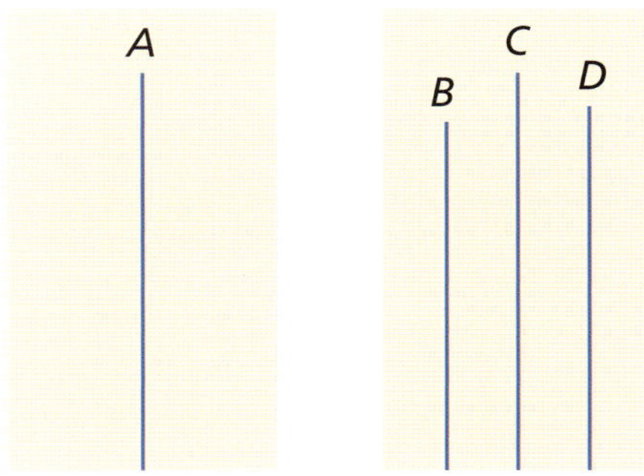

If you were asked to say which of the lines B, C, and D was the same length as line A, you would probably choose line C. But would you still make the same choice if several other people said it was line D?

COMPLIANCE

Another consequence of our desire to be accepted by others is that we often comply when we are asked to do things. We find it particularly hard to refuse when friends ask us to do a favor, for example, and we may even struggle to deny requests from complete strangers. Compliance is a part of everyday life: Employers want it from their employees, parents want it from their children, and salespeople want it from their customers. So why is it so difficult to say "no"? As we have seen, one reason is our natural desire to fit in: Most of us would prefer to be described as a can-do person rather than as a dissident. Another reason, however, is that the people making the requests often use powerful techniques to make us agree with them.

In 1978, building on the work of other researchers such as Sherif and Ned Jones, social psychologist Robert Cialdini went undercover for three years to learn what kind of compliance techniques people use in work-related situations. He enrolled in a variety of training programs to learn how to sell everything from vacuum cleaners and encyclopedias to real estate and cars; posed as an aspiring professional in advertising, fund-raising organizations, and public relations; and talked to religious cult members and political lobbyists. At the end of all this research he concluded that as well as consensus (agreeing with others), five other principles influence people's compliance: liking, reciprocity, consistency, scarcity, and authority.

Liking

We are more likely to comply with requests from people we like than from those we don't. Salespeople realize this and use a wide range of ingratiation techniques to encourage customers to like them. They may dress well to appear attractive, smile a lot to seem friendly, and try to find things in common with the customer (for example, they might talk about the fact that they grew up in the same city). They might also try to develop a rapport by finding ways to flatter or compliment the customer. Ingratiation is certainly effective, but it works only for as long as people believe the perpetrator is sincere: There are few worse turnoffs than false friendliness.

Reciprocity

Cialdini also found that we are more willing to comply with a request if the person making it has already done us some kind of favor. We often feel a strong need to reciprocate, or return the favor. One common persuasion method based on this tendency is called the door-in-the-face technique: People make a huge request, which they expect to be refused (equivalent to the door being shut in their face), then follow it up with a far smaller one. For example, a salesperson might ask a customer to buy a computer for $3,000. If the customer says that is too much, the salesperson "talks to the manager" about reducing the cost and offers a greatly reduced price of $1,500. The customer then recognizes that the salesperson has made a concession by reducing the price

> ***"Upon further investigation and research I noticed that influence was not just an art. There was a science to it as well."***
> ***—Robert Cialdini, 2001***

KEY POINTS

- We are naturally social creatures, tending to behave in ways that ensure the acceptance and liking of others.
- Many of us go to great lengths to conform to group opinion, even going against our better judgment.
- Complying with requests is also common, and we use various techniques to make compliance more likely.
- We tend to obey people whom we perceive as having authority over us, and those figures who are hugely successful at influencing others often become leaders.
- As members of society, we develop attitudes that can influence our behavior. When we behave in ways that contradict our attitudes, we suffer cognitive dissonance.
- Other people can persuade us to change our attitudes.
- We are often guilty of stereotyping; and if we evaluate certain groups unfavorably, we are displaying prejudice.
- Prejudice can be reduced if opposing groups work together to achieve a common goal. An example is the Jigsaw Classroom, where cooperation is vital for success.
- Helping others is generally part of our social nature, although sometimes an aspect of the situation we are in will prevent us from helping someone.
- Sometimes we behave antisocially by being aggressive. That may be because we hope to achieve something, or because we are angry, emotional, or even drunk.

Have you ever been persuaded to take part in a survey? And if so, how were you convinced? Market researchers often try to ensure your cooperation by dressing smartly, smiling a lot, and by trying to develop a friendly rapport—all ways of encouraging you to like them.

and feels obliged to return the favor by buying the computer, which may have been worth $1,500 all along.

A related tactic is the "and that's-not-all" technique. For example, a salesperson may describe all the features of an item and tell the customer the price, but wait until the very end to offer some kind of bonus, saying something like ". . . and if you buy this computer today, I'll even give you a printer for free." Once again this makes customers think the salesperson has done them a good turn and makes them feel they should return the favor.

Consistency

Other compliance techniques play on our desire to be consistent with choices we have already made. The foot-in-the-door technique involves making a small request and then following it up with a much larger one. For instance, market survey researchers may say their questions will take about 10 minutes; but once they have entered someone's house, they can often spin out an interview for an hour without objection. Why? Because asking them to leave would be inconsistent with the original choice to cooperate.

The lowball technique operates on a similar principle. A salesperson might begin by offering a customer a good deal, such as a cheap price on an item; and after the customer has agreed to buy the item, he or she raises the price, saying something like "I forgot about the delivery fee I have to charge." At this point the customer has already agreed to buy the item and will often continue with the purchase even though the price has been raised.

Scarcity

Other compliance techniques are based on the principle that we are more willing to comply with a request if we feel we are being offered an opportunity that won't last long. For example, a salesperson wanting to sell a computer might say something like "I don't know how much longer I'll have this computer...yesterday a couple of people said they would return to buy it this afternoon." In this case the salesperson is using the fast-approaching-deadline technique, which gives customers the impression that if they don't buy the goods immediately, they may miss out.

We may also comply with a request if we think we are being offered a rare opportunity, because we don't want to miss out. For example, a salesperson who can convince customers that a particular product is not available in any other stores will often increase his or her chances of selling the product. This is known as the hard-to-get technique.

Compliance in everyday life

Cialdini established the six principles by studying business professionals, but most of us use compliance techniques. As social beings, we have to make requests all the time. Parents, children, wives, husbands, employers, employees, and teachers all require others to comply. For example, parents may use the door-in-the-face technique to persuade their teenagers to come home at a reasonable time. If a mother wants her son home at 10:00 p.m. and feels sure he will ask to come home at midnight, she might tell him to be in by 8:00 p.m. When he objects, she may then appear to compromise by saying, "Well, OK, but make sure you're home by 10:00 p.m." Her son will then feel she has made a concession by extending her original deadline and feel obliged to make a similar concession by agreeing.

Similarly, the son may use the foot-in-the-door technique to persuade a friend to give him a ride to two stores. He might begin by asking for a ride to one store that isn't too far away; then if his friend says yes, he may ask to go to another store that isn't too far from the first one.

> ***"The thing that impresses me most about America is the way parents obey their children."***
>
> ***—Edward VIII, 1957***

Like most people, his friend will feel some pressure to make consistent decisions and will probably end up agreeing to the second request, since it is similar to the first one.

AUTHORITY FIGURES

Cialdini listed authority as the sixth principle—and various studies of conformity and compliance have shown how we try to make our opinions and behavior similar to those of other people when asked to do so by an authority figure.

Most us comply readily with instructions from people we regard as authority figures, such as police officers, school teachers, and government officials—and uniforms can be important symbols of this authority. Leonard Bickman, professor of psychology at Vanderbilt University, demonstrated this in 1974. His research assistant approached people on the sidewalks of New York City and asked them to pick a small paper bag off the ground. When the assistant was dressed in a police-style uniform, almost everyone complied with his request; but when he was dressed in a milk-delivery uniform or in regular civilian clothes, far fewer people did as he asked of them.

Some of the most famous research projects in social psychology were designed to study people's obedience—several experiments resulting from observations of what happened during World War II (1939–1945), when thousands of Nazis murdered millions of Jews. Were they insane or just ordinary people following the orders of a higher authority?

People tend to comply more readily with requests from authority figures, and wearing a uniform is a clear way of demonstrating that authority. Leonard Bickman found that people dressed in police uniform were particularly effective in gaining compliance.

FOCUS ON

STANLEY MILGRAM

Stanley Milgram (1933–1984) began studying social psychology at Harvard, where he worked under Solomon Asch. After graduating in 1960, he spent seven years teaching at Harvard and Yale Universities before accepting a position at the City University of New York.

Much of Milgram's research focused on obedience and the psychology of living in large cities, and he was known for his creative approach. His most controversial studies were concerned with obedience (*see* main text), and they provoked a great deal of criticism about the ethics of deceiving participants. Despite this, most psychologists would agree that Milgram's experiments revealed an important truth about human nature: Most people will sometimes do cruel things to obey a higher authority.

Milgram was also famous for an experiment researching community attitudes that employed what became known as the lost-letter technique. He and his colleagues dropped addressed envelopes all around New Haven, Connecticut, to see whether people would help by putting the letters in the mail. They found that people helped more when the letters were addressed to groups that seemed benign—such as "Research Associates"—than when the letters were addressed to more controversial groups such as "Friends of the Nazis."

In 1961 and 1962 Stanley Milgram (*see* box above) conducted a controversial series of experiments at Yale University to see just how willing ordinary people were to obey an authority figure. In the first set of experiments he invited some men to participate in what they thought was a study of learning and punishment. They were told that during the experiment they would be "teachers," that a man in another room would be the learner, and that they would have to administer electric shocks to the learner each time he gave an incorrect answer. Throughout the study the teachers sat in front of an electricity generator with a series of switches that supposedly administered increasingly painful shocks: The setup was realistic, but no real shocks were administered, and the learner was an actor.

Shocking results

During the experiment the learner gave many wrong answers. Every time he made a mistake, the teacher—who was the real subject of the research—was asked to administer increasingly stronger shocks. After a few shocks the learner began objecting: "Experimenter, get me out of here! I won't be in the experiment anymore! I refuse to go on!" But each time he protested, the experimenter ignored him and told the teacher to continue. The results were alarming: 63 percent of the teachers went all the way up to the maximum 450-volt shock switch.

The results surprised mental health experts. When Milgram described the experiment to psychiatrists without revealing the results, they predicted that most of the participants would quit before administering the 450-volt shock.

> ***"Often it is not so much the kind of person a man is as the kind of situation in which he finds himself that determines how he will act."***
> ***—Stanley Milgram, 1974***

Even Milgram was surprised at his volunteers' willingness to do whatever was asked of them, so he went on to try and identify the factors that influenced such remarkable obedience. In later studies he found that the teachers quit the experiment sooner if the learner could be seen and heard, presumably because they saw him suffering. He also found that they quit sooner if the experimenter instructed them over the telephone rather than while standing in the same room. Apparently the closer an authority figure is, the more likely people are to obey.

One of the most important lessons of Milgram's experiments is that ordinary people under the influence of a higher authority sometimes act against their better judgment. Like the participants in Asch's experiments on conformity, they found it difficult to resist the pressure of a social situation. While it is tempting to think that people who conform to group norms or who obey authority figures are lacking in conscience, there is a better explanation—they do these things because they desire social acceptance and thus find it difficult to resist the influence of others.

Leadership

Successful leadership requires a certain kind of authority that depends on several factors, including personality. In the 1980s psychologists such as Robert House, Jay Conger, and Jane Howell researched the powerful influence that a particular type of leader—called a transformational leader—can have over his or her followers. They cited examples such as Mohandas K. Gandhi and Winston Churchill, describing how they influenced huge groups of loyal followers, inspiring them to work hard and make personal sacrifices for a cause.

One of the best-known transformational leaders in U.S. history is Martin Luther King, Jr., who campaigned for racial equality. He inspired people to pursue this goal with impassioned speeches and letters. By setting a clear personal example, he taught people how to draw attention to the cause by engaging in peaceful protest.

Transformational leaders motivate their followers by setting clear goals, explaining the benefits in ways that make the goals seem deeply important and meaningful, and by teaching their followers the specific things they need to do to accomplish these goals. Gandhi, for instance, campaigned for an independent and unified India, making it clear how millions of people would benefit and encouraging his followers to march in rallies and boycott certain non-Indian products.

> ***"Leadership defines what the future should look like, aligns people with that vision, and inspires them to make it happen."***
> ***—John Kotter, 1996***

Transformational leaders also have particular personality traits. They usually have excellent communication skills that they use to motivate and teach people, perhaps making stirring speeches or writing moving letters that inspire their followers to work toward a goal. They have high levels of self-confidence and believe in their own ability to succeed, which inspires others to believe in them. They are energetic and hard-working, and they can demonstrate that they care sincerely about their followers.

Transformational leaders do not always inspire their followers to do good things, however. Adolf Hitler convinced millions of Germans to support his campaign to eliminate Jews from German society by appealing to people's sense of patriotism and by describing what he thought was needed to restore the country's economy.

Some leaders may find it difficult to reconcile the conflicting requirements of achieving their goals and caring for their followers or subordinates. Consequently, they may choose to become one of two types of leader: task-oriented (concerned primarily with getting the job done) or relationship-oriented (preoccupied with the feelings of their followers and with maintaining good relations). In 1967 Fred Fiedler of the University of Washington was the first to present an elaborate theory explaining the relative effectiveness of these two leadership styles in business.

Fiedler suggested that task-oriented leaders do the best job in a company in which the leader has good relations with all the employees, and the company has a clear goal. Because things are going well, the leader can focus on getting the job done. Task-oriented leaders also perform well if things are going badly because they can take charge and organize things. They do not perform so well when things are going moderately well, however. If the company has a reasonably clear goal and only some people are getting along with the leader, a relationship-oriented leader will do the best job by building strong relationships with the other employees.

ATTITUDES AND PERSUASION

One unavoidable aspect of being a member of society is that we constantly have to evaluate things as either good or bad, and these judgments can affect how we think, feel, and behave (*see* box above right). These evaluations are called attitudes, and our attitudes can develop in many different ways.

One way that we develop attitudes is through classical conditioning (*see* Vol. 1, pp. 74–89). If one stimulus frequently precedes another, the two can become associated in our minds. For instance, if a young boy always sees his mother react in a distressed or negative manner when she encounters a particular person, he will come to associate that person with negative feelings. Eventually that person will elicit the same negative feelings in the boy, even though he has no personal reasons for disliking the person. Positive attitudes can form in a similar way: If the mother always responds to another person in a positive way, her son may ultimately come to like that person, too.

We also develop attitudes through the process known as operant conditioning (see Vol. 1, pp. 74–89). If you express a certain attitude and are rewarded for it, you are likely to continue expressing that attitude. For example, if someone sees you with a copy of *The Catcher in the Rye* and says, "I'm so glad you are reading J. D. Salinger," you might develop a favorable attitude to that author's work. Conversely, if someone says, "Why are you reading that stupid book?" you might develop an unfavorable attitude toward J. D. Salinger. The negative remark seems to criticize you for your choice of reading material, and you probably don't like doing things for which you get criticized.

But we do not need punishments or rewards to develop attitudes. If we see other people deriving pleasure from listening to the work of Beethoven and Mozart, we might decide that listening to classical music is rewarding and begin to like it. Or if we see that other people suffer after drinking alcohol, we might learn to dislike beer, wine, and spirits.

CASE STUDY

From Attitude to Action

According to research by Russell Fazio published in 1989, the path from attitudes to behavior involves four steps:

1 You find yourself in a place where you are reminded of your attitude toward something.

2 You think about that thing in a manner consistent with the attitude you already hold: If you have a favorable attitude, you will tend to see many positive things about it; if you have an unfavorable attitude, you will tend to see many negative things about it.

3 You think about what others normally do when they find themselves in the same situation.

4 You behave in a way that is consistent with the kind of attitude you have.

Smoking and drinking are unlikely to be consistent with a positive concern about health. To avoid the cognitive dissonance caused by such mutually exclusive desires, people who are unable to give up such habits may find their attitudes to being healthy changing over time.

On other occasions our attitudes may develop from watching our own behavior. In 1967 Daryl Bem of Cornell University published several papers explaining how, if we are unsure about something, we monitor our own behavior before we decide what to think. For example, you may not know whether you like a certain type of music until the point at which you say to yourself, "Well, I've been listening to this for an hour now, and I haven't turned it off. I guess I must like it." Or you may see a movie and form no particular impression about it at the time; but if images and snippets of dialogue stay with you for a long while afterward, you may decide that it has had an influence and that you must have liked it.

> ***"How can I know what I think 'til I see what I say?"***
> ***—Graham Wallas, 1926***

Good intentions

Of course, many different experiences combine to influence our ideas about the outside world; and the more experiences we have to reinforce a particular attitude, the greater the influence that attitude may have on our behavior. But do attitudes always predict behavior? Not necessarily. Sometimes we behave in ways that are inconsistent with our attitudes. We might feel that recycling paper is a good thing, for example, yet seldom recycle it.

In their 1975 book *Belief, Attitude, Intention, and Behavior* Martin Fishbein of the University of Pennsylvania and Icek Ajzen of the University of Massachusetts proposed that a more important influence on behavior is not attitude but intention. If we want to know if people will recycle paper, we should ask them if they intend to do so, or how determined they are. Fishbein and Ajzen suggested three things that could influence intention: attitude (whether individuals believe recycling is a good thing), approval (whether other people will approve if an individual recycles paper), and capability (whether recycling is a practical possibility).

Cognitive dissonance

Because attitudes can influence behavior, social psychologists are also interested in how people's attitudes change. Leon Festinger (1919–1989) studied situations in which people change their attitudes without any direct pressure from others. His hypothesis, which became known as cognitive dissonance theory, was based on the idea that we feel discomfort when we become aware of inconsistencies in our thoughts and behavior. Cigarette smokers who think taking care of their bodies is important, for example, might experience cognitive dissonance because smoking is inconsistent with their beliefs.

> ***"Without doubt it is a delightful harmony when doing and saying go together."***
> ***—Michel de Montaigne, 1588***

Cognitive dissonance is an unsettling experience, so we might try to get rid of it by changing our behavior. Changing our behavior can be difficult, however (it is difficult to quit smoking, for example), so we might find our attitudes changing instead. Smokers who experience cognitive dissonance might find that taking care of their bodies becomes less important and thus avoid the problem of stopping.

Another way to get rid of cognitive dissonance is to justify our behavior (*see* box right). This is especially likely when we have to make choices between two good things. If you have only enough money to buy one CD but you really like two, you will be faced with the choice of which one to buy. You might feel cognitive dissonance because whichever one you choose, the positive qualities of the rejected CD are inconsistent with the fact that you rejected it. After choosing one CD, you might find yourself thinking about all the reasons that the one you chose is better than the other one, or that the other one is not as good as you previously thought. Often we like the things we choose even more after we have chosen them. Thinking in this way helps us reduce cognitive dissonance by justifying the choices we have made.

Persuasion

Changing our attitudes to avoid cognitive dissonance is something we do ourselves. But we might also change our attitudes because someone else persuades us to do so. In 1986, in an effort to explain how we let others persuade us, Richard Petty and John Cacioppo published a revised form of their elaboration likelihood model. According to this model, we can be

CASE STUDY

TAKE THE MONEY AND RUN

We experience cognitive dissonance when we cannot justify our behavior. To study this dilemma, researchers usually require participants to do something that is the opposite of what they really believe. For example, in a study conducted at Stanford University in 1959 Leon Festinger and James M. Carlsmith asked some of their participants to tell the rest that a boring exercise was fun. Half of the first group were paid $20 to do this, while the other half were paid only $1.

At the end of the study—which gave the participants time to change their attitudes to make them more consistent with their behavior—Festinger and his colleagues asked them how much they had enjoyed the boring exercise. They found that those participants who were paid only $1 seemed to convince themselves that the exercise really was fun because they had no reasonable way to justify what they had told other people. In contrast, those who were paid $20 maintained that the experience was boring. They seemed to experience less cognitive dissonance because they were able to justify what they had told other people by telling themselves they had done it purely for the money.

persuaded in two different ways: centrally and peripherally. Central persuasion requires considered thought: We weigh all the facts presented and come to a logical conclusion. For example, if you read a magazine article describing several scientific studies that have established a link between loud music and hearing loss, you might be persuaded that loud music is bad for your health. On the other hand, if you read the magazine article and found that the writer looked attractive and wrote in an intelligent manner, you might be persuaded to reach the same conclusion in a peripheral way: You would be influenced less by the facts presented and more by other, largely irrelevant matters.

We sometimes switch back and forth between peripheral and central ways of being persuaded. But which lasts longer? Research has shown that although people persuaded in a peripheral way are just as likely to change their attitudes as those persuaded in a central way, the effects of peripheral persuasion wear off more quickly. Attitudes are more likely to persist if we have thought carefully about the facts than if we are persuaded by someone's status or attractiveness, for example.

PREJUDICE AND DISCRIMINATION

Although we are social animals, we want to relate to only a limited number of other people. Consequently, we tend to choose just a few social groups to belong to, which we usually feel good about. Unfortunately, some of us find it difficult to like our own groups without disliking those to which we do not belong, even if we have little real knowledge of them. Forming a hostile

Which factors are more likely to cause you to change your attitudes about a subject? Initially you may be influenced by a lecturer's charisma, but in the long term you are more likely to be persuaded by a clear and well-reasoned argument.

Social prejudice can lead to extreme forms of discrimination. Between 1231 and 1834 many people suffered at the hands of the Inquisition—a tribunal authorized by the pope that tried to stamp out all heresy. Spain's first Grand Inquisitor was Thomás de Torquemada (see left), who turned his attention to local Jews, Protestants, and Moors. He dragged thousands of people before his brutal courts, torturing them to renounce their faith and burning many "false converts" at the stake. Even the pope could not stop the inquisitor, and in 1492 Thomás expelled all unconverted Jews from the country.

view about such a social group is called prejudice. Part of being prejudiced involves looking down on other people, which helps us feel better about ourselves. Thus we may find it particularly difficult to avoid being prejudiced when we feel threatened because it helps us maintain our sense of self-esteem.

Psychologists Steven Fein and Steven Spencer demonstrated this tendency in a series of experiments published in 1997. In one of them they asked participants to take a fake intelligence test and gave them fake scores, saying either that they failed or that they did very well. The study was conducted at a U.S. university where it was relatively common for students to harbor negative feelings toward Jewish women. After the partipants received their results, they were asked to evaluate either a Jewish woman's personality or a non-Jewish woman's personality. Fein and Spencer found that those participants who had failed the intelligence test evaluated the Jewish woman negatively, while those who had passed were positive about her. They also observed that participants who failed the intelligence test experienced a corresponding increase in self-esteem after they had evaluated the Jewish woman negatively. Their results suggested that people compensate for their own failures by putting down people from other groups.

Culture and society

Another reason that we hold prejudices is because they help us believe that our own culture is better than others (*see* Vol. 1, pp. 152–161). We usually value our culture because we rely on it to give our lives meaning and purpose and to provide us with a sense of identity. We might also want to feel that our culture is superior and reassure ourselves by denigrating other people's cultures.

> ***"I am free of all prejudice. I hate everyone equally."***
> ***—W. C. Fields, 1890–1946***

Prejudice may also result from friction between social groups. These groups often compete for wealth and power in society, and when members of one group are less successful than they believe they should be, they may take out their frustrations on the members of another group. In 1940

CASE STUDY

Unconscious Stereotypes

Some psychologists are interested in the possibility that people can hold stereotypes (generalized views about groups of people based on very few facts, *see* Vol. 1, pp. 152–161) without being aware of them.

In a 1989 paper Patricia Devine proposed that even people who are not normally prejudiced can store negative stereotypes about certain groups in their minds, and that these stereotypes can influence the way they think. In a study conducted at Ohio State University Devine presented participants with words to make them think about African Americans. None of the participants in the study was an African American, and people with both high and low scores on a previously conducted prejudice test took part. All the words were presented subliminally—shown rapidly on a computer screen so that the participants were not aware they had seen them.

Half of the research participants were subliminally exposed to words that related to stereotypes about African Americans, such as "poor," "welfare," and "lazy." The other half were subliminally exposed to words that had nothing to do with these stereotypes. Later the participants read a story about a man (whose race was not identified) who behaved in a forceful or assertive way and were asked to rate how hostilely he had behaved. Because many Anglo Americans tend to believe that African Americans are hostile, Devine predicted that the participants who had been subliminally exposed to the African-American related words would use this stereotype when judging the forceful man.

That is exactly what she observed. Regardless of whether the participants had scored high or low on the prejudice test, those who had been subliminally presented with the African American stereotype rated the man as more hostile than those who were presented with other unrelated words. This suggests that even people who are not consciously prejudiced can store stereotyped information in their minds and that it can affect their judgments without their even being aware of it.

Many of us are guilty of stereotyping others, although we don't always realize we are doing so. It is particularly easy to become prejudiced against people who are obviously different from ourselves. We might judge these Muslim women by their clothes, for example, and assume they have been coerced into covering themselves. But many young Muslim women choose to wear their hejab *(head covering) to show pride in their religion and heritage.*

Carl Hovland and Robert Sears of Yale University published a study illustrating this tendency. They examined old records of economic conditions and lynchings of African Americans in the southern United States between 1882 and 1930. At that time the economy of the southern states depended heavily on cotton, and a good economic indicator was the value of cotton each year. They found that in years in which the price was low, the number of lynchings was much higher. It appeared white farmers had vented their frustration by responding violently to alleged sexual offenses and petty crimes committed by their African American neighbors.

> ***"A great many people think they are thinking when they are merely rearranging their prejudices."***
> ***—William James, 1890***

It is easy to be prejudiced. We might dislike people of a particular religion, race, sex, age, or even those who dress differently from the way we do. We may even discriminate against other people when we think we aren't (*see* box p. 62). Although such prejudice may be subtle, it can still make a huge difference in society, affecting the decisions people make every day in places such as schools, courtrooms, and offices. This makes it difficult to create societies in which we can all get along with each other peacefully. Despite this, social psychologists have learned that there are some things that can be done to reduce prejudice in society.

Reducing prejudice

For many years people thought the most effective way to reduce prejudice between two groups of people was to bring them into contact with each other. According to this theory, if people are made to coexist under the right conditions, they will learn more about each other and come to like or at least tolerate each other. But that does not always happen. Sometimes bringing together groups with negative attitudes toward each other merely cements their prejudices and may lead to fighting.

When two groups desire the same thing, prejudice can lead to fighting. Since Israel was established in the Middle East in 1948, the Palestinians and the Israelis have been fighting over land that both groups believe is rightfully theirs.

Most social psychologists believe that for two groups to get along, both must support the idea of equality. If one group thinks it should be dominant, however, the two are unlikely to coexist peacefully. They also suggest that if two groups are encouraged to work together toward a

PSYCHOLOGY & SOCIETY

THE JIGSAW CLASSROOM

In 1971 the public schools in Austin, Texas, were in trouble. They had recently been desegregated, but African American, Hispanic American, and Anglo American students were not accustomed to attending school together. After just a few weeks students throughout the city were getting into serious fights. As the fighting increased, school supervisors called on social psychologists at the University of Texas at Austin for help. Elliot Aronson and his colleagues responded and spent several days observing students and interviewing them about the difficulties they experienced getting along with each other.

The root of the problem seemed clear. Most of the classrooms they observed seemed to maintain a competitive atmosphere. Usually the teacher would ask students questions, and students would compete with each other to give the right answers. For example, they might raise their hands in the hope they would be called on instead of other students. Students from poorer schools (who were generally African Americans and Hispanic Americans) felt uncomfortable competing with students who seemed to have had a more privileged education, however, and were less inclined to try to answer the teachers' questions. As a result, many of the African American and Hispanic American students participated less frequently in class. The ultimate effect of this was that some Anglo American students began to think that the African American and Hispanic American students were stupid, while many of the African American and Hispanic American students began to resent the Anglo American students. The students' prejudices toward each other quickly flared into violence.

Aronson and his colleagues looked at this difficult situation and realized that for things to improve, the atmosphere at the school would have to change from one of competition to one of cooperation. If they could get the students to cooperate with each other in the classroom, the students might learn to get along better. With this goal in mind, Aronson and his colleagues developed the Jigsaw Classroom.

The idea behind the Jigsaw Classroom is relatively simple. In a Jigsaw Classroom groups are created so that each one is composed of students from many different ethnic groups. To create an atmosphere of cooperation, each group is given a project that requires several pieces of information to complete. Each student in each group is given a part of the information, which means every group member has to participate for their group to complete the project. In other words, each member is given a "part of the puzzle," and they have to cooperate to "complete the puzzle." As the students cooperate, they gradually learn to get along with each other.

common goal, it will make them depend on each other and foster mutual feelings of trust. They also agree that prejudice can be reduced if minority group members are given a chance—by being placed in the right kind of situations—to disprove the negative stereotypes that other groups might hold about them. Finally, they point out that groups that have certain things in common, such as similar backgrounds, are more likely to get along with each other than those that do not.

Muzafer Sherif (*see* box p. 51) carried out one of the earliest studies exploring how groups can learn to get along in 1954. He organized a camp for boys at Robbers Cave State Park, Oklahoma. None of them knew each other previously, and Sherif deliberately picked boys with similar backgrounds and physical characteristics, dividing them into two random groups. He made the two groups compete with each other for prizes, and before long they began to behave aggressively toward each other. Then Sherif set up various emergency situations in the camp. Both groups had to work together to handle these emergencies, and by the end of the study he found that prejudice between the two groups had decreased significantly.

Using the same principle in 1971, Elliot Aronson and his colleagues at the University of Texas at Austin developed a program called the Jigsaw Classroom to reduce prejudice among students in class (*see* box above). In the ideal Jigsaw Classroom students work in groups made up of girls and boys from different ethnic groups. Each student is given a unique part of the solution to a problem, so that they all have to cooperate to arrive at the complete answer. By cooperating in this way, the students learn to get along. Researchers have conducted many studies using the Jigsaw Classroom program and have found that students who go through Jigsaw Classrooms become less prejudiced, score higher on exams, and develop higher self-esteem than students who do not.

HELPING AND ALTRUISM

In order to get along with other people in society, we have to help each other from time to time, although many different things can influence how much and how often we do so. Some of us seem to have personalities that makes us more inclined to help than others, but even those of us who normally help can sometimes find ourselves in situations that make us less helpful than usual.

One of the best illustrations of this was a 1970 experiment in which psychologists John Darley and Daniel Batson asked students of religion to give a talk. They asked half of the students to give a talk on "The Good Samaritan," a biblical story about helping and asked the other half to give a talk about employment. After they had given the students their topic, they told them that they would have to walk to another building to give the talk. They also told the students one of three things: that they were on time, that they were a

Most of us help others from time to time, but we usually have limits. The biblical story of the Good Samaritan (used in an experiment on helping in 1970) was intended to show the nature of real altruism. When bandits beat a Jewish traveler and leave him at the roadside, a priest and a Levite both pass by. It is a Samaritan—a traditional enemy of the Jews—who stops to help the injured man.

few minutes ahead of schedule, or that they were a few minutes late.

On the way to the other building all the students passed a man coughing and groaning, who was really an actor working for the psychologists. Surprisingly, the topic that the students were thinking about made almost no difference to how much they helped the man: Students thinking about the Good Samaritan were no more helpful than students thinking about jobs. On the other hand, time pressure made a big difference. Out of the total number of students who thought they were early, 63 percent stopped and helped; 45 percent of the students who thought they were on schedule helped; while only 10 percent of the students who thought they were late helped.

Darley and Batson's study suggests that even a simple aspect of a situation can be strong enough to influence the amount that we help. For example, people who live in big cities are not necessarily less helpful than people in small towns (as is often thought): It is just that they might be too preoccupied with their own concerns to notice when others need assistance.

Crowd behavior

Social psychologists have also shown that we tend to help less when more people are present. Bibb Latané and John Darley of Princeton University (*see* box below) conducted a series of experiments investigating helping behavior. In 1968, for example, they asked volunteers to discuss the problems of university life with one, two, or five other people, assuring them of anonymity by putting them in separate rooms and asking them to talk over an intercom. After they had been speaking for several minutes, one of the "participants" began making choking noises, said that he was having a seizure, and pleaded for help. Latané and Darley found that the size of the discussion group made a big difference in whether or not participants decided to help. When they believed they were the only other person

PSYCHOLOGY & SOCIETY

Neighborhood Watch

Bibb Latané and John Darley became famous for their studies of the effects of group size on helping. But how did they get interested in the idea that having more people around might make helping less likely? One of the things that prompted them to do this research was a terrible event that occurred at approximately 3:20 A.M. on March 13, 1964.

On this morning 28-year-old Kitty Genovese was making her way back to her home in Queens, New York. As she walked toward her second-floor apartment, a man under a streetlight suddenly grabbed her and stabbed her. Kitty screamed and woke up many of her sleeping neighbors. She yelled, "He stabbed me! Please help me!" Windows opened, and someone shouted at the man to leave her alone. Her attacker walked away.

Kitty struggled to her feet and looked around for help, but no one came to her assistance. A while later her attacker came back and stabbed her again. This time she cried out, "I'm dying! I'm dying!" A few people looked out their windows, and her attacker got into his car and drove away. But still no one came down to help Kitty, and no one called the police.

Kitty managed to crawl into a doorway, but at 3:35 A.M. her attacker returned and stabbed her a third time. Someone finally called the police at 3:50 A.M.; but when they arrived a couple of minutes later, Kitty was already dead. The person who called the police was a neighbor. He told them that he had dialed 911 only after thinking carefully about the situation and talking about it briefly with a friend. He told the police that he wasn't sure he wanted to get involved. Later it was learned that 38 people had witnessed at least one of the attacks over the half-hour period.

Were Kitty's neighbors evil? Latané and Darley didn't think so. They believed that Kitty's neighbors might have hesitated to help because of the number of people involved. Each of Kitty's neighbors probably expected one of the others to get involved. But since almost all of her neighbors expected someone else to help, no one did help Kitty until it was too late.

in the discussion, 85 percent of them left the room to seek help. But when they believed four other people were involved in the discussion, only 31 percent of the participants went to fetch help.

> ***"Without question, when people are uncertain they are more likely to use others' actions to decide how they themselves should act."***
> ***—Robert Cialdini, 1988***

Why are people in larger groups less helpful? One reason seems to be that they feel less responsibility to help since there are other people around who are equally or even better qualified to do so. They may also rely on the reactions of others to decide whether a situation requires assistance. If other people remain calm or fail to offer help, they may assume that the situation is not a real emergency.

How likely would you be to help if someone collapsed in the street? Research suggests that your reactions would probably be influenced by the number of other people present. In a large crowd you would probably feel less obliged to help. If other people failed to appear concerned, you might even assume that the situation was not sufficiently serious to warrant intervention.

Deciding to help

Psychologists have also wondered whether mood may influence whether we decide to help. In experiments researchers have attempted to put people in good moods by making them watch comedy films, eat cookies, or smell pleasant odors. In these cases participants seem to be more helpful in emergency situations. Evidence of the opposite effect is inconclusive, however. Some research has suggested that people in bad moods are less helpful, but other studies have produced conflicting results. It is also possible that we help others because we think we will improve our mood by doing so.

Empathy—or feeling what someone else feels—may also influence our decision when we encounter someone in trouble. When we feel empathy for someone, we are much more likely to help.

Because there are many different factors that can influence whether we will help or not, we sometimes have trouble making up our minds whether to take any action at all. So how do we make these decisions? Latané and Darley described five steps that we must go through as we decide to help. First, we must notice that something has happened. Second, we have to realize that there is an emergency. Third, we have to feel responsible in some way—if we think it is someone else's duty to help, we will probably do nothing. Fourth, we have to know what to do—there may be no point in stopping to help someone who is choking, for example, if we have no idea of emergency procedures. Fifth, we have to convince ourselves that helping will not be dangerous or embarrassing.

Theoretically, soldiers in combat are fighting for a specific cause, so their acts of violence should be committed due to instrumental aggression. In reality, however, they are likely to experience many intense emotions during a battle, so it would be difficult to differentiate between instrumental and angry aggression when analyzing the motives for their behavior.

ANTISOCIAL BEHAVIOR

Although societies thrive when people help each other, it is also an unfortunate fact of life that we often hurt each other. Behavior intended to coerce or harm other people is called aggression. Social psychologists often distinguish between two types: instrumental aggression, which is committed for the sake of some reward, such as money, power, or defense; and angry aggression, an emotional type of behavior committed with the intention of harming another person.

> ***"Anger is a great force. If you control it, it can be transmuted into a power that can move the whole world."***
> ***—Sri Swami Sivananda, 1953***

Feeling frustrated and unable to exert any control in a situation can cause people to behave aggressively even when the object of their anger may not be the cause. People stuck in a traffic jam, for example, may take out their anger on other drivers. But it is unlikely that such acts of angry aggression will make them feel any better.

We can be aggressive for many reasons, and some aggressive behavior might be categorized as both instrumental and angry. If you insult people in a high-status position, for example, they might respond aggressively to remind you that they have power over you, but they might also respond aggressively because your behavior has made them angry. In such cases instrumental and angry aggression cannot really be differentiated.

Frustration

We often act aggressively because we feel frustrated. In their 1939 book *Frustration and Aggression* John Dollard and his colleagues at Yale University suggested that all aggression is caused by some kind of frustration, and that frustration always leads to some kind of aggression. It is easy to think how we might become aggressive when we feel frustrated. Children who fight in the playroom, for example, might feel frustrated because they are unable to claim exclusive rights to toys they regard as their own. But it is just as easy to think of exceptions: Professional boxers do not fight because they are frustrated with their opponents; they fight for money. So, they commit instrumental aggression. Indeed, many people who commit instrumental aggression are not at all frustrated.

We can also respond to frustration in other ways that have nothing to do with aggression. In 1980 a clinical psychologist at the University of Pennsylvania, Martin Seligman, published *Human Helplessness: Theory and Applications*, in which he showed that when people repeatedly encounter situations over which they have little or no control, they suffer from stress and may become depressed.

Neither do we always commit acts of aggression against those who frustrate us. Sometimes we behave aggressively toward someone or something else instead. If we are frustrated by someone who has power over us, for example, we might decide it is

better to take out our frustration in some other way. Drivers who get a traffic ticket might displace their aggression toward the police officer who caught them by hitting the steering wheel. That allows them to express their anger without assaulting the officer, which they know would be a bad idea. Frustration may also exacerbate prejudice, as discussed on page 63.

Feeling aggressive

Does displacing our aggression make us behave less aggressively later? Can drivers who pound their fists on the steering wheel actually get rid of their aggression in this way? Dollard and his colleagues thought so, but subsequent research has shown that this idea is probably mistaken. In 1999, for example, Brad Bushman and his colleagues at Iowa State University conducted an experiment in which they provoked student volunteers by writing critical comments on their essays. They encouraged one group of students to let out their aggression by hitting a punching bag, while the second group was simply left to cool its heels. By the end of this exercise the first group of students had worked themselves into more of a rage and had become far more aggressive than the second group of students. So it seems that those of us who express our anger in a physical way, watch violent television programs, or react angrily to others do not feel less aggressive afterward; on the contrary, we may become more combative and perhaps even violent.

> ***"Punching a pillow to reduce anger is like using gasoline to put out a fire—it only makes matters worse."***
> ***—Brad Bushman, 1999***

Sometimes we become aggressive because our feelings become confused.

Boxers in training generally behave aggressively because they hope to gain money or status by fighting well—so they commit instrumental aggression rather than reacting to feelings of anger or frustration. But if people attack a punching bag to try to release pent-up feelings, they are more likely to end up in an angry aggressive mood because they have focused on their anger and worked themselves into a state of physical arousal.

Leonard Berkowitz became a professor at the University of Wisconsin in 1959, and it was there that he became interested in aggression research. He has published many papers on the subject, and his books include Aggression: Its Causes, Consequences, and Control *(1993) and* Causes and Consequences of Feelings *(2000). He has served as an expert advisor to the U.S. government, and he has also been an outspoken advocate of gun control.*

If we are insulted at the same time as we are experiencing a strong but unconnected emotion, we might confuse that emotion with anger and react aggressively toward the person who provoked us. In 1964 Stanley Schachter showed that if we are provoked while our heart is pumping rapidly after exercise, for example, we might confuse this state of arousal with a feeling of intense anger.

In 1990 Leonard Berkowitz of the University of Wisconsin proposed that different kinds of negative emotions and negative thoughts are connected in our minds, which means that when we are experiencing one negative emotion, it is fairly easy for us to start feeling another. We might become angry more easily if we are in pain, for example; and if we are feeling irritable, we might behave more aggressively than someone who is not. Other researchers have shown how stimuli such as loud noises, disgusting smells, hot temperatures, and even cigarette smoke can make people aggressive.

Mental images can play an important role, too. Berkowitz and his colleagues showed that aggressive thoughts can be created just by showing people images of weapons, and that these thoughts can lead to aggressive behavior. In one experiment they asked angry participants to administer electric shocks to another person. Half of the participants administered the shocks while a gun was in the room; the other half while a badminton racket was beside them. As anticipated, they found that the first group administered stronger shocks. Researchers have also found that people who watch violent television programs behave more aggressively.

Although certain ways of thinking can lead to more aggression, anger may also be triggered by the inability to think clearly, and alcohol and other drugs can greatly influence our state of mind. Research by Claude Steele and his colleagues at Stanford University (1990) has shown that alcohol makes people less cautious than they would normally be. Instead of considering the consequences of their behavior, they tend to react to the immediate aspects of a situation—perhaps focusing on an insult they have just received or the fact that everyone else is fighting.

Although we usually prefer to get along with other people, it seems most of us believe aggression is justified in certain circumstances, which may explain why people in societies throughout history have behaved aggressively from time to time. We are generally social creatures, but aggression is also part of our makeup.

CONNECTIONS

- Behaviorism: Volume 1, pp. 74–89
- Cross-cultural Psychology: Volume 1, pp. 152–161
- Emotion and Motivation: Volume 2, pp. 86–109
- Learning by Association: Volume 3, pp. 44–63
- Social Development: Volume 4, pp. 130–149
- People as Social Animals: pp. 6–27
- Relating to Others: pp. 28–49
- Mental Disorders and Society: Volume 6, pp. 142–163

Communication

"There's language in her eye, her cheek, her lip . . ."

William Shakespeare

Interpersonal communication is such a pervasive part of our lives that we often communicate without realizing it. From the words we speak to the tone of our voice to the expressions and gestures we use we continually send out messages to the people around us. In contrast, mass communication consciously uses some of these techniques to reach much larger audiences.

Communication can be defined quite simply as the transmission of a message from one person (the sender) to another person (the receiver) through some form of medium. When two people talk by telephone, one sends messages to the other by speaking words through the medium of the telephone line. And when a corporation prints advertisements in a national newspaper, it sends messages to potentially thousands or even millions of receivers at the same time through the medium of the printed word.

Defined like this, communication may seem simple. But bearing in mind the huge variety of ways in which people communicate, it turns out to be a much richer and more complex topic extending far beyond the realms of psychology. Anthropologists have much to say about how different cultures communicate, while musicians probably know more

BIOGRAPHY

Claude Elwood Shannon

From the design of cellular telephones to the art of delivering political speeches most modern theories of communication owe something to the work of U.S. mathematician and electronics engineer Claude Elwood Shannon, born in Gaylord, Michigan, on April 30, 1916.

After attending the University of Michigan in 1940, Shannon gained his doctorate from the Massachusetts Institute of Technology (MIT). The following year he joined Bell Laboratories, an institution that had long been at the forefront of research into electronics and communications technology. While there, he published his seminal 1948 paper "The Mathematical Theory of Communication," in which he argued that information is a physical quantity that can be measured just like any other. Usually known as "information theory," Shannon's ideas sought to put communications on a more clearly defined mathematical footing, using quantitative measurements of how efficiently information can be transmitted and received.

Information theory found its major application in the design of telecommunications equipment, and it was later applied to various other disciplines, from linguistics to psychology and from artificial intelligence to cryptology (the study of codes). Shannon did not always agree with his ideas being stretched so far. As he once wrote modestly: "Information theory has perhaps ballooned to an importance beyond its actual accomplishments."

Shannon returned to MIT in 1956 and remained there until 1978, when he became professor emeritus. He died on February 24, 2001, in Medford, Massachusetts.

In social psychology Claude Shannon is well known for his mathematical theory of communication, but in his spare time he enjoyed a variety of hobbies, one of which was juggling.

than most about how to communicate emotion. Teachers are adept at explaining complex ideas effectively, while advertising copywriters (who write TV commercials and billboards) know how to persuade.

Psychologists are interested in studying communication for numerous reasons. From the point of view of cognitive psychology language reveals much about how people's minds process information —how they think, reason, and remember. For social psychologists studying language and nonverbal communication sheds light on how people interact with one another, what different cultures have in common, and how the communication methods used by humans and other animals differ from one another. Finally, studying mass communications (advertising, TV, and other forms of large-scale communication) helps psychologists and sociologists understand the workings of modern culture and society, which can help them investigate the various factors involved in persuasion and attitude formation, and answer questions such as whether violent films make children more aggressive.

Communication theory

Theories and models of how people communicate often draw extensively on ideas from electronics and computer science. One of the best-known theories of communication evolved from the work of U.S. mathematician Claude Elwood Shannon (*see* box p. 72). Also known as information theory, it explained how messages are transmitted between a sender and a receiver through a fixed-capacity channel (a communication channel of limited capacity, much like a pipe with a certain width that limits the rate at which water can flow through it). Although

> ***"The fundamental problem of communication is that of reproducing at one point either exactly or approximately a message selected at another point."***
> ***—Claude Shannon, 1948***

Shannon's mathematical theory proved most influential in the design of telecommunications equipment, it also proved useful as a metaphor for human communication. So when copywriters speak of "channels of communication," they might be loosely referring to words and images (on a billboard) or music (conveying emotions through the soundtrack to a TV commercial).

Shannon's theory may seem little different from the basic definition of

KEY POINTS

- Communication involves the transmission of messages from a sender to a receiver through a medium (sometimes known as a communication channel). Communication channels include everything from spoken language to the clothes and perfumes people wear.
- The two main types of communication are verbal (written and spoken language) and nonverbal (things such as body posture, hand gestures, and eye contact).
- Verbal communication (or language) involves a speaker and a listener, who take it in turns to use words to exchange "mental models" of the world.
- Nonverbal communication often complements or reinforces the messages sent by verbal communication. On other occasions it contradicts people's verbal messages, such as when they lie.
- Some forms of nonverbal communication, such as facial expressions, seem to be universally understood; others, such as gestures, depend much more on culture.
- Not all languages consist of words. American Sign Language (ASL) is a comprehensive language for deaf people based entirely on gestures.
- Interpersonal communication (between one person and another) usually involves a two-way conversation: an exchange of verbal and nonverbal messages according to a set of well-defined but unwritten rules.
- Mass communication involves communicating messages to a large section of society at the same time. Although it is usually a one-way process, market research and other techniques can be used to find out if the communication has been successful.

communication proposed at the start of this chapter, but it also introduced extra concepts. For instance, the message being transmitted is usually referred to as the signal, and for the communication to be successful, the receiver must distinguish it from any distracting background "noise." Such an idea is easy to understand in the context of a telephone call, but for other forms of communication signal and noise may be less obvious. For a billboard the signal is clearly the persuasive advertising message that the copywriter is trying to convey. Noise is anything that keeps the message from getting through, and that could include competition from other billboards put up nearby, trees along the highway that keep the billboard from being seen, confusion in the way the copywriter has worded the headline, or various other things that work against the effectiveness of the communication.

Stimulated by his observations of advertising, Marshall McLuhan began writing books about technology, media, and communications at the age of 40. His outrageous statements about the media and its aftereffects led to many reexaminations of the consequences of digital multimedia.

In truth, human communication is much richer and more complex than Shannon's simple model might suggest. When two people talk, for example, they do not simply exchange words. Talking one on one, they also send messages by the tone of their voice, by their use of facial expressions, through their body language, and in other ways. Human communication, then, is multichanneled. Although some forms of communication, such as the cry of a baby, seem to be inborn, others are clearly learned, such as the gestures or other conventions that vary from culture to culture. So human communication is not hard wired (programmed at birth) in the same way as a telephone switching office.

In Shannon's theory messages are simply packets of information transmitted from the sender to the receiver, but the information that the messages contain is irrelevant. In human communication the message content strongly influences how the information should be transmitted. Thus educational "messages" are delivered by teachers standing at their blackboards, persuasive messages are delivered through TV commercials and billboards, and emotional messages might be delivered by singers on stage. In everyday life the context in which communication occurs is vitally important. The message "Where's the beef?" means something quite different when it is spoken by a housewife in a supermarket, by a presidential candidate attacking his opponent, or by the voiceover on a TV advertisement for hamburgers. Canadian communications theorist Marshall McLuhan (1911–1980) even went so far as to suggest that the medium strongly influences the message people receive with his famous pronouncement "the medium is the message."

For all its complexity, communication can also be considered in much simpler terms. All forms of communication can be divided into two kinds: verbal (using either written or spoken language) and nonverbal (including sounds, gestures, and other body language). Interpersonal communication (two-way communication between two people) is also very different from mass communication (one-way communication between one person and a large section of society).

VERBAL COMMUNICATION

People generally believe that written and spoken language is the most important form of human communication, and it certainly plays a central part in much of human culture. Consider how difficult it would be trying to mime a comprehensive summary of human knowledge, such as the *Encyclopedia Britannica*, for example. Yet language is not always as essential as it seems. Shakespeare's emotionally charged play *Romeo and Juliet* is often performed as a ballet. Not a single word is spoken, yet the music and the actions of the dancers communicate the essence of the story quite adequately. The conversations of everyday life are spoken not just in words, but in looks, gestures, touches, and tones of the voice—and even in perfumes, clothes, body piercings, and tattoos.

> ***"Language, like consciousness, only arises from the need, the necessity, of intercourse with others."***
> ***—Karl Marx, 1846***

Psychologists have long studied verbal and nonverbal communication as though they were completely separate subjects, reflecting the influential 1960s work of U.S. linguist and anthropologist Charles Hockett (1916–2000), who made a clear distinction between "paralanguage" (nonverbal communication) on the one hand and written and spoken language on the other. Yet some researchers see no real distinction between the two. The U.S. anthropologist Adam Kendon has argued that speech and gestures are of equal value as communication tools, while U.S. linguist Dwight Bolinger (1907–1992) believed "language is speech embedded in gesture," by which he meant that gestures (including tone of voice) fundamentally determine the meaning of spoken words. U.S. researchers David McNeill and Susan Duncan have also rejected this distinction, arguing that human language production and comprehension can only be properly understood if nonverbal communication is also taken into account.

Jonathan Cope and Darcy Bussell of the Royal Ballet, UK, dance the roles of Romeo and Juliet in a 1995 performance. Although ballet lacks the subtle nuances of a verbal rendition of Shakespeare's great tragedy, the dancers can still convey much of the emotion and drama of the story by using body language and facial expressions.

Thanks to a complex system we can now use the telephone to contact people all around the world. But while this channel of communication is international, we only communicate successfully if we speak the same language as the person at the other end of the line.

Language as communication

Many philosophers and psychologists have wondered about the relationship between thought and spoken language, some proposing that thought depends on language, some suggesting that language depends on thought, and others believing that they are separate activities. The way humans process and understand spoken and written and language is covered in depth in Vol. 3 (pp. 114–135), so in this chapter we look more specifically at how language works as a communication tool.

If language were purely a tool that aided thinking, we might all walk around talking to ourselves in our own languages, but never actually speak to one another. Yet the essential features of language make it especially suitable for communication with other people, enabling us to express and communicate a more complex range of thoughts and ideas than would be possible by nonverbal communication alone. Language is governed by rules and highly structured, and these things make it possible for other people to decode what we say and mean. But it is also highly creative: We don't store in our minds everything we are likely to say in our lives because we cannot possibly know what we will need to say at every moment in the future. Rather, we think up new things to say when we need to say them, and we can even invent new words, such as "Internet" or "cowabunga," when we need to describe new ideas or emotions. Thus much of our language is explicitly designed for communication, for sharing information, for making and maintaining social relationships through conversation, and for expressing emotions.

Language can bridge the gap between two people like the wires that connect their telephones. A complex system of international cooperation and regulation ensures that any given telephone can send calls to or receive calls from any other given telephone anywhere in the world. But people are not telephones. They are all different: They may be raised in different countries, brought up in different social backgrounds, and specialized in different professions. So language has to work in a much more dynamic and flexible way than a telephone wire to make a connection and permit successful communication.

Language and meaning

In his 1983 book *Mental Models* British psycholinguist Philip Johnson-Laird described how people think and reason about the world according to "mental models" that they construct in their own minds. Communication is thus a matter of what Johnson-Laird calls "the symbolic transmission of a mental representation," sharing these mental models with other people. So conversations become a kind of trading game in which mental models, described in words and embellished with various nonverbal "cues" (signals), pass back and forth between people. If speakers want or need to say something about an aspect of the world, they first construct a mental model so they understand the thing, then they describe it in words that take account of what a listener is already likely to know about it. Listeners then decode the words and construct their own mental model (or modify their existing mental model) of the subject in question. As a speaker and listener converse, they continually swap roles, exchanging ideas about each other's mental models and modifying their own models accordingly.

One thing makes it possible for people to communicate in this way more than any other: Language is not just meaningful to each individual, it is meaningful to all the people who use it. In other words, it is a system of shared meanings. Each word printed on this page means more or less the same thing to you, the reader, as it means to me, the writer. So if I write the word "limousine," you will probably understand that I'm referring to a large automobile used to chauffeur around rock stars and world leaders, not to a pickup used on a cattle ranch.

However, verbal communication is complicated by the fact that the same words do not always mean exactly the same things to everyone. Sometimes a certain word may mean different things to different people, and even different dictionaries may define the word in slightly different ways. Each word conjures up a mental model based on the unique things people have experienced in their lives. If you have been to a high school prom, the word "limousine" might take you back to an enjoyable evening spent with friends. But if you've ever watched a film about the assassination of President John F. Kennedy in 1963, "limousine" might take on an altogether different and more negative meaning. And if someone in your family is a chauffeur, "limousine" might evoke something different again.

> ***"In all communities and at all times, humans are alike in having language. This essential connection, between having language and being human is one reason why those interested in the nature of human minds have always been particularly intrigued by language."***
>
> ***—Lila R. & Henry Gleitman, 1970***

Theories of meaning

Meaning, therefore, is the foundation of how languages communicate. But what does "meaning" really mean? The simplest explanation is that words have meanings because they refer to things in the world. So, "limousine" has a different meaning than "pickup" because they refer to two types of automobile. Yet meaning cannot be quite this simple because abstract words such as "truth," "love," and "justice" do not refer to tangible things in the world even though they have reasonably clear (albeit rather complex) meanings.

One theory of meaning is that complex words are defined in terms of simpler ones, which is essentially how dictionaries work. Thus Merriam-Webster's *Collegiate Dictionary* defines "limousine" as "a large, luxurious, often chauffeur-driven sedan that sometimes has a glass partition separating the driver's seat from the passenger compartment." Another theory of meaning is that some words work as prototypes or typical examples of things. Asked to draw a house, for example, most North American children would draw a rectangle with four windows, a central door, a roof, and a chimney. The word "house" is thus defined in terms of a set of key features. Other words, such as "brownstone," "shack," "apartment," and "cabin," are examples of the prototype, or exemplars, not all of which share all the features of the prototype.

Hierarchies of meaning

But it is not just the individual words of a language that communicate meaning. A sentence consists of words and has an overall meaning made up of the collective meanings of these individual words. Similarly, paragraphs express wider thoughts, while essay-length collections of paragraphs may express another scale of meaning. This hierarchy has no obvious equivalent in nonverbal communication. A flirt can communicate his or her intentions to another by stringing together a whole series of gestures, postures, and looks; but these individual components of

BIOGRAPHY

Wittgenstein and the Meaning of Language

Modern ideas about the meaning of language and how it works as a tool of communication and thought were influenced greatly by the work of Austrian-born British philosopher Ludwig Wittgenstein (1889–1951). Originally Wittgenstein trained as a mathematician, but he took up philosophy when he moved to Cambridge University, England, in 1911, where he soon began thinking about the problems of language.

While serving as an artillery officer in World War I (1914–1918), Wittgenstein began work on his first major book, *Tractatus Logico-Philosophicus* (1922). One of its major themes—and one of Wittgenstein's preoccupations throughout his life—was his attempt to understand what language is, how people use it to think their thoughts, and how it communicates ideas between different people. Wittgenstein believed our thoughts are limited by the language we use; as he once wrote, "Whereof one cannot speak, thereof one must be silent." He also argued that meaningful language must be based on "pictures of reality" or straightforward descriptions of simple facts about the world around us. According to this idea, much of our language, including much of philosophy, is quite literally meaningless.

But the idea that language has this underlying order and simplicity came to bother Wittgenstein in his later years. After a long break from philosophy, when he worked in Austria as a schoolteacher and a gardener, he returned to Cambridge in 1929. In the second major phase of his career he wrote a more complex and less coherent work known as *Philosophical Investigations* (published posthumously in 1953). In this book he explored the idea that language is used in a wide variety of ways in different social situations. Far from just being used to "picture" facts about the world, it is also used for such things as prayer, criminal interrogation, social conversation, and so on. Wittgenstein referred to these different situations as "language games." In marked contrast to his arguments in *Tractatus*, he came to believe that language games are not related by a simple underlying logic; they just happen to have things in common. Wittgenstein also realized that the meaning of language depends greatly on the game being played or, in other words, on the context in which words are being used. (A judge who says, "I give you five years," to a prisoner means something very different from a doctor who says the same thing to a terminally ill patient.)

Wittgenstein died in Cambridge in 1951. But more than half a century after his death his ideas continue to exert a powerful influence on the psychologists and philosophers working to unravel the mysteries of language.

nonverbal communication do not build up into layers of meaning in the same way that words, sentences, and paragraphs do. Perhaps this is the ultimate indication of the power of language as a communication tool: It can be used for everything from the one-word hellos and goodbyes of everyday life to the speeches of Martin Luther King and the plays of Shakespeare.

NONVERBAL COMMUNICATION

People are constantly sending out nonverbal signals, but how many of these "transmissions" (to use the language of communications theory) are actually received? There is a major distinction between nonverbal behavior (sending out signals) and nonverbal communication (sending out signals that are received and interpreted by other people).

Nonverbal communication is quite different, in this respect, from verbal communication. Generally, when a person speaks to someone else, they do so with the intention of communicating a precise message. Nonverbal communication is much more of a hit-and-miss affair. For one thing, people are often unaware that

FOCUS ON

COMMUNICATING WITH THE EYES

It is often said that "the eyes are the windows to the soul," and some psychological research seems to confirm this. Our eyes convey an enormous amount of nonverbal information, both in where they choose to look and in the appearance they give to the people we are talking to.

Early in the 1960s researchers Eckhard H. Hess and J. M. Polt suggested that the size of the pupils in a person's eyes reveals something of what they are thinking: When people look at interesting pictures, their pupils dilate (become larger). When Hess and Polt showed pictures of nude women to a group of men, the men's pupils dilated significantly; women's pupils dilated when they were shown pictures of nude men or photos of mothers and babies. (Other researchers have disputed this, however.)

In a later study Hess showed two almost identical pictures of an attractive woman to a group of young men. The only difference between the pictures was that in one picture the woman's pupils were very dilated, while in the other her pupils had been altered photographically to appear much smaller. Hess found that the men's pupils dilated much more when they looked at the woman with dilated pupils, and they tended to describe her as pretty, feminine, soft, and attractive. When they looked at the woman with smaller pupils, their pupils dilated less, and they described her as cold, selfish, and hard. Interestingly, most of the young men who took part in the experiment believed the two photographs were identical.

The amount of eye contact people make during conversation is another important form of nonverbal communication. If a person makes too little eye contact, they may seem distant, shifty, or untrustworthy; if they make too much eye contact, they can seem unnerving, offensive, or aggressive. There also seem to be important differences in eye contact both between genders and between cultures. Women generally seem to make less eye contact than men, for example. In some cultures it is acceptable to gaze at people for a long time; elsewhere staring is considered rude. Looking someone in the eye is considered a mark of respect in some countries; in others it is considered more respectful not to look at them.

Eyebrows also play a significant role in nonverbal communication. Zoologists have found that both humans and other primates show dominance by lowering their eyebrows. And greeting someone with a briefly raised eyebrow is a greeting understood by most cultures throughout the world.

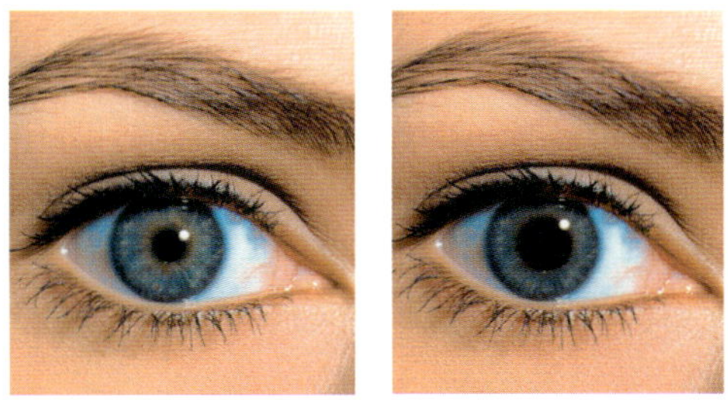

Our eyes can convey a great deal of nonverbal information even though we may be unaware of it. Pupil dilation (as in the eye on the right) is usually a sign of interest or attraction, and we also respond subconsciously to dilated pupils in others.

British naturalist Charles Darwin was the first scientist to propose a theory of evolution. He also studied nonverbal communication, concluding that it was important for survival in many species.

they are communicating at all. Students slouched over their desks may not realize they are communicating "boredom" to their teacher; friends touching or gazing into one another's eyes may not realize they are communicating "love." These nonverbal messages are often transmitted automatically by the sender, but whether or not these subtle signals are received is a different matter. The teacher might not realize just how boring the lesson has become; the two friends may never realize that they are actually in love.

Early studies

One of the first people to study the importance of nonverbal communication was British naturalist Charles Darwin (1809–1882). In his book *The Expression of the Emotions in Man and Animals* (1872) he outlined the importance of facial expressions and other types of nonverbal communication in various animal species. Darwin argued strongly that much of human communication was innately determined and that it served the interests of humans as a species.

Radical though they seemed at the time, some of Darwin's ideas had long been anticipated in other cultures. The Chinese, for example, had evolved rules over thousands of years for judging people's character from their physiognomy (the size and shape of their face). Later, the ancient Greek playwright Theophrastus (about 372–287 B.C.) compiled a catalog of 30 human personalities called characters, which he described in terms of their particular characteristics, including their body language. Similar ideas can be found in Indian culture, too. The modern equivalent of these "spotter's guides" to nonverbal communication is *Manwatching*, a best-selling 1970s study of how people relate to one another written by British zoologist Desmond Morris (born 1928).

Sometimes these ideas were taken to extremes by people who thought they could detect meaningful communication channels when none were really there. The phrenologists, for example, believed that feeling for bumps on a person's skull could shed insight on their character (*see* Vol. 1, pp. 30–39). And in 1895 Italian physician Cesare Lombroso (1836–1909)

"The power of communication between the members of the same tribe by means of language has been of paramount importance in the development of man; and the force of language is much aided by the expressive movements of the face and body."

—Charles Darwin, 1872

famously published his study *Criminal Anthropology*. Lombroso believed it was possible to detect whether or not people were likely to be criminals from their bodily and facial characteristics, arguing that people with long fingers were more likely to be pickpockets, while murderers tended to have large jaws.

These ideas seem preposterous today, yet most of us regularly misinterpret signals of nonverbal communication or leap to similarly absurd conclusions. How many of us, for example, have a mental image of the classic "egg-headed" professor, with his balding pate, thin face, and mean eyeglasses? And how many professors correspond to this stereotype? Sometimes our haste to generalize from nonverbal cues can lead to surprising results. In a 1988 experiment that illustrates this point well, psychologists Diane Berry and Leslie McArthur showed that juries are less likely to judge people with "baby faces" (round face, large eyes, high eyebrows, small chin) as guilty of criminal behavior than people with other facial types.

Nature or nurture?

Charles Darwin argued that nonverbal communication was adaptive: It conferred an advantage that helped species survive (*see* Vol. 1, pp. 134–143). It is easy to see why this should be the case. A dog that barks loudly or otherwise displays its aggression to warn other dogs away from its patch is less likely to have to fight for its territory than a dog that does not, and a dog that avoids fighting is more likely to survive than a dog that does not. A baby that cries whenever it is hungry or in pain is more likely to be suckled than a baby that never cries. Darwin contended that nonverbal communication serves various other useful purposes, most notably in attracting mates, and several psychologists have since supported his view.

An impressive demonstration that nonverbal communication is more a product of nature than of nurture has come from the work of U.S. psychologist Paul Ekman and his collaborators. In a classic study carried out in 1971, Ekman and his colleague Wallace Friesen asked members of an isolated New Guinea tribe to make facial expressions to match a set of basic emotions such as "you are happy," "your child has died," and "you are angry and about to fight." They photographed the expressions and showed the pictures to people in the United States, who could recognize which expression was which with a high degree of accuracy. The same experiment also worked in reverse: The New Guinea subjects proved equally able to recognize expressions on the faces of Americans. In a 1987 study Ekman and his colleagues carried out a more extensive experiment using six different facial expressions in a mixture of ten western and nonwestern countries (*see* p. 83). They found that people across all these cultures were remarkably successful in correctly identifying the six expressions.

We do not always realize when and how we are communicating. For example, close friends often show their affection subconsciously, using nonverbal messages. They may touch frequently or gaze into each other's eyes, although they may not be consciously aware that they are communicating love.

Types of nonverbal communications

Although people communicate through many different nonverbal channels, some are particularly important in the sense that they carry more useful information.

Sign Language

FOCUS ON

When we think of language, we tend to think of written and spoken words, yet not everyone communicates in this way. North American Plains Indians developed a system of gestures called sign language so they could communicate with tribes who used different languages. Their sign language includes gestures for naming each tribe, for emotions, for types of weather, and for elements of the landscape such as rivers and trees. Sign language is also common among the native peoples of India and Australia.

Perhaps the best known sign languages are those used by deaf people. Some involve spelling out words letter by letter, while a system called cued speech is based on emphasizing word sounds. A widely used system called American Sign Language (ASL), or "signing," is a fully fledged language with gestures that represent words and concepts. Now used by around 500,000 people in North America, it was developed in the 19th century by American educator Thomas Gallaudet (1787–1851) from a French sign language (FSL) invented in the 18th century.

Research by psychologists suggests ASL behaves more like a written or spoken language than ordinary nonverbal gestures. Instead of simply being translated from English or another language, ASL gestures originate independently within communities of deaf people, even to the extent that different regional communities evolve their own words and slang. ASL has its own grammar and syntax for combining individual words into sentences. And tellingly, children born to parents who use ASL pick up the gestures in much the same way that other children pick up languages such as spoken English.

American sign language has gestures for both words and concepts but, in many ways, is more like a spoken language.

Thus people's body language typically says more than their hairstyle or perfume, while the tone of their voice may, on occasion, say more than the words they speak. As a consequence, psychologists have studied some types of nonverbal communication more than others: notably kinesics (body language), paralinguistics (the tone of people's voices and other things that color the way their words are understood), and proxemics (how near people place themselves to others).

Most people have heard of "body language" since the publication of Julius Fast's 1970 book of the same name. Body language is also referred to as kinesics thanks to psychologist Ray Birdwhistell. Kinesics includes people's basic posture, the gestures they make, their facial expressions, their eye movements, whether they touch the people near to them, and various other communication channels.

People who adopt similar postures while they converse are unconsciously showing liking, so they are more likely to be friends or to be sharing similar views than two people with different postures.

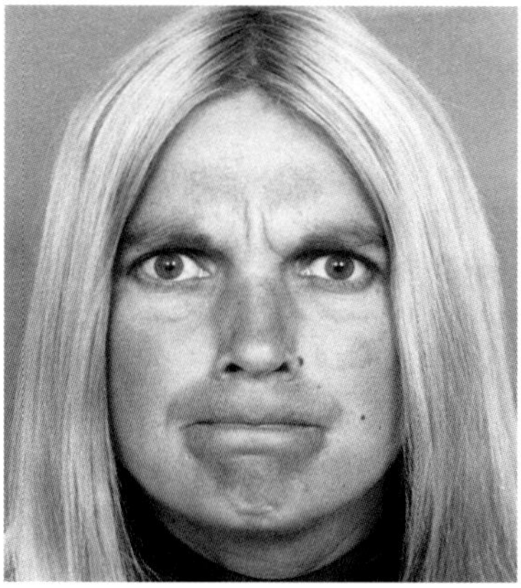

Anger

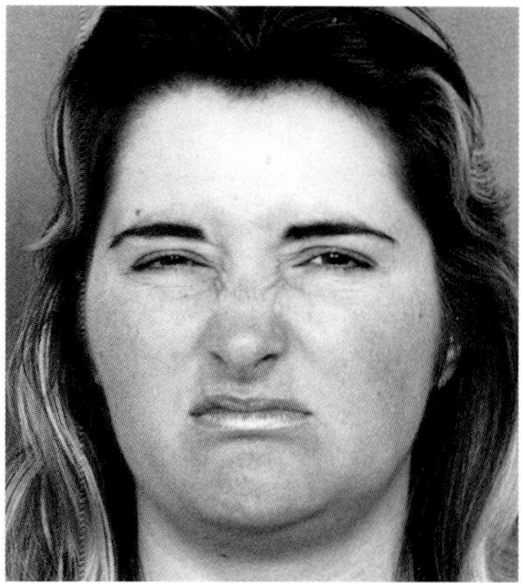

Disgust

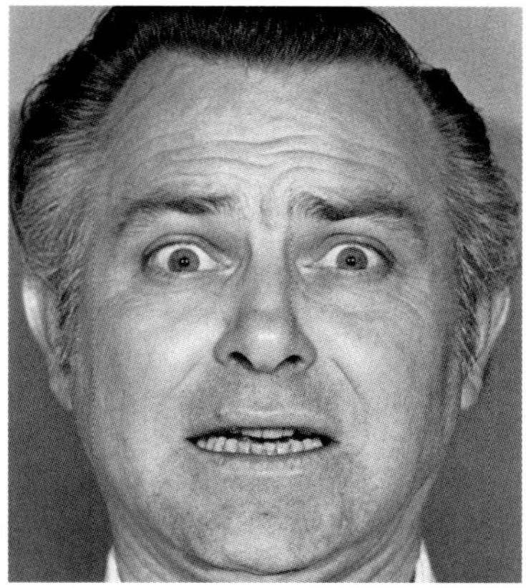

Fear

Happiness

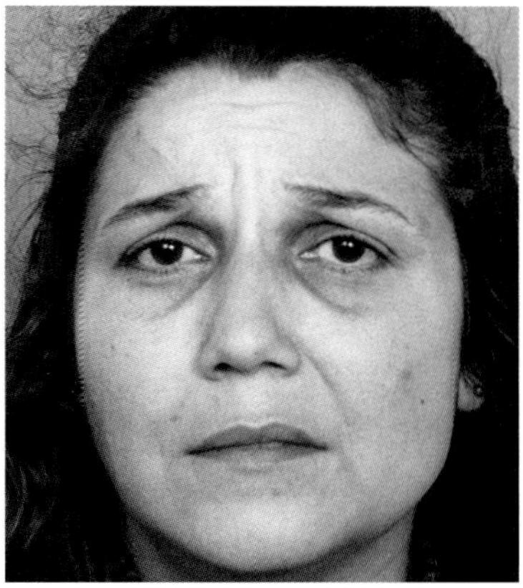

Sadness

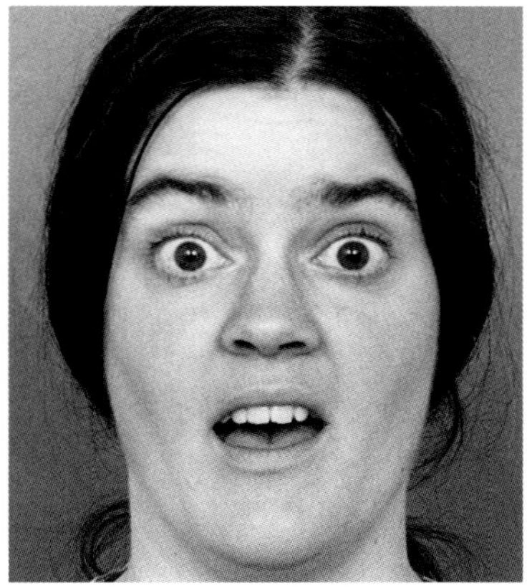

Surprise

Paul Ekman and his colleagues showed that people have a basic set of universally recognizable facial expressions. They include the six shown above: anger, disgust, fear, happiness, sadness, and surprise.

A person taking part in a job interview will adopt a very different posture than a person relaxing on the couch at home, while two lovers are likely to engage in much more open and sexually provocative body language than two work colleagues. One interesting observation about posture is the way friends and lovers tend to mimic one another's postures when they are talking. Sometimes known as postural congruence, it can be a reliable indication of whether two people generally get along. People who adopt similar postures when they sit or stand near one another are most likely to be getting along and sharing similar views; those who adopt different postures are quite likely to disagree.

Facial expressions have been studied more than most other types of body language. The work of Ekman and his colleagues seems to show that there is a basic set of facial expressions that is understood around much of the world, a minilanguage in which thousands of words are swapped for the six basic expressions of happiness, sadness, fear, surprise, disgust, and anger. But do people make faces to communicate or simply to express their emotions? A 1979 study by social psychologists R. E. Kraut and R. E. Johnston measured when people were likely to smile in different social settings, such as in bowling matches. They found that when bowlers successfully knocked down the pins, they were much more likely to smile if they were facing toward their friends than if they were facing down the alley. Thus in social situations smiling seems to be more about communication than simply showing feelings. When we

Gestures vary widely between cultures, and certain gestures can mean quite different things depending on where they are used. In the United States, for example, making a circle with your index finger and thumb signifies something is OK. In Japan the same gesture means money, and in France it means zero or worthless. In Australia, Spain, Germany, the Middle East, and Latin America this gesture is considered insulting.

smile at other people, they are likely to smile back and to feel some of the original emotion that made us smile to begin with.

Considering how long we spend looking at other people's faces when they talk to us, it is hardly surprising that facial expressions have become an important form of communication, and the fact that there appears to be a region of the brain's right hemisphere specialized in face recognition confirms just how important face recognition is (*see* Vol. 4, pp. 40–57). Less obvious, but no less important, however, are the gestures people make. While the ability to make and understand facial expressions seems to be hard-wired in our brains, a 1979 study by Desmond Morris and his colleagues suggests that gestures are much more a product of people's individual culture. In Thailand, for example, it is rude to point the sole of your foot or shoe toward another person; in other countries that gesture might pass unnoticed. In the United States extending two fingers from your hand and pointing them upward signals victory no matter which way your palm is facing. But in the UK that gesture is highly offensive if you keep your palm pointing toward you. Although many gestures depend on local culture, some do seem to be universally understood. Smiling at someone usually indicates friendliness, for example.

Proxemics, or the space people feel they need to leave between themselves and others around them, is another type of nonverbal communication that varies widely from culture to culture. Just as dogs tend to feel threatened by incursions into their territory, so humans can feel uncomfortable if their space is violated. Dogs may bark; people may back away until they feel comfortable again. Research by anthropologist Edward Hall in the

Culture dictates how close you can come to another person without invading their personal space, and this distance will also vary according to the type of relationship you have with that person. In the United States a casual conversation would usually take place at a distance of between 4 feet (1.2m) and 18 inches (0.4m).

1960s suggested there are four zones of increasing intimacy for typical North Americans. More or less anyone is allowed in the most distant zone, which ranges outward from 12 feet (3.7 m). From 4 to 12 feet (1.22–3.7 m) people will allow in strangers who have some connection with them, such as other guests at a cocktail party. From 18 inches to 4 feet (0.5–1.2 m) is a more personal zone in which casual conversations take place. But only lovers, close friends, and relations or children are allowed into the most intimate zone at distances closer than 18 inches (0.5 m). These distances vary between cultures.

Why communicate nonverbally?

Given that most people have the ability to communicate verbally, what possible use is nonverbal communication? The question may be obvious, but it is also something of a red herring, since we cannot help but communicate by nonverbal as well as verbal means. It is more enlightening, therefore, to ask how verbal and nonverbal communication relate to one another.

According to Paul Ekman, there are five possible relationships between verbal and nonverbal communication. Nonverbal communication can take the place of verbal communication, for example, when successful bowlers smile instead of saying "Yeah!" Nonverbal communication can agree with verbal communication, such as when we say yes and nod our heads at the same time. Equally, it can disagree, such as when we speak a lie but our guilty body language gives us away (*see* box p.

> ***"If the spoken language is stripped away and the only communication left is body language, the truth will find some way of poking through."***
> ***—Julius Fast, 1970***

FOCUS ON

Can You Tell When Someone Is Lying?

Nonverbal communication often complements the messages we send when we speak, but sometimes we transmit quite different messages in our verbal and nonverbal channels. The most obvious example of this discrepancy is when we tell lies. What gives us away is the difference between the verbal and nonverbal signals we send out. When we lie, we may adopt an unusually tense posture, wring our hands, behave nervously and shiftily, use a higher pitched voice than usual, make more errors in our speech, or display other signs of fear. We may be able to lie with words, but there's usually less we can do to keep our gestures from telling the truth.

In a 1974 experiment Paul Ekman showed emotional films to nurses and then asked them either to reveal their true feelings or to try to conceal them. Ekman made videotapes of the nurses as they spoke and then showed them to other people, who had to judge whether the nurses were telling the truth or lying. Some of the tapes focused on the nurses faces, while others focused on their body language. Ekman found that the judges who saw the body language tapes were much more effective at figuring out when the nurses were lying than those who were shown the tapes of facial expressions. Ekman describes the way the truth leaks out in situations such as this as "nonverbal leakage."

Law enforcement officers become practiced at working out whether people are telling the truth. They often use a scientific gadget called a polygraph (or lie detector), which is based on the idea that nonverbal communication can reveal when a person is telling lies. Wired up to a criminal suspect, it measures breathing, pulse rate, and fingertip perspiration and displays the results on a moving graph. Initially a trained operator asks some reference questions (ones to which the answers can be verified) and then begins to ask real questions about the crime that the suspect may have committed. By comparing the graph traces generated for the reference questions with those generated for the real questions, it is theoretically possible to figure out whether the suspect is telling the truth. In practice, however, lie detectors can be unreliable. For this reason evidence from lie detectors cannot be used in court in some countries, such as the UK.

FOCUS ON

Gender Differences

Women and men show a wide range of differences in their ability both to transmit and receive nonverbal communication. Women, for example, are consistently better at sending out nonverbal signals, and they are generally more "touchy-feely" than men. And both men and women find it easier to decode women's nonverbal communications, especially women's facial expressions.

A wide range of studies has also found that women are consistently better at responding to nonverbal communications than men. In 1978 U.S. psychologist Judith Hall reviewed 75 separate scientific studies of gender differences in nonverbal communication. Twenty-four of the studies showed differences between the sexes, and 23 of them were differences that favored women. In 1984 Hall reviewed another 50 studies and found 11 more sex differences, 10 of which favored women.

Women, for example, seem to be slightly better than men at detecting lying from nonverbal cues, and there is some evidence to suggest they are born with a natural gift for nonverbal communication. Some studies, for example, have found that baby girls are more likely to cry than baby boys when they hear another baby crying nearby. It also seems that boys learn not to cry when they are upset, while girls do not behave in the same way. Generally studies find that girls are better than boys at transmitting and receiving nonverbal communication, just as women are better than men in later life.

Although the differences between the sexes are small, they are statistically significant. Quite why women should be better than men at nonverbal communication remains a mystery. It may simply be that women have a better understanding of their emotions or that they generally pay more attention to their (and therefore other people's) appearance. Or it may have something to do with the woman's traditional role as a caregiver. A woman who has to devote much of her life to bringing up children, who are entirely dependent on nonverbal communication during the first part of their lives, is likely to become much more attuned to nonverbal cues. Another explanation suggests that because women enjoy lesser status than men in many societies, they have to pay more attention to the people around them, and that nonverbal communication helps them do so.

Women are not just better at nonverbal communication; they also seem more accomplished at conversation than men, disclosing more personal information and feeling more at ease discussing intimate topics. Women are generally much more polite than men, they interrupt less, behave in a less dominant way, and smile much more. They are much more accomplished at using intonation, varying the pitch of their voice sometimes up to twice as much as men. According to British social psychologist Michael Argyle (1979), these differences between men and women reflect the two very different functions of conversation: Women are usually much more concerned with conversation as a means of maintaining a social relationship, while men are generally preoccupied simply with transmitting information.

85). During public speaking nonverbal communication often complements or highlights a verbal message, such as when a politician wags a finger in time with a spoken warning. Finally, nonverbal communication provides a useful way for listeners to relate to speakers without interrupting. We often nod while we're being spoken to, for example, to indicate we are paying attention to the speaker.

INTERPERSONAL COMMUNICATION

Whether we're buying things in stores, calling up friends on the telephone, or talking to people in the street, most of the interpersonal communication we engage in involves two-way conversations with others; and these conversations may be verbal or they may be conducted without a word being spoken. Some conversations are conducted with a specific purpose in mind. During a job or college interview, for example, the interviewers ask most of the questions, and the interviewee is generally expected to talk at much greater length than they do. In a doctor–patient interview the purpose of the conversation is for the doctor to find out why the patient is ill. Other conversations, such as chance encounters with friends in the street, are conducted on a more equal basis and are as much about maintaining interpersonal relationships as exchanging information. Indeed, the word "conversation" comes from a Latin word that means association with other people.

The rules of conversation

Every conversation involves an exchange of information according to socially determined rules. The most important rule of conversation is that at any given time, one person is the speaker and the other is the listener; two people do not generally talk at the same time, and—obviously—both people cannot listen at the same time. Another rule is that people take turns at being speaker and listener, switching roles smoothly and predictably for the duration of the conversation. These rules of conversation are not usually written down or taught, but picked up as people gain practice at speaking and listening in social situations.

Although there are general rules of conversation, they depend substantially on the social context. In a doctor-patient interview it is both socially acceptable and pragmatically necessary for a doctor to ask all the questions and to behave in a manner that may be brusque. But if a doctor behaved in the same way at a cocktail party, he or she might be regarded as rude and domineering. When a woman talks to a small boy, she may have to ask several questions to begin with simply to overcome the boy's shyness, and she will probably have to persist until the boy begins to talk. But if a man behaved in the same way when talking to a woman, he would probably be considered rude or aggressive, and it is unlikely the woman would talk to him for long.

Sometimes nonverbal communication can take the place of a verbal exchange. Instead of cheering, for example, bowlers might celebrate their success by smiling and raising a clenched fist.

> ***"The rules of conversation are taken very much for granted. We are only aware of them if they are broken."***
> ***—Michael Argyle, 1979***

Nonverbal conversation

Conversations are mostly about the exchange of verbal information, but nonverbal communications also play a vital role. No matter how quickly people talk or whether they barely know one another, they can usually synchronize the roles of speaker and listener accurately without either person leaving long pauses between utterances or interrupting the other. The secret is the nonverbal cues that they give to one another. As speakers complete their sentences, they may lower their voice, make appropriate hand gestures, or look for some time at the other person. If listeners want to begin speaking, they may nod vigorously, begin to move their lips, or show other signs of impatience. Generally, the most important forms of nonverbal communication for speakers are tone of voice, pauses between words and sentences, gestures of different kinds, and use of eye contact. Listeners rely on vocalizations (such as "uh-huh"), gestures (nodding heads), eye contact, facial expressions, and posture.

Some conversations can be conducted entirely using nonverbal communication, without a single word ever being spoken. The rituals of greeting and goodbye, for example, are complete miniconversations. In different cultures people may hug, kiss, bow, or "high-five" in sometimes lengthy exchanges of nonverbal communication. Petting and mating rituals are nonverbal conversations, too, which are conducted according to socially determined rules, albeit ones that are very different from those governing verbal conversation.

Restricted conversations

Most conversations involve a combination of verbal and nonverbal communication, although the limitations of technology sometimes restrict the communication channels available to people. The most obvious example of this is when people talk over the telephone, during which nonverbal channels such as eye contact, posture, gestures, and facial expressions cannot be transmitted or received. Perhaps surprisingly, most people adapt easily to talking by telephone, and many find it a much more efficient way to communicate precisely because nonverbal signals do not distract from the information being conveyed. One study, for example, found

FOCUS ON

INTERNET CHAT

One of the things that guaranteed the growth of the Internet was its use of ASCII (the American Standard Code for Information Interchange), a type of least-common denominator, universal alphabet that virtually all computers can understand. Most Internet chat rooms, in which people converse by typing sentences onto their computer keyboards, are still based on nothing more than exchanges of plain ASCII text.

Despite this apparent limitation, highly emotional conversations can take place in chat rooms. The most obvious way in which people communicate emotions is by using combinations of ordinary keyboard symbols called emoticons or smileys. Thus a colon followed by a hyphen and a parenthesis :-) is equivalent to a smile (sideways) and usually indicates that the speaker means no offense. Other smileys include ;-) for a wink, :-(to indicate a sad face, and :oP~~ to indicate drooling.

With such limited channels of communication Internet chat should, in theory, make for cold and impersonal exchanges. Yet the opposite is often the case. In her 1999 book *The Psychology of the Internet* U.S. psychologist Patricia Wallace reviews studies of how the Internet can lead to strong friendships and even to lasting romance. As Wallace demonstrates, one thing that chat rooms do very successfully is entirely subvert our normal nonverbal communications. In a chat room everyone gets an equal shot at talking and being heard; in comparable situations in everyday life (such as at parties) only the best-looking, loudest, funniest, or smartest people might get a chance.

The Internet has opened up a whole new channel of communication, and despite its apparent limitations, people still use it to hold emotional conversations.

that people talk for longer, leave shorter pauses, and interrupt less often and for less time when they speak on the telephone than when they speak face to face.

The gains that telephones offer in efficiency of conversation have to be paid for somewhere, and the price seems to be a loss in emotional communication, with people usually reporting that telephone conversations have much less warmth than face-to-face ones. Yet the loss of communication channels does not always reduce emotion. People who use Internet chat rooms (in which people can converse by typing things on their computers) often form close friendships or even intimate online relationships, despite—or perhaps because of—the limited communication channels available (*see* box p. 88).

> ***"The Internet pulls the rug out from under our tendency to rely on good looks in interpersonal attraction."***
> ***—Patricia Wallace, 1999***

Conversation as social skill

It should be clear from the content of many conversations (or the lack of it) that communication of information is not always the primary concern. The fact that people are talking (about absolutely anything) is often more important than what they are talking about. And the way people converse—the way they follow the rules of polite conversation—says a great deal about them. People who are good at conversation make an effort to be friendly, to avoid confrontations, and to stick to the accepted rules (not interrupting a speaker, for example, and apologizing when they must do so). Good listeners (people who pay attention, ask sensible questions, and provide a sympathetic ear) are more likely to become friends than poor listeners.

When two computer modems or two fax machines first connect to one another, there is a brief period of what is called "handshaking" before any real information is transmitted or sent. During this period the two machines assess one another's transmission speeds and other capabilities and agree on a mode of communication that both can use. People accommodate one another in a similar way during a successful communication. Adults adapt to the inadequacies of children, for example, people with harsh accents may moderate them, and people trying to converse in a different culture will adapt to use either more or less nonverbal communication as appropriate. In short, people try to meet their conversational partners half way.

Conversation can bring and keep people together, but not all conversations are successful ones. They can fail for a variety of reasons, usually because one of the speakers violates one or more of the unwritten rules. People may speak too much or too little, leave lengthy pauses between utterances, constantly interrupt the speaker, talk only about themselves, fail to listen to the other person, or make various other mistakes. Conversation is one of the most important social skills, and people who fail to master it can pay a high price in their interpersonal relationships.

> ***"'My idea of good company, Mr. Elliot, is the company of clever, well-informed people, who have a great deal of conversation; that is what I call good company.' 'You are mistaken,' said he gently, 'that is not good company, that is the best.'"***
> ***—Jane Austen, 1818***

MASS COMMUNICATION

Conversations are fine for talking to our friends and families, but what happens when we need to send the same message to many different people at the same time?

President Clinton addresses a joint session of Congress. If you watch a political speech like this on TV, you will notice that the speakers use similar words, expressions, and gestures as when they are having a normal conversation. This type of mass communication is entirely a one-way process, however, and is more consciously planned than a personal interaction.

Mass communication is the name usually given to the technique of communicating with a whole section of society and can include anything from TV speeches by politicians to billboard advertisements from manufacturers. Indeed, much of everyday modern life relies on the careful application of mass-communication techniques: Margarine manufacturers use advertising campaigns to persuade consumers that their products taste "just like butter," politicians consult experts in nonverbal communication to sharpen their body language, and governments use public information campaigns to inform people about the dangers of smoking. Unlike interpersonal communication, however, mass communication is usually a one-way process conducted according to a very different set of rules.

Mass communication often uses strategies similar to the techniques that individuals would use in a conversation. When politicians make speeches on TV, for example, they often speak as though they are standing in your home, making gestures, looking at the camera, adopting certain postures, and so on. But unlike a normal conversation, mass communication is almost invariably one-way, which has benefits and drawbacks for both parties. Someone who delivers a speech on TV, or writes a billboard ad, or puts on a radio play can put a lot of thought into what messages they want to deliver and how best to do that. But they get no direct feedback from the people who receive them, and often they have no idea whether their messages have been received at all. Listeners, too, may find it easier to pay attention to a mass communication or to switch off completely in a way that would be socially unacceptable in a face-to-face conversation. But they cannot interrupt a TV politician, ask questions of a billboard, or join in with the dialogue of a radio play in the same way that they can interact in interpersonal communications.

The art of persuasion

Some forms of mass communication are designed purely to inform or entertain, while others—such as advertising—are designed deliberately to change people's attitudes. Although many advertisements are both entertaining and creative, every effective advertiser recognizes that the main purpose of advertising is to sell.

PSYCHOLOGY & SOCIETY

The Hidden Persuaders

One of the first people to shine a spotlight on the dark and sometimes disturbing psychological communication tricks employed by the advertising industry was U.S. journalist Vance Packard. In his alarming 1957 bestseller called *The Hidden Persuaders* he set out a catalogue of evidence to back up his contention that "Americans have become the most manipulated people outside the Iron Curtain."

People generally behave much less rationally than they would like to believe. They do one thing, but claim they do another; they behave in one way, but justify their behavior in elaborate ways so they appear better in their own eyes and in the eyes of other people. If people are so irrational, there is often little point in trying to sell them products by appealing to their rational minds through rational arguments. According to Packard, that is exactly what led advertising men in the 1950s to become "depth men"—employing psychologists and psychoanalysts so they could understand how to make their communications work more successfully on a subconscious level. The eminent behavioral psychologist J. B. Watson (*see* Vol. 1, pp. 74–89), for example, was hired to work as a consultant to the J. Walter Thompson advertising agency in New York City.

Packard cited many examples of hidden persuasion. In the early 1950s, when consumers first became aware of the effects on their teeth of eating sugary foods, sales of candy began to fall substantially. Sensing a problem, the manufacturers of some candy bars began to sell their products as a reward that could be given to children for being good, and promptly experienced a doubling in sales. Other products are also sold by hidden persuasion. According to Packard, toothpastes have always been sold by playing on people's guilt that they do not keep their teeth clean enough. Automobiles are deliberately styled and advertised to communicate all the kinds of virtues that their prospective buyers are likely to cherish. And sunglasses can even be sold in the dead of winter with appropriate communication techniques.

Although Packard's ideas remain interesting today, and techniques such as the ones he revealed still play a major role in advertising and marketing communications, things have moved on. Much of the suggestive Freudian thinking employed by early advertising campaigns has gone the same way as Freudian psychology. And consumers are now much more aware of how they are being manipulated.

Copywriters increasingly take account of just how conscious of advertising culture modern consumers have become, for example, by parodying 1950s ads or by making references to one well-known advertisement in another. Sophisticated advertisements such as these do not simply communicate the message "We're trying to sell you a product"; rather, they say, "We know that you know that we're trying to sell you a product. But by crediting you with more intelligence, we hope you're more likely to buy it." The fact that advertising remains one of the world's largest industries suggests that "the hidden persuaders" are still as successful today as they were in Vance Packard's day.

Although researchers have reached a better understanding of how people communicate, there is much they do not know. For this reason communication remains more art than science, one that some people seem to use instinctively to popular effect. Elvis Presley was thought to be a great communicator, prompting devotion from thousands of fans around the world.

Sales staff in stores are trained to engage customers in conversations that conclude with the purchase of a product (*see* pp. 52–54). But advertisements on TV, the movies, billboards, and in newspapers are not smart and cheerful sales staff who can talk people around. How, then, do they communicate, and how do they persuade?

Just as face-to-face conversations involve a process of accommodation, so advertising campaigns typically start with market research that establishes exactly who the consumers of a product are likely to be—the so-called "target audience" of the campaign. Next follows some serious thinking about the product and the key benefits that it offers. Often these benefits are encapsulated in a single key thought known as a proposition. If the product offers something that no other product can match, so much the better. This is known as a unique selling proposition (USP). It is then the job of copywriters to communicate this selling proposition to the target audience in an emotionally appealing, creative, and memorable way so that people are persuaded that they really need the product. Copywriters use a variety of techniques to help them do this, from inducing feelings of guilt (you must use deodorant X, or people will think you smell) to using endorsements by famous TV figures so that their status or credibility rubs off on the product. In a sense these tricks of "hidden persuasion" (and many others like them) are the equivalents of nonverbal communication in everyday conversations.

One of the hardest things about mass communication is knowing whether the message has gotten through. Psychologists working for advertising agencies usually test TV commercials with "focus groups" of typical consumers before they are run for real. Market research organizations also question typical consumers in the street (carefully selecting only members of their target audience) to see whether they have seen campaigns and whether these campaigns have been effective. Ultimately, however, the true test of mass communication is whether sales of a product increase or whether a politician gets elected. Armed with this kind of feedback, product manufacturers and advertisers can then modify their future campaigns. Over a long period mass communication campaigns and feedback devices such as opinion polls and market research amount to what is effectively a long and complex conversation between the communicators and their audiences.

> ***"Advertising may be described as the science of arresting human intelligence long enough to get money from it."***
> ***—Stephen Leacock, 1924***

A MYSTERIOUS ART

Everyone communicates information every minute of the day, whether they intend to do so or not. Most people are also constantly receiving information, either in conversations with people around them or through mass communication. Interpersonal relationships are built and maintained through conversations, while relationships between consumers and the goods they buy are built and maintained through more elaborate conversations involving mass communication and market research. Communication is to social psychology what money is to trade and commerce; it makes the world of interpersonal relationships go round.

Although communication is important, it remains more art than science, since psychologists still know relatively little about how people communicate. It remains unclear how and why people generate language, for example, or why people produce such a complex mixture of verbal and nonverbal communication during conversations. No one is skilled enough in nonverbal communication to be able to detect with 100 percent reliability when the people around them are lying, telling the truth, happy, sad, or sexually attracted. Similarly, no copywriter is skillful enough to write advertisements that sell products to everyone. Great progress has been made in teaching computers to understand "natural language" (the words we use in everyday life), but we still do not know enough to program computers that can understand anything but a limited range of commands or that generate completely convincing conversations. Despite all we know about communication, much more about it remains a mystery.

> ***"Communication is not simple . . . it is profoundly complicated; and the revelation of its hidden complexity is one of the great discoveries of the 20th century."***
> ***—Philip Johnson-Laird, 1990***

CONNECTIONS

- Evolutionary Psychology: Volume 1, pp. 134–143
- Cross-cultural Psychology: Volume 1, pp. 152–161
- Emotion and Motivation: Volume 2, pp. 86–109
- Language Processing: Volume 3, pp. 114–135
- Social Development: Volume 4: pp. 130–149
- Relating to Others: pp. 28–49
- Relating to Society: pp. 50–71

Personality

". . . dispositions, impulses, tendencies, appetites, and instincts . . ."

Morton Prince

Personality refers both to people's inner personalities and to their public personas; it consists of aspects such as motives, goals, beliefs, and values. Both perspectives are enduring and affect the ways that people think, feel, and act. Personality psychologists try to categorize people's mental characteristics, explain how childhood and other life experiences cause them to become the way they are, and predict how their personalities might influence their lives.

Personality is the characteristic and distinctive behavior, emotions, and thoughts that comprise an individual's response to his or her circumstances and environment. It affects the way people think and feel about themselves and others; it also influences the choices they make about careers, family lives, romances, and social relationships. How people think and feel about themselves affects how they relate to others, so studying the individual is a vital part of social psychology.

There are many theories of personality—possible explanations of why we are the way we are—and these can themselves influence our attitudes and behavior. A fashionable theory of personality, for example, can affect the way schools are run, the choices parents make when raising their children, and even social policy and government decisions. A theory can also help shape the approaches used by psychological counselors and therapists.

Personalities differ for various reasons. Family environment, culture, and life experiences all play a part; genetics is important, too. Behavior geneticists have tried to estimate the amount of variability due to genetic or environmental causes by comparing the behavior of children raised by their biological parents with that of adopted children (see pp. 142–163). The best and most easily interpreted studies of this type are those involving identical twins who were adopted and raised apart in unrelated families. In spite of their separate upbringings, these twin pairs tend to achieve remarkably similar scores in personality trait tests.

The big five

The aspects of personality that are most commonly measured are extroversion (gregariousness), emotional stability (degree of neuroticism), agreeableness

Some of the most informative data about the formation and nature of human personality have been gathered from studies of identical and non-identical twins.

KEY POINTS

- Personality refers both to people's public personas and to their inner personalities.
- Personality is partly inherited and partly a result of environment, culture, and life experience.
- Personality tests usually measure specific traits such as agreeableness; they are not definitive.
- Sigmund Freud believed unconscious conflicts between powerful instincts motivated behavior and he focused attention on the crucial role of emotional development during infancy and early childhood.
- Ego psychologists studied the role of infant attachment patterns in personality formation. Mary Ainsworth identified three types: secure, anxious/avoidant, and anxious/resistant (*see* Vol. 4, pp. 112–129). Mary Main found that adults' views of their childhood relationships with their parents correlated with their own infants' behavior.
- Traditional behaviorists argued that behavior is shaped by the environment and people's learning history. Albert Bandura proposed a more modern form called social learning theory, in which children learn by observing the consequences of other people's behavior.
- Humanistic psychologists suggested that a central, organizing motive guides human behavior: the actualizing tendency. People thrive when this propensity is allowed to flourish and suffer when external influences exert excessive controls. Susan Harter and Patricia Waters found that people who perceived approval as being based on certain high expectations were more likely to engage in false behavior. Diana Baumrind identified three parenting styles—permissive, authoritarian, and authoritative—that produce different outcomes.
- Sociocultural theorists believe that more sophisticated arguments are needed to capture the complexities of personality. Alfred Adler asserted that personality is inextricably linked to social psychology, suggesting that development is influenced by the way children deal with feelings of inferiority, and by birth order. Harry Stack Sullivan stressed the importance of "chumships" in personality transformation. Karen Horney identified three basic trends present in all people: the tendency to move toward others, the tendency to move away from others, or the tendency to move against others.

(warmth, friendliness, and social closeness), intellect or imagination (openness to new ideas), and conscientiousness. These are known as "the big five." Psychologists have estimated that about 50 percent of people's variability on the traits of extraversion and emotional stability are influenced by genetics and constitutional factors. Their lowest estimates for genetic effects on the big five are about 30 percent for the dimension of agreeableness. So, although personal and social experiences during childhood and adolescence play a part in influencing adult personality (which usually becomes stable and consistent at around age 30), they may account for only about 50 percent of the variation.

You may already have in mind elements of your own theory of personality. Your views may be explicit and well thought out, or they may be a set of implicit assumptions that guide the ways in which you think about yourself and other people. In either case you will probably realize that simple theories are unlikely to account adequately for the variety and complexity of human personality. Today, personality psychologists take account of historical theories and link them to contemporary findings in personality assessment and research in an effort to explain how each person is simultaneously like all other people, like some other people, and like no one else in the world.

> ***"Every single hysteric and neurotic remembers painful experiences of the remote past [and] still clings to them emotionally."***
>
> ***—Sigmund Freud, 1909***

Most personality psychologists of the 20th century developed their theories when there was much less information than we have today about the genetic and biological bases of personality. Some of them simply assumed that biology was fundamentally important, while others focused on the influence of the social environment (*see* table p. 97). Yet although their research was inhibited by lack of data, it still provides a useful foundation for the modern study of personality structure, development, and dynamics. Sigmund Freud (1856–1939) (*see* Vol. 1, pp. 52–65), for example, proposed that unconscious conflicts between powerful instincts motivate human behavior, and that these conflicts stem from experiences early in life. The U.S. psychologist John B. Watson (1878–1958) thought this theory was unscientific (*see* p. 106), and rejected the idea of the unconscious mind. Watson argued that behavior is shaped by the environment (external determinism) and people's learning history, and he was optimistic about the possibility of changing bad habits. Humanistic psychologists such as Carl Rogers (1902–1987) emphasized internal causes of behavior, and regarded environmental pressures as a potential source of maladjustment. Sociocultural theorists such as Alfred Adler (1870–1937) (*see* Vol. 1, pp. 52–65) believed these were simplistic arguments that failed to capture the complexities of personality.

FREUD AND PSYCHOANALYSIS

Freud provided the first comprehensive theory of personality development. His ideas subsequently influenced almost every aspect of psychology and much of people's everyday understanding of human personality. Several of the names

FOCUS ON

Personality Testing

There are many different types of personality test, but they all end up describing their subjects in terms such as extrovert, friendly, reliable, calm, and creative. (Almost 15,000 words in English language—about 3 percent of the total number—refer to personality traits.)

Raymond Cattell used a statistical procedure called factor analysis to devise 16 basic personality dimensions, in which everyone occupies some point on a spectrum between two extremes. His categories were reserved/outgoing, less intelligent/more intelligent, emotionally unstable/emotionally stable, humble/assertive, sober/happy-go-lucky, expedient/conscientious, shy/venturesome, tough minded/tender minded, trusting/suspicious, practical/imaginative, forthright/shrewd, self-assured/apprehensive, conservative/experimenting, group dependent/self-sufficient, undisciplined/controlled, relaxed/tense.

Other psychologists have come up with different categories. Hans Eysenck, for example, believed that only two broad factors were needed to capture the structure of personality: extroversion and neuroticism. Researchers agree that personality comprises the big five dimensions: Openness to new ideas; Conscientiousness; Extroversion; Agreeableness; Neuroticism (OCEAN).

Many tests require subjects to indicate which of a number of different statements they think best describes them. When testing the big five, subjects might be asked which of the following statements they agree with:

Openness to new ideas

- I have a vivid imagination.
- I am quick to understand things.
- I have difficulty understanding abstract ideas.
- I try to avoid complex people.

Conscientiousness

- I pay attention to details.
- I make plans and stick to them.
- I leave my belongings around.
- I find it difficult to get down to work.

Extroversion

- I feel comfortable around people.
- I don't mind being the center of attention.
- I don't talk a lot.
- I keep in the background.

Agreeableness

- I sympathize with others' feelings.
- I take time out for others.
- I insult people.
- I feel little concern for others.

Neuroticism

- I am relaxed most of the time.
- I seldom feel blue.
- I worry about things.
- I take offense easily.

In some tests researchers study the impressions people make on others (their public personas), and so subjects may be asked to rate the personalities of their friends.

Major Approaches in Personality Psychology

	NATURE AT BIRTH	INNER/OUTER CAUSES OF BEHAVIOR	DETERMINISM/FREE WILL MOLDS PERSONALITY	IMPORTANCE OF EARLY CHILDHOOD EXPERIENCES
Psychoanalytic (Freud)	selfish (sex and aggression urges)	unconscious/ inner	determinism	high
Behaviorist (Watson, Skinner, social learning theorists)	neutral (blank slate, or *tabula rasa*)	environmental/ outer	determinism	medium
Humanistic (Maslow, Rogers)	good (self-actualization motive)	conscious/ inner	free will	low
Sociocultural and biosocial theorists (Adler, Horney)	mix of positive and negative motives	mix of inner and outer	mix	medium to varied

he coined to describe his observations have found their way into everyday language: terms such as "Oedipus complex" and "the unconscious," for example, were invented by Freud, and their common usage in the modern world is testimony to the pervasiveness of his influence. Freud's psychoanalytic theory included three important areas: the tripartite structure of the mind, the psychosexual stages of development, and the operation of defense mechanisms.

Tripartite structure of the mind

Freud divided the adult mind into three parts, which he named the id, the ego, and the superego. The id comprises raw instincts such as hunger, sex, and aggression. Its sole function is to seek immediate gratification, and it operates on an unconscious, irrational level. Its unremitting pursuit of pleasure and avoidance of "unpleasure" (anxiety) provide the mental energy that fuels the ego and the superego.

The ego operates on both unconscious and conscious levels, and is governed by the reality principle. The ego attempts to satisfy the id by engaging in a process of reality testing. For example, if the id alerts an infant to hunger, the ego will prompt the child to place objects in his or her mouth until a food supply is found.

The superego develops when children are about five years old. It embodies family and cultural values. In other words, it is conscience—the part of our mind that gives us an idea of good and evil and guides us toward the former and away from the latter. The superego draws its energy from the id but controls it by acting as a brake on the id's most extreme and socially unacceptable desires.

> ***"Every normal person, in fact, is only normal on the average. His ego approximates to that of the psychotic in some part or other and to a greater or lesser extent."***
> ***—Sigmund Freud, 1923***

Freud's theory is based on the notion of internal forces locked in conflict. The id

Why do infants put objects in their mouths? Some people believe it is oral gratification, to compensate for the absence of the mother's breast.

says, "Do it now!" The superego says, "Never do it!" and the ego is left to settle the argument. So, the ego must balance the competing demands of three taskmasters: the id, the superego, and reality. The ego also provides the id with its only link to reality, one of its main tasks being to create a diversion that will appease the id and alleviate the anxiety caused by frustrated instinctual impulses. Defense mechanisms are a method of avoiding the pain caused by conflict; they operate by distorting reality to make it more palatable or less painful (*see* box p. 100).

The psychosexual stages

Freud's theories are closely tied to biological and maturational processes. He built the five psychosexual stages (oral, anal, phallic, latency, and genital) around physiological features such as the sucking instinct, the eruption of teeth, and the achievement of muscular control. He also placed emphasis on infantile sexuality, which he described as polymorphously perverse. By that he meant all areas of the body are experienced as sexually pleasing. To Freud infants are all id, and their instinctual needs seek a new outlet at each psychosexual stage. Thus personality development is a progressive shift from the polymorphous perversity of the newborn to focused zones of eroticism. Patterns of frustration and satisfaction of instinctual (libidinal) urges at each stage contribute to the permutations of adult personality.

In the oral stage the mouth is the primary erogenous (erotic) zone. In the early phase (up to approximately eight months) infants find gratification in feeding, sucking, and swallowing. In the later phase (during teething) they derive pleasure from biting and chewing. Satisfaction of these impulses contributes to their sense of trust and independence, but frustration or excessive gratification may increase the traumatic impact of weaning and produce a fixation on oral stimuli. Freud described fixation by likening the ego to an army. Becoming fixated at one particular stage is like leaving troops behind at a distant outpost, and the net effect is a weakening of the army. Thus fixations have consequences for later personality development (*see* table, below). For example, excessive gratification of sucking and swallowing needs may promote unrealistic optimism based on the early experience that one need only ask in order to receive. Frustration of urges to bite and chew may contribute to pessimism and the belief that a person's efforts are in vain. Fixations in the oral stage have been associated with seemingly mundane habits such as cigarette smoking, chewing pencils, and a preference for soft, milky foods as opposed to hot, spicy ones. They have also been linked to interpersonal styles such as high sociability and even the desire to acquire knowledge.

In the anal stage attention shifts from the mouth to the anal region as sphincter control becomes a physiological possibility and arouses the child's interest. In the early phase libidinal pleasure is focused on the expulsion of feces, and a delight in defecation and urination is typical in the toddler. The later phase is characterized by anal retention, and toilet training represents the first of society's attempts to control the child's instinctual impulses.

The phallic stage occurs between the ages of three and five. During this phase many children like to "play doctor," one of the most striking expressions of the shift in focus to the genitals. According to Freud, it is at about this time that children abandon hope of possessing the opposite-sex parent as a love object and start to identify with the same-sex parent. Prior to this stage boys view their mother as the primary object of their love and resent the father's competition for her affection—a resentment that takes the form of an

Psychosexual Stages and Personality Characteristics

STAGE NAME	FOCUS OF LIBIDO	SATISFYING BEHAVIORS	OUTCOME OF GRATIFICATION	CONSEQUENCES OF FIXATION
Early oral	mouth	sucking, swallowing	trust	gullibility, passivity, oral optimism
Late oral	mouth	biting, chewing	independence	oral pessimism, manipulativeness, sarcasm
Early anal	anus	expulsion of feces	self-control	obstinacy, cruelty, messiness, destructiveness
Late anal	anus	retention of feces	mastery of the environment	excessive conscientiousness, punctuality, orderliness, thriftiness, cleanliness
Phallic	genital organs	sexual curiosity, self-examination, and manipulation	sexual identity, superego formation (healthy conscience)	problems with authority figures, sexual maladjustment
Latency	—	—	—	—
Genital	genital organs and sublimation	sexual intercourse, intimacy, sublimation in work and art	fulfilling work, delay of gratification	—

unconscious desire to possess the mother and depose the father. Fear of retaliation leads to castration anxiety, causing boys to identify with their fathers both as a defense mechanism and as a vicarious source of instinctual gratification. By identifying with the same-sex parent, boys internalize cultural and family taboos against incest and develop a superego that is part ego ideal and part conscience.

For girls, realizing that their genitals are different from boys' produces penis envy. They become disenchanted with their mothers for depriving them of a penis and turn their affections toward their fathers. To possess her father, however, a daughter risks losing her mother's love, so to defend herself against this threat, she identifies with her mother. According to Freud, the prohibition against incestuous longings in girls is weaker than the fear of castration in boys, resulting in a weaker female superego. Many psychologists have criticized this view of female development, however. For example, Karen Horney (*see* pp. 114–115) asked whether penis envy in might not have a counterpart called "womb envy" in boys.

During the latency stage sexual instincts lie dormant (inactive), as children undergo a solidification of the superego formed during the phallic stage.

The genital stage begins with the onset of puberty. As sexual intimacy becomes possible, individuals seek new objects of affection and learn to sublimate other id impulses into productive channels, striking a balance between love and work. Often there is an unconscious tendency to seek a sexual partner reminiscent of the

FOCUS ON

Defense Mechanisms

Freud proposed the concept of defense mechanisms, and his daughter Anna provided a more complete elaboration of the various types, which include:

Repression protects the ego from consciously experiencing the anxiety of unacceptable thoughts ranging from taboo id wishes to painful memories. The ego keeps these thoughts in the unconscious—away from conscious awareness—where they continue to exert an influence over behavior.

Displacement replaces one way of satisfying an id impulse with another. For example, playing defenseman on an ice hockey team might be an acceptable form of displacement for aggression. When displacement takes a socially productive form, as in the ice hockey example, it is known as sublimation.

Projection attributes unacceptable, anxiety-producing facts about oneself to someone or something else. For example, instead of thinking "I can't dance," an anxious woman might convert her worry into the thought "He is a terrible dance partner" or "This music has no beat."

Reaction formation this defense mechanism transforms an objectionable thought into its opposite. For example, a man who is drawn to sexual perversions may become an evangelist who preaches against the wickedness of the flesh.

Sigmund Freud expressed what many others had previously thought, in this case that people who participate in violent sports must be giving vent to feelings that might otherwise erupt unacceptably in other contexts.

opposite-sex parent. When Freud described this tendency, he used the phrase "object finding is object refinding."

The goal of socialization, according to Freud, is to gain control of the perverse and murderously aggressive id impulses by exercising the superego (conscience) and invoking a system of defenses (*see* box p. 100) against the anxieties of id frustration and consciousness of painful memories. People do this in unique ways depending on the extent to which they have been satisfied or frustrated at each psychosexual stage of development; these different approaches combine with the superego to form an individual's personality.

Ego psychology

Despite the criticism of and controversy surrounding many of his theories, Freud succeeded in focusing attention on the crucial role in personality of emotional development during infancy and early childhood. He had many followers, some of whom developed their own versions of psychoanalytic theory, resulting in an approach called ego psychology.

Ego psychologists stress the importance of the ego from birth and propose a more optimistic vision of infancy than Freud. In their view infants are not simply a mass of unconscious id impulses but social creatures with an innate urge to interreact with others. This is the premise on which German-born American ego psychologist Erik Erikson (1902–1994) based his reinterpretation of Freud's psychosexual stages into a psychosocial model of personality development.

ATTACHMENT THEORY

In the 1960s British psychologist Donald Winnicott (1896–1971) described the relationship between newborn babies and their caregivers as a state of "fusion" in which mother and child experience such intense feelings of connection and attachment that the boundary between them seems blurred. The importance of this bonding has been supported by studies of early attachment patterns in orphaned monkeys. When given a choice between a wire "mother" with a feeding bottle and a cloth "mother," infant monkeys sought out the wire mother only to satisfy hunger but at other times clung to the cloth mother, presumably to satisfy their needs for contact comfort.

A baby monkey seeks comfort from a "mother" made of reassuringly soft cloth in an experiment by Harry Harlow. These studies influenced Donald Winnicott's theory of bonding between human mothers and infants.

> ***"The average family is all the time preventing and clearing up the disturbances in this and that child."***
> ***—Donald Winnicott, 1965***

The same desire seems evident in humans. Compelling evidence for the importance of maternal attachment in infancy was drawn in the 1940s from filmed studies of orphanages in which American researcher Rene Spitz found that after long periods in institutions, motherless children developed a type of depression he called "hospitalism." A typical child, he wrote, had "wide-open,

Attachment Histories and Interpersonal Styles

	SECURE	INSECURE	
		Anxious/avoidant	**Anxious/resistant (ambivalent)**
Toddler	easily soothed on reunion with mother; seeks proximity to mother	on reunion with mother looks or pulls away, ignores mother, or mixes proximity-seeking with avoidance; as easily soothed by a stranger as by mother	on reunion with mother mixes proximity-seeking and resistance (hits, kicks, cries); seeks contact prior to separation; inconsolable when separated from mother
3-and-a-half-year-old	greater persistence in problem-solving; greater enthusiasm and affective sharing with peers; greater peer competence and ego strength than other two groups	less peer competence and ego strength than "secures"; less freedom in exploring environment	less peer competence and ego strength than "secures"; may passively resist exploring environment
4- to 5-year-old	moderate ego control (flexibility in peer interactions); handles emotions of peers with greater ease, greater curiosity than other attachment groups	tends toward ego overcontrol (constrained); avoids contact with peers; low expression of emotion	tends toward ego undercontrol (high expression of distress, anger, fear); inappropriate reactions to peer interactions (impulsive, helpless)
6-year-old	in doll play, accepting, tolerant of others' imperfections; on reunion with parent, relaxed, responsive (initiates positive interactions)	in doll play, defensive, dismissing of attachment; on reunion with parent, maintains distance (ignores parent, continues to play)	in doll play, overt anger, hostility; on reunion with parent may exaggerate dependency/intimacy or spurn parent in overt or covert way (leaning against parent then jerking away)

expressionless eyes, frozen immobile face, and a faraway expression as if in a daze."

As interesting as these findings are, according to U.S. psychologist Shari Thurer, they led to the assumption that what was true in extreme cases applied equally to average mothers, and produced "researchers who were baby watchers."

Despite Thurer's reservations, it still seems that attachment affects infants' ability to thrive at a profound level that Freud did not explore. This type of research stresses the importance of infants' experiences of "felt security" as emphasized by British developmental psychologist John Bowlby (1907–1990), who suggested that such feelings arise out of parents' sensitivity and responsiveness to infants' signals or "affective" cues of feelings such as distress, happiness, and fatigue. The quality of young children's relationships with their caregivers also has implications for their ability to explore their physical and social environment.

Attachment patterns

Many theorists take the view that early attachment patterns may set the tone for basic personality styles, including people's emotional regulation in social settings. By observing mothers and their infants, and by introducing infants to what was called the "strange situation" (which involved mothers leaving the room and returning),

Canadian psychologist Mary Ainsworth (1913–1999) and her colleagues identified three styles of infant attachment to a caregiver: secure, anxious/avoidant, and anxious/resistant. These varying responses influenced childrens' relationships and their social development (*see* table p. 102).

Mothers of securely attached toddlers tend to be sensitive to the wishes and needs of their children but encourage them to actively explore their environment. Consequently securely attached toddlers engage in social interactions with delight and enthusiasm, and use their mothers as a "secure base"of operations when striking out into unfamiliar territory. As they grow, securely attached children demonstrate greater flexibility in their interactions with other preschoolers and tend to smile more and interact with greater emotional expressiveness than their peers. Preschool teachers have observed that such children display more positive emotions and handle negative emotion in others with greater ease. Children with a history of secure attachment are also more curious, have higher levels of self-esteem, and are more willing to initiate positive interactions with their mothers. They are highly adaptive, displaying social competence, enthusiasm and flexibility in problem solving.

Like securely attached children, infants with anxious/avoidant attachments have little difficulty in separating from their mothers to explore the environment and show relatively little avoidance of strangers in the presence of their parents. However, their interactions are marked by relatively little affective sharing, and when distressed, they are easily consoled by strangers. After a brief separation period these infants generally ignore or turn away from their mothers, although they may intermittently seek proximity. As preschoolers they tend to be excessively controlled by their egos: avoiding inconsistent or ambiguous situations, appearing less demonstrative, relating to others in a more constrained and conforming manner, and lacking much social spontaneity.

> ***"John Bowlby and Mary Ainsworth revolutionized the way in which we think about and observe young children and their parents."***
> ***—S. Goldberg, 2000***

According to Mary Ainsworth, a young child clinging to or screaming not to be parted from a parent is displaying anxious/ resistant tendencies.

Infants with anxious/resistant attachments find it harder than either of the other groups to separate from their mothers to explore their surroundings. They are wary in the presence of strangers and in novel situations, lack confidence in others, and in times of distress neither the mother nor a stranger can provide ready relief. They may react with extreme passivity to a reunion or show angry ambivalence, alternately seeking proximity and expressing themselves aggressively and emotionally. At preschool age such children continue to demonstrate general wariness in exploring the environment and tend toward ego undercontrol. They react to stressful situations with a high degree of emotion, have difficulty delaying gratification, and are typically more distractible, with generally short-lived interests and enthusiasms. After a brief separation from their parents they mix exaggerated bids for dependency with angry expressions of rejection.

This preschool child is having a tantrum, displaying anxious/resistant tendencies by reacting to a stressful situation with a high degree of emotion.

Internal working models

But how do attachment patterns such as these affect children's behavior in peer and school settings? Many theorists believe a child's early experience of attachment forms an internal working model that is integrated into the personality and invoked as a guide for behavior in subsequent social interactions. These attachment experiences are internalized by the child, but are subject to change and elaboration as a result of new experience. Thus, they are considered to be "working" models that provide a general guide or template for interpersonal interaction.

The notion of internal working models remains inferential, however. Researchers have not asked children how they structure their approach to others but have drawn inferences based upon the similarities observed between children's interactions with their primary caregivers and their interactions with peers and strangers.

Studies that have followed infants into the childhood years suggest anxiously attached infants experience more problems in peer relationships than those who are securely attached, and that these difficulties have adverse effects on the development of social competence. Current research suggests internal working models operate continuously, but longitudinal studies (research following the same people over time) extending beyond childhood are needed to clarify the stability or variability of people's interpersonal relations, and to test the importance of early attachments for personality development.

Researchers interested in internal working models have begun to explore the links between adults' perceptions of their childhood relationships with their parents and their own children's attachment styles. In the 1980s, for example, after identifying secure, avoidant, and resistant patterns using the subjects' retrospective accounts of their early attachment histories, Mary Main and her colleagues at the University of California at Berkeley found that mothers' responses to adult attachment interviews (AAI) correlated significantly with the behavior of their infants. For example, women who reported a history of avoidant attachment to their mothers had children who demonstrated similar attachment patterns. This suggests patterns of attachment may pass from generation to generation. In a comprehensive review of numerous studies, Marinus van Ijzendoorn of the University of Leiden, Netherlands also observed consistent relationships between parental AAI accounts and the quality of attachment to their children. This correlation was seen most strongly with maternal attachment patterns; but the older the children, the weaker the connection seemed to be.

Later, however, the use of AAI and other retrospective methods to access information about the continuity of attachment relations across generations came under scrutiny. For example, in the 1990s Nathan Fox of the University of Maryland suggested that the interviewees' temperament and current psychological state may have a greater influence on their responses than the actual quality of their early relationships with caregivers. Until longitudinal work proceeds to the point where adolescents who were observed as infants can be interviewed as adults, insights into the stability of attachment patterns will remain largely inferential.

> ***"The predictive validity of the AAI is a fact, [but] there is only partial knowledge of how attachment representations are transmitted."***
> ***—Marinus van Ijzendoorn, 1995***

FOCUS ON

Relationships and Attachment Styles

In 1987, Cindy Hazan of Cornell University and Philip Shaver of the University of California, Davis investigated potential links between adults' attitudes toward attachment and the quality of their attachments to intimate partners. They observed that the incidence of each of the three attachment styles appeared to be roughly the same in adulthood as in infancy: just over half (56 percent) of the adults in their intimacy study were classified as securely attached, while the rest were distributed evenly between anxious/resistant (20 percent) and anxious/avoidant (24 percent). These proportions were similar to those obtained in infant research, which classified 62 percent of infants as secure, 15 percent as anxious/resistant, and 23 percent as avoidant.

This woman's facial expression and physical pose seem to suggest she is pulling away from the man behind her. Superficially, she does not seem to be comfortable with his display of affection or concern.

Also in the 1980s, Mary Main suggested that avoidant adults may deny the importance of attachments, favoring compulsive self-reliance instead—a pattern reminiscent of the ego overcontrol of anxious/avoidant infants. Studies of college students suggest that anxious/avoidants tend to be afraid of closeness and to doubt the existence or the durability of romantic love. Moreover, they do not consider romantic love to be necessary for happiness. In contrast, anxious/resistant students describe love as a preoccupation, viewing intimate relationships as "painfully exciting." And just as anxious/resistant preschoolers tend to be ego undercontrolled (highly spontaneous, but unable to sustain interest and enthusiasm), anxious/resistant students have a personality style that enables them to fall in love more easily and more frequently than their peers, but makes it difficult for them to find "true love." They are full of self-doubt and are at ease disclosing feelings of insecurity.

Attachment and intimacy

Psychologists have also questioned whether persistent attachment styles extend beyond the family and early peer group. Do people apply their internal working model of attachment to other attachment relationships, such as those with intimate partners (see box p. 105). Researchers have used various experimental methods in their attempts to answer this question, such as retrospective self-reports and ratings by the subjects' friends. They have also studied adolescents' current relationships with their parents and compared them with those they have with their peers. AAI has also been used as a measure of adolescents' perceptions of their early relationships. Both methods have suggested that adolescents who indicate a secure attachment are more socially adept and better adjusted than those who report insecure attachments.

Personality characteristics also appear to reflect the three attachment groups described previously. Securely attached adults appear to expect close relationships to endure and to find others trustworthy. They tend to view themselves as likable and are described by others as emotionally expressive—patterns closely parallel to the higher social competence and freedom of emotional expression noted among securely attached children. Other people's evaluations of anxious/avoidant and anxious/resistant adults portray them as less socially adept than secure adults, although only anxious/resistant adults see themselves as less socially competent.

Psychologists still debate the extent—if any—to which the style of developing and maintaining attachments becomes integrated into the core personality. But the similarities between mother-infant attachment patterns, peer interaction styles, and adult attachments suggest that there may well be a link between them.

BEHAVIORISM AND SOCIALIZATION

John B. Watson tried to change the definition of psychology from the study of mental life to the science of behavior (*see* Vol. 1, pp. 74–89). He wanted to exclude Freud's concept of the unconscious and omit any reference to the conscious mind, which he considered to be an unscientific, philosophical abstraction. Instead, he proposed that psychology's primary goal should be the prediction and control of observable behavior, gained largely through laboratory experiments using animals and people as research subjects. Watson rejected the idea that instincts and heredity influence personality development, suggesting that all behavior patterns are learned entirely through environmental experience. He even suggested that the word "personality" could be usefully replaced by the neutral term "habit system."

Thus behaviorism is not so much a theory of personality as a general theory of behavior that rejects all explanations of the internal processes of a person. Watson assumed that human infants are a "blank slate" at birth, and whether they become adults with good or bad habits is determined by their environment.

Watson believed that most adult behavior is the product of classical conditioning—or simple association learning—as demonstrated by Pavlov's famous experiment with dogs (*see* Vol. 1, pp. 74–89). Watson explained how classical conditioning is crucial for human emotional development. An infant has no innate fear of a furry animal such as a rabbit, but does fear unexpected loud noises. In an experiment with a young boy, Watson classically conditioned fear of a rabbit by pairing a loud noise with presentation of a rabbit. This learning pattern also became more generalized so that the infant feared other, similar objects such as a fur coat. He concluded that over the years such experiences accumulate into a complex set of emotional habits.

Watson believed emotional dependency was the worst habit a person could acquire, so he advised mothers never to kiss their infants but to shake their hand and treat them as objectively as possible. By avoiding "love conditioning," he

Concepts of Learning

THEORIST	TYPE OF LEARNING	CHARACTERISTICS
Watson	classical conditioning	passive, association learning
Skinner	instrumental/operant conditioning	active response selection through reinforcement and chaining of series of responses
Bandura	observational learning	modeling and vicarious reinforcement
Bandura and Mischel	learning rules and symbols	concepts, strategies, expectancies

proposed that parents would encourage their children to grow up as efficient, self-reliant adults. Although Watson's childcare manual was influential in the 1930s, subsequent research on attachment has contradicted his advice. Meanwhile, his attempts to explain adult behavior through a history of classical conditioning came to be seen as too simplistic, causing later behaviorists to shift their focus to more complex types of learning.

B. F. Skinner (1904–1990) (*see* Vol. 1, pp. 74–89) concentrated on instrumental or operant conditioning. Rejecting the idea of free will, he concluded that behavior is a function of its consequences. Humans and other animals are active organisms, so any response or behavior pattern that is rewarded will be selectively strengthened, and whatever is ignored will tend to be eliminated. Skinner showed that, in this way, even pigeons could learn remarkably complex behaviors.

Research into operant conditioning in childrearing has demonstrated that consistent punishment inhibits aggression among elementary school boys. Skinnerian schedules of reinforcement have also been successfully applied in the treatment of autistic and mentally retarded children. However, complex human behavior, such as learning to drive a car or speak a language, required psychologists to look for higher levels of explanation on the hierarchy of learning.

Social learning theory

Albert Bandura (born 1925) helped pioneer the transition from traditional behaviorism to social learning theory by studying the role of observational learning. He noted that children who saw a role model being rewarded for acting aggressively, behaved more aggressively than those who saw a model punished for such behavior. Learning from the consequences of other people's behavior is known as vicarious reinforcement. What is observed is learned, but behavior that people think will be positively reinforced is more likely to be copied.

> ***"Most of the images of reality on which we base our actions are really based on vicarious experience."***
> ***—Albert Bandura, 1976***

Bandura and others extended this theory to encompass the most advanced types of learning (cognitive learning, *see* Vol. 1, pp. 104–117), which regulate complex behavior by using internalized goals, strategies, and expectancies. For example, Walter Mischel of Columbia University showed that specific mental representations of potential rewards helped children delay gratification in a laboratory test. Another key determinant of self-regulated behavior is perceived self-efficacy: the things people believe they are capable of accomplishing. It appears many variables influence this perception, including personal successes and failures, encouragement from other people, and adequate role models. Bandura believes that self-efficacy expectancy is a central feature of personality, and that people's expectations have direct consequences on their behavior. For example, a cigarette smoker's self-efficacy expectancies may cause him or her to say, "I'd like to quit smoking, but it's hard. I've tried before, and I don't think I can." But another smoker might say, "I'd like to quit smoking, and I know if I really put my mind to it, I can." The expectation of success or failure influences their level of persistence and may shape the outcome of their efforts.

> ***"People's beliefs about their efficacy affect the sorts of choices they make. In particular, it affects their levels of motivation and perseverance in the face of obstacles. Most success requires persistent effort, so low self-efficacy becomes a self-limiting process . . . to succeed, people need a sense of self-efficacy, strung together with resilience to meet the inevitable obstacles and inequities of life."***
>
> ***—Albert Bandura, 1976***

Bandura and Mischel have come a long way from Watson's radical behaviorism, but their focus on situationally specific behaviors still puts them at odds with theorists who assume a more coherent and consistent integration of a person's personality. However, some researchers continue to predict that cognitive social learning theory will emerge as a widely recognized, global theory.

THE HUMANIST APPROACH

In the 1940s and 1950s U.S. psychologists Carl Rogers (1902–1987) and Abraham Maslow (1908–1970) introduced a new personality perspective called humanistic psychology (*see* Vol. 1, pp. 66–73). Unlike Freud, they believed in people's innate goodness and basic integrity, suggesting that a central, organizing motive guides human behavior: the actualizing tendency. Rogers summed it up as the natural human urge "to maintain and enhance the experiencing organism." In his view, the actualizing tendency is generally positive and growth promoting—people thrive when it is allowed to flourish and suffer when external influences exert excessive controls or restrictions.

Rogers believed that personality development is influenced by people's interpretation of their unique experiences. They have a basically positive direction but may act in undesirable ways because of the distortions and defensiveness that result from conflicts between inner experience and the need to be held in positive regard by others. In an ideal world this need is satisfied by parents' unfailing expressions of acceptance, sympathy, care, and warmth. Children who live in a state of "unconditional positive regard" learn to trust their feelings and experiences, and use these evaluations to guide their future actions; this brings them closer to fulfilling their innate potential. As such children mature, the unconditional positive regard they have received from parents and others may be internalized as unconditional positive self-regard; this fosters a healthy self-concept that allows individuals to trust in their own experience and act on the basis of that trust.

Conditional positive regard

In reality, of course, most families extend "conditional positive regard" to their children. In other words, parents' acceptance of their children is partially dependent (conditional) on the children behaving appropriately. These "conditions of worth" are mutually understood. For example, Amy knows that if she hits her little brother, her mother may get angry and tell her she is bad. At the same time, she may really feel like hitting her little brother. Perhaps he's been teasing her all day. Confronted with the choice between hitting him (which would please her) and satisfying the conditions of worth (which would preserve her mother's acceptance and love), Amy experiences a classic conflict: "Shall I do what I want or what I know I should do?" In most instances children act on the basis of "shoulds" because the need for positive regard is so strong. However, Rogers views this need as the most serious obstacle to the course of actualization because it leads people to deny or distort their true feelings. The price is alienation from their true selves.

Amy has only a few options to resolve the conflict. She can hit her little brother, but that would produce a withdrawal of positive regard and be damaging to her developing self-concept ("I am a bad person because I hit my little brother"). Alternatively, she could distort her valuation of the experience ("I love my little brother and would never do anything to hurt him") and thus preserve her mother's positive regard at the expense of denying her true feelings. In an ideal situation Amy's mother would continue to express unconditional positive regard by acknowledging the validity of Amy's feelings but she would make a distinction between her daughter's feelings and the appropriateness of her behavior. She might tell Amy: "Sometimes we all get angry," suggesting it is understandable that she wants to hit her little brother, but explaining that he does not want to be hit and has a right to his feelings, too.

According to Rogers, treating a child with unconditional positive regard lays the foundation for healthy personality development. Acknowledging children's right to evaluate their experiences in their own way and providing a democratic, mutually respectful family atmosphere are the keys to producing fully functioning people. In fully functioning people the self-concept is built on trial-and-error evaluations; they can correct their mistakes, since they perceive them clearly and without distortions, and are notably free of the anxiety and confusion that plagues people who operate on the basis of conditions of worth.

At some time or another, all children feel the desire to hit someone. Whether they give in to the urge or resist it, their decision is often influenced by what other people may think of them. They are particularly concerned about the possibility that their actions may affect the level of affection they receive from their parents or carers.

True and false behavior

In the 1990s researchers such as Susan Harter and Patricia Waters of the University of Denver noted links between parental conditions of worth, distortions in the true self (false self-behavior), and self-esteem. In a series of studies Harter and her colleagues examined the level and quality of parental and peer support and adolescents' tendency to engage in false self-behavior. They anticipated that those who perceived approval as being based on certain high expectations (conditional support) would be more likely to engage in false behavior than those who were accustomed to unconditional approval.

They observed strong links between the conditionality of parents' support and the adolescents' sense of hopefulness about their ability to gain the future support of others. This, in turn, seemed to influence the adolescents' willingness to engage in true self-behavior. Those who received only conditional support were more likely to feel hopeless and to resort to false self-behavior to gain the unconditional support they sought. Those who received unconditional support maintained confidence (hopefulness) in their ability to gain support in the future, engaging more readily in true self-behavior (in other words, being honest about themselves, their virtues, their faults, and their sins of commission and omission). This work suggests that adolescents' subjective reactions to parental conditions motivates them to engage in either true or false self behavior, a finding that both corroborates and refines Rogers' earlier assertion that parental conditions of worth contribute to the development of the self.

Parenting styles

Other research also appears to support Rogers' contention that ideal parenting involves democratic family processes,

CASE STUDY

Unconditional Positive Regard and Creativity

According to Rogers, an environment that fosters constructive creativity provides children with both psychological safety—in which they experience unconditional worth but have no external evaluations imposed—and psychological freedom, prompting them to engage in unrestrained symbolic expression.

In recent years efforts have been made to test these assertions empirically. Using data from their longitudinal study of 100 people's psychological makeup (begun in 1968 at Berkeley, California when the participants were three years old), David Harrington and Jack and Jean Block developed three indices to measure the extent to which parents' child-rearing techniques conformed to Rogers' descriptions of creativity-fostering environments. They were compared with a composite of children's creative potential drawn from assessments conducted during their preschool years and during early adolescence. They found that parents who used Rogerian-style child-rearing practices with their preschoolers produced young adolescents who had higher measures of creative potential than their peers. Even after accounting for initial differences in the intellectual abilities and creative potential of the preschoolers, it seemed a history of Rogerian-style child-rearing increased creativity. In contrast, children raised in more restrictive (authoritarian) or chaotic (permissive) environments showed less creative potential.

Many psychologists believe that human creativity of any order can flourish only in an atmosphere of security that breeds self-confidence and in which failure will not be deprecated or punished.

unconditional warmth, and acceptance. In the 1960s Diana Baumrind of the University of California at Berkeley found that children with high levels of competence in social situations—those who were self-assertive, independent, and socially responsible—tended to have parents who combined nurturance and warmth with discipline and clear parent-child communication strategies.

Baumrind identified three parenting styles—permissive, authoritarian, and authoritative—which produce distinctly different developmental outcomes. Permissive parents are high on nurturance and warmth, and their communications with their children are characterized as very clear (*see* table right), but they tend to exert low levels of control and place few maturity demands on their children. Thus the permissive household is typified by the fewest external restrictions on the child. Despite this atmosphere of nurturing acceptance, however, the children of permissive parents tend to be less self-controlled and self-reliant and more dependent on their parents than those with authoritative parents.

In the authoritarian household parenting practices are the reverse of permissive. The clarity of parent-child communications is low, there is little nurturance, and parental control and maturity demands on the child are high. Children brought up in this environment are often shy and withdrawn, lacking in vitality and self-assertion, and low in motivation. Although children raised in permissive environments tend to engage in activities with greater vitality and a more positive mood than the products of authoritarian households, they otherwise behave in remarkably similar ways, exhibiting greater dependency on their parents and less self-control in their interactions with others.

Authoritative parents combine warmth, nurturance, and clear communication with relatively high levels of discipline and control. They expect their children to act maturely, and their children respond accordingly, tending to be self-assured, independent, highly motivated to achieve, and socially responsible. So their tendency toward actualization is socially apparent.

Baumrind's Parenting Styles

	AUTHORITARIAN	AUTHORITATIVE	PERMISSIVE
Control/discipline	high	high	low
Clarity of parent-child communication	low	high	high
Maturity demands	high	high	low
Nurturance/warmth	low	high	high

While Baumrind's data support Rogers' idea that nurturance, acceptance, and warmth are essential to children's healthy personality development, they are less clear about whether this acceptance must be unconditional. Indeed, Baumrind's studies tend to suggest that the best possible child-rearing style combines dependable warmth with clearly stated and realistic demands.

THE SOCIOCULTURAL INDIVIDUAL

Psychoanalytic, behavioral, and humanistic approaches have all produced theories of personality development in which people's preoccupation with selfish instinct gratification (Freud's id) is the primary instigator of human action. However, some of the pioneer theorists of interpersonal orientation, such as Alfred Adler, Harry Stack Sullivan (1892–1949), and Karen Horney (1885–1952), shifted attention away from these ideas toward the influence of social relationships and cultural contexts.

Adler and the inferiority complex

Adler defined his theory as individual psychology, describing people's striving for superiority as "the fundamental fact of life." He asserted that individual psychology was inextricably linked to social psychology—people strive not for themselves alone, but for the perfection of society. A lack of social interest is considered abnormal. Ideally, mothers should encourage their children to develop this natural propensity by acting as the first link to the social world, and helping them extend this interest to others. The role of the father, in Adler's view, is to foster feelings of self-reliance and courage and stress the need to establish a career.

Coping with inferiority

Adler believed that feelings of inferiority are the natural consequence of being a small, helpless infant. Children are aware of their parents' great size and relative strength, and much of their activity attempts to compensate for the feelings of inadequacy this awareness produces. Thus striving for superiority, excellence, and mastery is a natural propensity that can be enhanced or constrained depending on the circumstances of children's lives, especially their family environment.

In Adler's view feelings of inferiority can be a force for good or evil—they have the potential to wreak havoc or inspire greatness. Depending on how a child interprets them, these feelings may become either the source of all human striving or the root of psychopathology. In optimum settings these feelings are an impetus to grow and change. But if inferiority feelings become accentuated, children may feel overwhelmed and ineffectual, thus developing what he termed an inferiority complex.

Inferiority complexes have various causes, most of which can be attributed to treatment in the first five years of life. Adler identified three primary sources: pampering, neglect, and organ inferiority. Pampering exacerbates children's feelings of inferiority by depriving them of opportunities to develop independence and initiative. Anticipation of their every need makes them feel overwhelmed by their perceived inadequacies and they are unable to develop strivings for excellence and mastery. Neglected children may develop inferiority complexes for the opposite reasons. Believing themselves to be unloved and unlovable, they renounce the necessity for love, and become hostile or withdrawn. Without parental guidance social interest gives way to self-centered strivings, resulting in a style of life that lacks the capacity for concern for others. Compassion is replaced by mercenary feelings—"What's in it for me?"

Physical or organic deficiencies are another risk factor. Children born with cerebral palsy, for example, may have normal or superior mental capacities, but because their delivery systems (the physical means by which they may express themselves) are impaired, such talents may be underestimated. In such cases a physiological handicap develops into a psychological one, with intensified feelings of inferiority that impair the individual's ability to strive for achievement. Organ inferiority develops in response to a physiological impairment; an inferiority complex may develop in response to early childhood experiences, but it is not inevitable. Although Adler believed that people's basic goals and personality characteristics are developed by the age of five, he conceded that growth and change were possible through concerted effort.

> ***"It is not the child's experiences which dictate his actions, it is the conclusions which he draws from his experiences."***
>
> ***—Alfred Adler, 1912***

Research on birth order

Adler also emphasized the importance of birth order in personality development (*see* box p. 113), which prompted other psychologists to study the influence of birth order on the choice of career and development of the drive to achieve. Important work in this area was carried

The Importance of Birth Order

FOCUS ON

Alfred Adler proposed that family structure can have a profound effect on the development of achievement motives, career choice, and interpersonal skills. First-born children are likely to fall prey to pampering, increasing their chance of developing an inferiority complex. These feelings of inferiority may be exacerbated after the birth of a sibling, which may lead to a painful dethroning. Adler suggested that the personality characteristics of first-borns show higher levels of social maladjustment, which may lead to neurotic tendencies, alcoholism, and even criminality. On the other hand, first-borns may assume a parental role with younger siblings and be more able to accept responsibility. They tend to choose careers involving a high degree of responsibility but which are relatively conformist, such as medicine or law, perhaps reflecting their dislike for disruption of the status quo. Middle children are in a favorable position because they are unlikely to be pampered. Furthermore, the presence of an older sibling acts as an impetus to excel. In Adler's view middle children tend to be socially adept, highly competitive, and able to assert themselves to overcome feelings of inferiority.

Although youngest children escape the pain of being dethroned by newly arriving siblings, they are in the unfortunate position of being pampered by both parents and older siblings, compounding any feelings of inadequacy they may already have. Although the presence of many older siblings may produce a high degree of ambition and a tendency to choose unique paths, pampering may deprive the youngest child of opportunities to set goals and strive for their achievement. Adler considered last-born children to be the second highest risk group for inferiority complexes, but added that the stimulation provided by older siblings may, in some instances, inspire last-borns to excel.

Only children are in the unique position of never being dethroned and may continue to be pampered by their parents to the end of their lives. The result, in Adler's opinion, is that only children sometimes overestimate their own importance. Consequently they may have difficulties interacting with peers.

First-born children learn mainly from their parents; subsequent offspring are typically nurtured and even taught not only by their parents but also by older siblings.

out by Frank J. Sulloway, whose 1997 book *Born To Rebel* adduced a wealth of evidence in support of his theory that birth order does indeed affect personality, although not always in the ways that Adler suggested. For example, while there is evidence that first-borns are more obedient and willing to accept positions of responsibility in social situations, instead of suffering from debilitating inferiority complexes, they are more likely to seek higher education and to achieve eminence in their professional lives. They also tend to score higher than their younger siblings on standardized intelligence tests. Some researchers have noted that mothers demand more of their first-borns, are more likely to withhold affection if they fail on tasks, yet are extremely warm and affectionate toward them if they do perform well: a pattern reminiscent of Baumrind's authoritative parenting style.

The situation with regard to later-borns appears to be significantly more complex. The second child might be the first girl in the family, for example, or the youngest child might be the youngest of 12 rather than the youngest of 3. There are so many possible permutations that it may be impossible to create a general model of first, middle, and last-borns that takes all these important variables into account.

Attempts have also been made to study the influence on families of cultural differences and socioeconomic status. Despite many other variations, however, it seems birth order remains an important influence on people's ability to get along with others. The youngest children tend to be perceived as more affable than either middle or firstborns, and while firstborns appear to initiate social interactions with greater frequency than their siblings, their attempts are less successful than those of either middle or youngest children.

Peer influences and chumships

Harry Stack Sullivan was one of the first theorists to emphasize the role of peers in the definition and development of a unique personality. He proposed that friendships formed in the preadolescent phase—particularly the development of close, same-sex friendships ("chumships") —help children adjust any maladaptive features of their personalities (those that produce behavior with negative effects) developed during early family interactions. Sullivan described chumship as a forum for the "clearing of warps." In the context of a secure relationship chums can share ideas, values, and opinions, and thus give each other important feedback about the appropriateness and desirability of their actions and beliefs. For example, children who were adored by their parents may develop a heightened sense of their own importance that may be less favorably received in a peer group. Chums can share that kind of information without the threat of abandonment, and having heard the others' opinions make appropriate adjustments to their own behavior and to their developing views of themselves and their place in the world.

The emergence of chumship in preadolescence is made possible, in part, by children's increased cognitive capacities (as noted by Jan Piaget, *see* Vol. 4, pp. 58–77). Whereas toddler and early childhood interactions tend to be centered on object play, propinquity (nearness in place), and shared interests, friendships in preadolescence and adolescence involve increasing levels of intimacy, mutual trust, self-disclosure, and loyalty. Although some of the interchanges between chums stay at a fairly mundane level (such as exchanges of opinion about appearance), the creative work of chumship lies in each child's capacity to understand the other's point of view. This capacity for taking multiple perspectives (seeing things from many different viewpoints) is both a cognitive accomplishment and a sign of emotional development (indicating the capacity for empathy). However, a child's willingness to adjust behaviors and beliefs in response to mutual exchanges in a trusting relationship is largely the product of an emotional investment in the peer. Sullivan observed that chumship differs from other friendships both in intensity and level of commitment. In chumships the two individuals care for the welfare of the other as much as—or even more than—they do for themselves. Thus emotional investment and mutual support are the core features that enable genuine personality transformation.

Karen Horney's approach

Karen Horney was an early-20th-century neo-Freudian who emphasized the importance of relationships in personality development. In contrast to Freud, who believed that human mental disturbance is born of the conflict between environmental factors and repressed instinctual impulses, she took the view that inner conflicts arise from contradictory and equally compelling needs such as the desire for both privacy and friendship. In Horney's theory the ability to mediate effectively between these disparate demands within the self is the hallmark of healthy adaptation.

Horney identified three basic human

In the first half of the 20th century, Harry Stack Sullivan developed a theory of psychology based on interpersonal relationships, especially close friendships that he called "chumships."

tendencies: to move toward others, to move away from others, and to move against others. Essentially these trends are mutually exclusive, requiring people to negotiate internally between competing urges. Much depends on context, so while it may be appropriate to move toward others in a new work environment, a normal person has the flexibility to move away from or against an assailant on the street. In a neurotic personality, one trend may be dominant, and all interactions approached from a single perspective; alternatively, some people may vacillate between one tendency and another.

Most people have encountered individuals who might be called extreme in their tendency to move against others. Often regarded as troublemakers or bullies by teachers and peers, or as hostile and volatile by employers, these individuals have a Machiavellian world-view grounded in their need for control and their tendency to exploit others for their own ends. Conversely, individuals who exhibit extreme tendencies to move toward others are often viewed as overly solicitous, compliant, and malleable in interpersonal interactions. Their need for love, approval, and affection is so pervasive that all other urges are subordinated to it. Individuals with extreme tendencies to move away from others are often identified as shy or withdrawn. This tendency toward isolation and detachment is a simultaneous source of both discomfort and solace to the individual, who may feel, on the one hand, that it is best to fend for oneself, since others cannot be relied on to provide security, but on the other still acknowledges the need to socialize out of a sense of propriety. In Horney's view these extreme stances are the result of children's early experiences of security and safety in interpersonal relationships.

Continuity

In a series of studies published in 1989, Avshalom Caspi, Glen Elder, and Daryl Bem suggested that two processes combine to increase the stability of these personality characteristics. The first, known as cumulative continuity, involves a self-selection process. For example, a boy who tends to move against the world and whose ill-temper leads him to drop out of school limits his future career opportunities. He thus selects a set of frustrating life circumstances that evoke a continued pattern of striking out against the world—the progressive accumulation of consequences produces cumulative continuity. The second process, termed interpersonal continuity, is a kind of self-fulfilling prophecy in which people who expect to be treated with hostility may act in ways that evoke aggressive or hostile reactions in others.

Caspi, Elder, and Bem examined archival data from the Berkeley study (*see* p. 111) that had identified children with explosive behavior patterns. Two follow-up interviews in the 1940s showed that those with childhood histories of aggression continued to exhibit aggressive behavior into their 30s and 40s and were more likely to be divorced than their even-tempered peers. Men with histories of aggressive behavior experienced erratic patterns of employment and a progressive deterioration of economic status. Women with explosive histories often married men from lower socioeconomic groups, tended to be ill-tempered in their interactions

Close "chumships" are generally formed during preadolescence. These friendships are characterized by high levels of intimacy, loyalty, mutual trust, and self-disclosure, and according to Harry Stack Sullivan, are an important way for participants to receive feedback about any maladaptive aspects of their personalities.

with their children, and often transmitted their explosive style to their offspring.

Then, in 1988 Caspi, Elder, and Bem identified another group of people from the 1940s' surveys who had childhood histories of shyness. They found that in adulthood the consequences were most striking in males. Men who had been shy during childhood delayed marriage and parenthood, experienced greater levels of marital disruption, and took longer to establish stable careers than their peers. Women identified as shy were more likely to conform to traditional marriage and childbirth patterns, although their shyness did not affect the timing of these events. Given that the data were collected in the 1940s, most of the women studied did not establish stable careers, and the range of occupational status was small. Despite that, however, it appeared that shy women were the most likely to have no work history or to cease employment after marriage or childbirth. Outgoing women averaged nine years in the labor force, and shy women only six years.

> ***"The shy man does have some slight revenge upon society: he frightens other people as much as they frighten him. He acts like a damper upon the whole room, and the most jovial spirits become, in his presence, depressed and nervous."***
> ***—Jerome K. Jerome, 1886***

Caspi and his colleagues suggested that shy children grow into adults who have difficulty in dealing with situations that require initiative, such as negotiating career steps or proposing marriage. The demands on women to take the initiative, particularly in career settings, have increased as the definitions of sex roles in society have broadened. In a recent study of college women, Karen Kelly noted that shyness appears to act as a restraining barrier to their educational and career aspirations, mirroring Caspi's observations of men's career aspirations in the 1940s. It appears the long-term consequences of shyness may be determined at least partly by the expectations of society.

The development and stability of personality characteristics such as shyness and aggression appear to be determined by a diverse range of factors. Culturally prescribed sex roles, the expectations that people carry into their interactions with

Since the 1940s, the number of female university graduates has risen enormously. It remains to be seen whether this change, and the corresponding increase in the number of women who work throughout their lives, will influence the results of longitudinal studies of personality traits. Are cultural changes making women less shy, and more aspirational and successful as adults?

FOCUS ON

An Equation for Adult Personality

Psychologists believe behavior (B) is a function (f) of complex interactions between a person (P) and a situation (S): a behavioral equation often written as B = f (P x S). Adult personality tendencies (APTs) form a key part of the person part of this equation, influencing the way different people perceive and interpret the same situation. These tendencies are the outgrowth of complex transactions between various biological, individual, and social elements during childhood and adolescence, which can be expressed as follows:

T = Temperament, including genetics, constitutional, and biological factors.

M = Motives, including needs and goals.

F = Family, including family dynamics and the unique way each child experiences them.

C = Culture, including the national culture and subcultures within it, such as ethnicity, religion, class, kinship, gender, and peer groups.

U = Unconscious, including traces of early personal experiences, family and cultural values, and the collective or sociobiological aspects of being a member of the human species.

SA = Self-awareness, including conscious self-concept and thoughts and feelings about the other five elements (T, M, F, C, and U), which create the possibility of choice and future change in developing the creative self.

All this gives the following equation:

APT = T x M x F x C x U x SA

others (interactional continuity), and the accumulation of consequences of an individual's social behavior (cumulative continuity), all influence the life course of personality characteristics.

FUTURE DIRECTIONS

Contemporary work in the psychology of personality has advanced beyond the simple assumptions that underlay traditional psychoanalytic, behaviorist, and humanistic approaches to personality development. Instead of arguments about good and bad human nature, inner and outer causes of behavior, and free will versus determinism, modern researchers are looking for a new model of adult personality tendencies that accounts for all the complex transactions between people and their social environment. This model must explain how people's biological building blocks become transformed through encounters with parents, siblings, peers, and the broader culture to form the dynamic structures of adult personality. No psychologist has yet constructed such a working model, but research into areas such as gender roles, self-concept, motives, traits, and responses to specific situations should continue to clarify the major elements of personality, the composition of which may even be expressible as a mathematical equation (*see* box above).

In conclusion, personality is a term that is hard to define. Every individual may be unique, or there may be some socializing tendency that tends to make some people more similar than others. Neither is it clear how personality changes over time and according to situation. Some deny that it exists at all, saying that we have no more than tendencies and traits. Finally, and most worryingly for those who look for certainties, as yet there is no perfectly reliable way of measuring all aspects of personality. But as with many other aspects of psychology, while there are no definitively right and wrong answers, the questions alone are interesting and often illuminating in themselves.

CONNECTIONS

- Phenomenology and Humanism: Volume 1, pp. 66–73
- Behaviorism: Volume 1, pp. 74–89
- Cognitive Psychology: Volume 1, pp. 104–117
- Problem Solving: Volume 3, pp. 136–163
- Stages of Development: Volume 4, pp. 58–77
- Emotional Development: Volume 4, pp. 112–129
- Nature and Nurture: pp. 142–163

Intelligence

"Intelligence in its various forms and activities is what makes a man."

James Harvey Robinson

What does it mean to be "intelligent"? Are some people just naturally more intelligent than others? If so, why? Can we measure these differences and use them to predict real-life outcomes, such as whether children will succeed as adults? How should we interpret any differences in the intelligence of men and women or of various ethnic groups?

Most people can distinguish intuitively between "clever" and "stupid," but they find it much harder to agree on a definition of intelligence. In 1921 researchers asked 14 scientists to define the term and got 14 different answers. Most definitions included the ability to solve problems and to learn from experience but had little else in common.

British psychologist Charles Spearman (1863–1945), whose name is almost synonymous with the term "general intelligence," commonly abbreviated to "g."

Many psychological researchers have defined intelligence simply as scores on intelligence tests. However, this definition has two problems. First, there is no general agreement about what intelligence tests really measure. Second, the argument in favor of their use is circular—intelligence tests were designed to measure intelligence, and therefore intelligence tests are the best measure of intelligence. Such a definition tells us nothing about the nature of intelligence itself.

After more than a century of research several questions about the nature of intelligence remain unanswered. Is intelligence a single ability that helps people perform well at any task, or is it made up of several different abilities? Can intelligence be increased with learning, or is it fixed at birth? What are the characteristics of intelligent people? Each of the major theories about the nature of intelligence answers these questions differently.

THEORIES OF INTELLIGENCE

In 1904 British psychologist Charles Spearman gave a set of tests to a group of English schoolboys and observed that their performance on each of the tests was highly correlated with their performance on the others. Correlation is a measure of how strongly things are related to each other. Spearman found that people with high scores on one test also had high scores on the other tests. Likewise, students with low scores on one test also had low scores on the other tests.

To explore these findings Spearman developed a statistical method known as factor analysis that can identify the underlying reasons for these correlations. Factor analysis is a statistical technique that reduces a large set of variables to a smaller set, based on an underlying connection between the variables. It is a bit like cooking—if you bake a cake, you will notice that the taste of each slice is highly correlated with the taste of every other slice. To explain this, we could say that high correlations occur because each slice contains the same ingredients.

> ***"The more intelligent one is, the more men of originality one finds. Ordinary people find no difference between men."***
> ***—Blaise Pascal, 1670***

Based on his factor analyses, Spearman identified two ingredients that explained individual differences in test scores. He called the first of them the general factor, or general intelligence, abbreviated to "g." Spearman believed that "g" represented overall cognitive ability. In other words, the tests were correlated with one another because they all tapped into a person's general intelligence. Spearman also identified a second, specific intelligence factor, abbreviated to "s." Specific intelligence refers to the thinking skills required for work in particular areas, such as math or verbal reasoning.

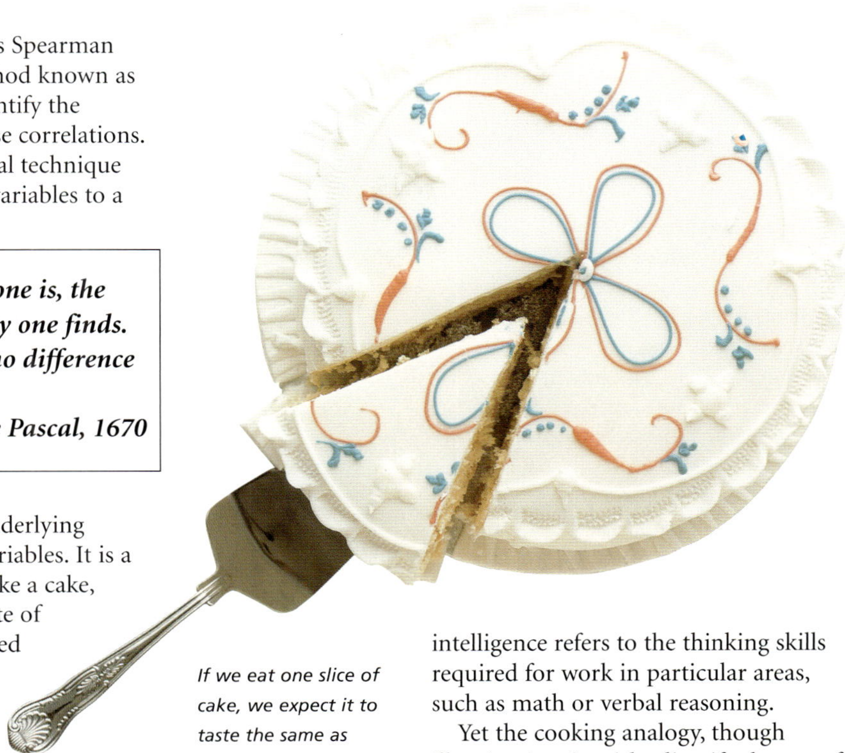

If we eat one slice of cake, we expect it to taste the same as every other slice. On the same principle, factor analysis can help us extrapolate the nature of a whole from knowledge of some of its parts.

Yet the cooking analogy, though illuminating, is misleading if taken too far. Cake ingredients are real, but Spearman's factors are abstract ideas. It is important to remember that the idea of "general intelligence" is based principally on the mathematics of factor analysis and does not give any insight into where "g" might come from. Factor analysis is difficult to interpret by itself. As we will see, slightly different methods of factor analysis can produce very different results.

Most scientists who study intelligence tend to study "g." Many researchers have made progress toward understanding the nature of "g." Some studies have found

KEY POINTS

- There is much debate about whether differences in intelligence are a product of nature or nurture and the extent to which they are influenced by factors such as culture, race, sex, and social status.
- According to Charles Spearman in 1904, specific cognitive abilities are informed by general intelligence.
- In 1938 Howard Gardner proposed seven types of intelligence (see p. 121) measuring different qualities.
- In 1941 Raymond Cattell suggested that general intelligence influences a number of specific intelligences.
- J. P. Guilford (1964) proposed that intelligence was made up of 150 interdependent components.
- The earliest intelligence tests were based on speed; Alfred Binet first made them tests of problem solving.
- Intelligence quotient (IQ) tests were first introduced in 1912 by German psychologist William Stern.
- The Scholastic Aptitude Test (SAT), now the Scholastic Assessment Test, was introduced in U.S. schools in 1926.

that "g" is related to measures of the efficiency of neural connections in the brain. Overall, people with higher levels of "g" tend to process and respond to stimuli more quickly than those with lower levels.

Specific intelligence

Spearman's critics took exception to the idea that intelligence could be reduced to a single number. They used different methods of factor analysis to identify more than one "specific" intelligence. For example, measures of verbal comprehension and verbal reasoning might correlate with each other, but not with measures of spatial awareness.

In 1938 U.S. psychologist Louis Thurstone proposed that intelligence was not a single entity but several primary mental abilities. To test this theory, Thurstone gave a collection of 56 tests to 240 college students. Using a new method of factor analysis on their scores, he identified seven underlying factors, which he called primary abilities. They are as follows: verbal comprehension (V), word fluency (W), number (N), spatial ability (S), associative memory (M), perceptual speed (P), and reasoning (R). He believed these results proved that Spearman's idea of a single intelligence was incorrect.

However, many scientists pointed out problems with Thurstone's categories. Each of his tests showed a positive correlation with every other test. These correlations were much lower than those Spearman had found, but they still suggested a common underlying factor that affected performance on all the tests. Thurstone's method of analysis made it difficult to identify a single underlying factor. When other researchers used different methods of analyzing the same data, they identified a "general intelligence" factor.

> ***"The invention of IQ does a great disservice to creativity in education."***
> ***—Joel Hildebrand, 1986***

The second problem with Thurstone's methods was the way he used only college students, who typically score higher on tests than the general population and thus do not represent the full range of ability.

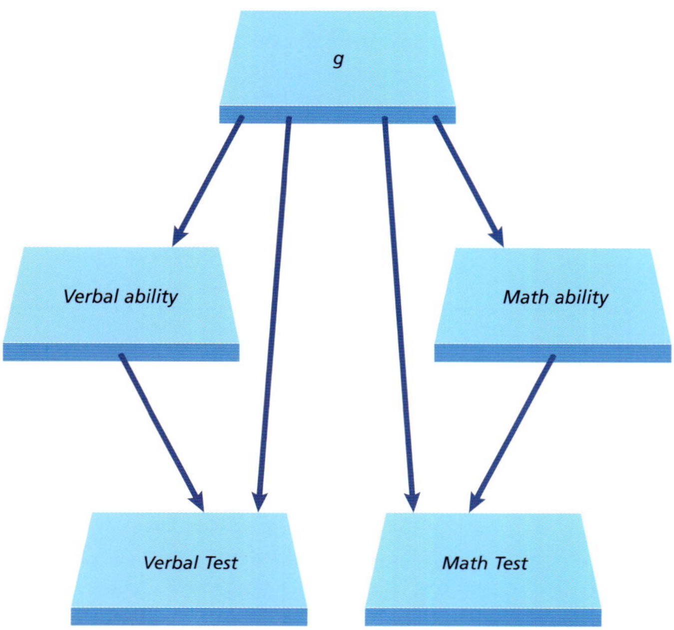

A hierarchical model of intelligence, with general intelligence ("g") at the top. The diagram reflects the fact that it is possible to perform well in math and verbal tests without having ability in either discipline.

Hierarchical model

By 1941 Thurstone realized that his results did not after all disprove Spearman's theory of general intelligence. Thurstone eventually tested people of a wider range of ability and could find no evidence for six specific intelligences. In the same year U.S. psychologist Raymond B. Cattell (1905–1998, *see* box p. 121) found a way to resolve the differences between Spearman's theory and Thurstone's. Based on a new method of factor analysis, Cattell argued that people have a general level of intelligence that affects how they perform on all tests. He concluded that this general intelligence affects specific intelligences, and that these specific intelligences affect how people perform on particular tests. For example, general intelligence affects performance on all tests, but math intelligence affects only performance on

CASE STUDY

Cattell's "Culture-Fair" Tests

Raymond B. Cattell divided general intelligence into two distinct types: crystallized and fluid. Crystallized intelligence represents knowledge acquired through experience. Tests of crystallized intelligence, such as verbal memory and general knowledge, are thought to reflect the influence of culture and schooling.

Fluid intelligence represents the biological ability to acquire knowledge and solve problems. Tests that reflect fluid intelligence, such as reasoning speed, spatial reasoning, and inductive reasoning (*see* Vol. 4, pp. 94–111), are thought to reflect intelligence independent of learning. Cattell developed a "culture-fair" test to measure fluid intelligence (*see* below—these problems should all be solvable by anyone, regardless of background, education or general knowledge).

In theory, changes in biology should affect fluid intelligence but not crystallized intelligence. In fact, brain damage, poor nutrition, and exposure to toxins in the uterus affect fluid but not crystallized intelligence. Moreover, fluid intelligence declines with age, but crystallized intelligence does not. Finally, changes in the quality of schooling can increase crystallized but not fluid intelligence.

It can be difficult to distinguish between what is learned and the biological basis for learning it. Cattell argued that some amount of ability (fluid intelligence) is required to gain knowledge (crystallized intelligence). However, most cognitive tests assess both types of intelligence, so fluid and crystallized intelligence are correlated with one another.

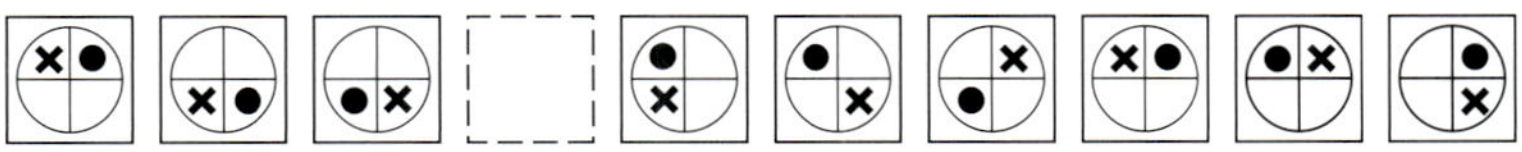

Series: *Choose one of the six figures on the right to fill the dotted square.*

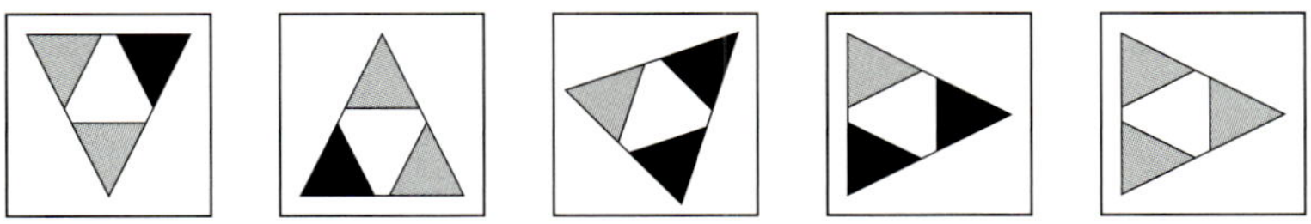

Classification: *Choose the figure that doesn't fit.*

Topology: *Choose the diagram in which a dot could be placed as in the one on the left.*

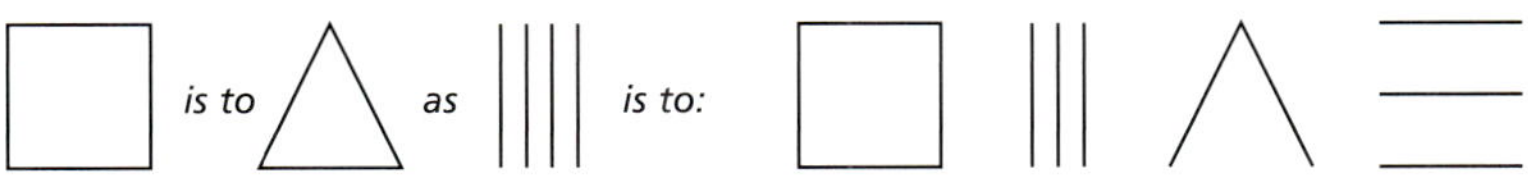

Analogies: *Choose one of the four diagrams to complete the analogy.*

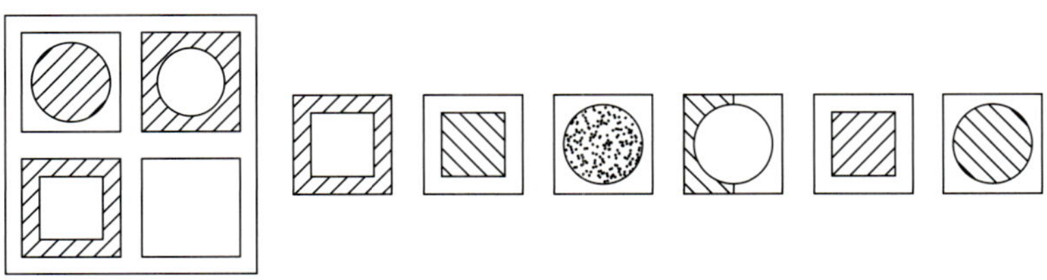

Matrices: *Choose one of the six figures to fill the empty square.*

math tests. This is referred to as a hierarchical model (*see* diagram p. 120).

In 1983 Harvard psychologist Howard Gardner argued that the traditional definitions of intelligence do not capture all of the ways in which humans can excel. We do not have one underlying general intelligence but multiple intelligences, each part of an independent system in the brain. Every person has a unique profile of strengths and weaknesses on each type of intelligence. To illustrate his theory, Gardner proposed seven unique types of intelligence and identified a famous person who demonstrated each one. Linguistic intelligence involves skill in using speech and language, and was demonstrated by the poet T. S. Eliot (1888–1965). Logical-mathematical intelligence is the ability to reason abstractly and solve mathematical and logical problems. Physicist Albert Einstein (1879–1955) was held up as a good example of this type of intelligence. Spatial intelligence is the ability to perceive visual information. The cubist painter Pablo Picasso (1881–1973) had a high level of spatial intelligence. Intrapersonal intelligence involves understanding one's own feelings and desires, and was seen in the Indian leader Mohandas K. Gandhi (1869–1948). Interpersonal intelligence involves understanding the feelings and motives of others, and acting on that understanding. According to Gardner, Sigmund Freud (1856–1939) had a high level of interpersonal intelligence. Bodily-kinesthetic intelligence is the ability to use one's body or portions of it in various physical activities, such as dancing, athletics, acting, surgery, and magic. Martha Graham (1894–1991), the famous dancer and choreographer, is a good example of bodily-kinesthetic intelligence. Finally, musical intelligence, the ability to perform and appreciate music, was represented by Russian-born U.S. composer Igor Stravinsky (1882–1971). In the 1990s Gardner added an eighth category: naturalist intelligence, the ability to recognize and classify plants, animals, and minerals. Charles Darwin (1809–1882) is an outstanding example of this form.

> ***"There are hundreds of ways to succeed and many different abilities that will get you there."***
> ***—Howard Gardner, 1986***

American Martha Graham was the central figure of the modern dance movement. Her special gift was taken by psychologist Howard Gardner as the epitome of what he termed bodily-kinesthetic intelligence.

Independence implies distinctness

In developing this theory, Gardner drew on many diverse sources of evidence to determine the number of intelligences. For example, he studied brain-damaged people who had lost one ability but retained others. The fact that abilities could operate independently of each other suggested the existence of separate intelligences. Gardner argued that evidence for multiple intelligences also came from prodigies and savants. Prodigies show an exceptional talent in a specific area from a young age but are normal in other respects. Savants are people who score low on IQ tests but who demonstrate some remarkable gift, such as outstanding mathematic or drawing ability.

To Gardner the presence of certain high-level abilities in the absence of others also suggested the existence of multiple intelligences. Educationists quickly adopted Gardner's theory because it embraced a wider definition of intelligence than had previously been accepted and implied that traditional schooling may ignore a large portion of human abilities. Also, it recognized that students considered "slow" by conventional academic measures might excel in other respects.

FOCUS ON

CREATIVITY

Robert Sternberg and others have defined creativity as the ability to produce work that is both novel (original) and appropriate (applicable to the situation). The relationship between creativity and intelligence is the subject of debate. Not everything that is considered "intelligent" is necessarily "creative." For example, going inside when it rains is commonly described as an intelligent thing to do, but it is not creative. Additionally, not everything "creative" is necessarily "intelligent." Painting an original work of art is creative, but it is not necessarily intelligent. Creativity is difficult to study in the laboratory, not least because it is likely to surface when people have complete freedom of response. Some of the best-known studies of creativity were conducted by German-born Briton Hans Eysenck (1916–1997) in numerous essays and the 1995 book *Genius: A Natural History of Creativity*.

A study in the 1920s by Catherine Cox and Lewis Terman focused on famous people and attempted to extrapolate their intelligence from biographical information. For example, they estimated an IQ of 165 for Charles Darwin and 150 for Abraham Lincoln. They estimated the highest IQ, 210, for Johann Wolfgang von Goethe, the German poet. The way in which these ratings were calculated was less than scientific.

Recent research has attempted to determine the origins of creativity. Since the 1980s the following factors have been widely accepted as the fundamental dimensions of the human personality: extroversion, agreeableness, conscientiousness, neuroticism, and openness to experience or intellect. Evidence for the big five, as these characteristics are known, was reviewed by Lewis R. Goldberg of the University of Oregon in an influential article published in the journal *American Psychologist* in 1993. Dean Simonton of the University of California, Davis, then argued that cultures that are more creative are more diverse and have more resources than less creative cultures. Social psychologists have shown that changing the instructions can increase creativity on a task. For example, open-ended questions produce responses that are more creative than strict, matter-of-fact questions. People are also more creative and come up with a wider range of solutions when encouraged to use trial-and-error than when instructed to stick to the existing rules.

Hans Eysenck tried to demonstrate that creativity coincides with several different personality variables. Some of the variables that he considered were self-confidence, the desire or capacity to take risks, attraction to complexity, and an individual's independence of judgment.

Three main criticisms have since been made of Gardner's theory. First, he based his ideas more on intuition than on empirical studies, and there are no tests available to identify or measure the intelligences. Second, he ignored research that shows a tendency for different abilities to correlate. Third, some of the intelligences Gardner identified, such as musical intelligence, should be viewed simply as talents because they are not usually required to adapt to the everyday demands of human life.

Triarchic theory

In the 1990s Yale University psychology professor Robert Sternberg criticized traditional definitions of intelligence for being narrow and unreliable predictors of real-life success. He proposed that intelligence consists of three related parts—creative, analytical, and practical. This has become known as the triarchic (three-part) theory of intelligence.

Creative intelligence is the ability to apply things learned from experience to new situations. People with creative intelligence are good at combining seemingly unrelated facts to form new ideas. According to Sternberg, traditional intelligence tests do not measure creative intelligence because it is possible for people to score high on an IQ test yet have trouble dealing with new situations.

Analytical intelligence is skill in reasoning, processing information, and solving problems. It involves the ability to evaluate, judge, and compare. Analytical intelligence is the part of Sternberg's theory that most closely resembles the traditional conception of general intelligence. Instead of defining intelligence as the skills needed to perform well on intelligence tests, Sternberg argues that these skills are only one part of intelligence.

Practical intelligence relates to people's ability to adapt to, select, and shape their real-world environment. It involves skill in adapting to life demands and reflects a person's ability to succeed in real-world settings. To demonstrate practical intelligence, Sternberg gave the example of an employee who loved his job but hated his boss. Instead of applying for a new job, the employee gave a recruiter the name of his boss, who was subsequently hired away from the company. By getting rid of the boss he hated instead of leaving the job he loved, the employee showed adaptation to his real-world environment. People with high practical intelligence may or may not perform well on standard IQ tests.

Sternberg's theory attempted to broaden the domain of intelligence to correspond more exactly to what people frequently think intelligence is. However, some critics believe that scientific studies do not support Sternberg's proposed triarchic division. They argue that practical intelligence is not a distinct aspect of intelligence, but rather a set of abilities that can be predicted by general intelligence.

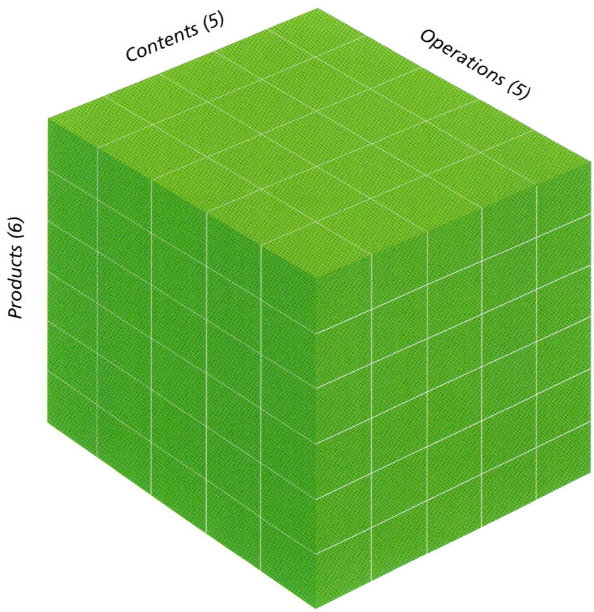

Guilford's Cube. According to J. P. Guilford, all mental tasks contain an element from each of three dimensions—operations, content, and product. Within each dimension there are five operations that are applicable to each of the five senses, and within each of them there are six possible products. This makes a total of 150 mental tasks, all of which are closely related, and many of which are practically interdependent. They can be visualized in the form of a cube.

Information processing

The theories of intelligence discussed so far propose different structures of intelligence. In 1964 U.S. psychologist J. P. Guilford put forward a theory that was concerned with how intelligence works. According to him, all intellectual tasks contain three basic components, which he called dimensions—mental operations, content, and products. He further assumed that the mind could perform any of five basic operations—cognition (knowing), memory, divergent production (thinking of alternatives), convergent production (drawing conclusions), and evaluation. These basic operations could be applied to five types of content—auditory, visual, symbolic, semantic (words), and behavioral. The result of applying an operation to a content type could be expressed as one of six products—units, classes (categories), relations, systems, transformations, and implications (*see* diagram left).

Guilford's idea was that all combinations were possible of these dimensions, operations, and contents. They resulted in 150 possible types of intellectual task. For example, memorizing details about a work of art might be described as memory for symbolic units. One of Guilford's tests, known as "Story Titles," was a measure of

KEY POINTS

Theory	Date	Theorist	Description
General intelligence	1904	Charles Spearman	• A general mental ability underlies performance on all intellectual tasks.
Specific intelligences	1938	Louis Thurstone	• Intelligence comprises seven primary abilities that influence performance on specific tasks.
Fluid and crystallized	1966	Raymond B. Cattell	• Intelligence is made up of two broad abilities: Fluid intelligence is biological and independent of learning; Crystallized intelligence reflects cultural experience.
Multiple intelligences	1983	Howard Gardner	• Intelligence has eight distinct types, each using a different system of the brain.
Triarchic theory	1985	Robert Sternberg	• Intelligence has three major parts: analytical (reasoning), creative, and practical.
Information processing	1964	J.P. Guilford	• All intellectual tasks are a combination of: (a) one of five types of operations; (b) one of five types of content; (c) resulting in one of six types of product. They add up to 150 types of intellectual task.

the evaluation of semantic transformation in which people were presented with a brief story and asked to choose the most appropriate of several possible titles. The test involves an evaluative judgment of semantic (verbal) material, and the product of the evaluation is a transformation (a story with a new title).

Guilford argued that his results disproved the existence of a general intelligence. That was because 17 percent of his tests showed almost no correlations. However, critics attached greater significance to the 83 percent of responses that did correlate. Guilford's theory was criticized on three other grounds. First, on some of the tests people's scores were inconsistent. Second, most of the subjects were U.S. Air Force officer trainees, selected for their intelligence so the results were not generalizable. Third, critics maintained that some of Guilford's tests did not tap into general intelligence, particularly behavioral measures.

INTELLIGENCE TESTS

When scientists talk about "intelligence," most of them mean scores on intelligence tests. Often tests are designed to measure both abstract reasoning skills and the ability to cope with everyday problems. David Wechsler, creator of one of the most widely used such tests, wrote in 1975 that intelligence tests "measure more than they measure." A test might ostensibly measure knowledge or spatial ability, but Wechsler believed that it can also tap into people's ability to understand and cope with the world around them.

Before the 20th century intelligence was measured either through tests of reaction time or by the physical dimensions of the brain. Samuel Morton (in the 1820s) and Paul Broca (in the 1860s) examined the skulls and brains of people from different races. They assumed that bigger brains meant higher intelligence and reported that northern Europeans had bigger brains than other people. However, these findings were largely subjective. In 1970 South African anthropologist Philip Tobias showed that all evidence of a link between human brain size and intelligence was flawed.

Francis Galton (1822–1911), a cousin of Charles Darwin, believed that intelligence was inherited and measurable. He reasoned that people of higher intelligence would be able to process and

Unusually for a psychologist of his time, the Frenchman Alfred Binet (1857–1911) was more interested in the workings of the healthy mind than in mental illness. He pioneered modern intelligence tests.

respond to the environment more quickly than less gifted people. In England in 1884 he created a laboratory in which he claimed to be able to measure intelligence from a series of sensory speed tests. This approach was criticized by French psychologist Alfred Binet, who held that intelligence should be measured by tests of abstract reasoning.

Reliance on sensory measures soon diminished. Scientists turned to intelligence testing to quantify differences between people and groups. Intelligence tests assume that intelligent people can process information more quickly than the unintelligent. In 1905 Binet designed a test to identify children in need of special education. The test consisted of a series of short, related tasks that involved basic processes of reasoning. The total score on these tasks told the tester the subject's mental age. Binet did not claim to measure an intelligence that was independent of learning and stressed that mental age had limited applications for extrapolating a person's overall ability. However, once Binet's test made it to the United States, it was applied much more widely than its originator had intended and triggered a national obsession with mental testing. Lewis Terman of Stanford University made small revisions to Binet's test and promoted it as a diagnostic of innate (inborn) intelligence. Terman's version of the test, the Stanford-Binet Intelligence Test (*see* box below), is currently one of the most widely used assessments of intelligence. The Stanford-Binet test emphasizes abstract reasoning

> ***"Intellectual qualities are not superposable, and therefore cannot be measured as linear surfaces are measured."***
>
> ***—Alfred Binet, quoted by Stephen Jay Gould, 1981***

CASE STUDY

The Stanford-Binet Intelligence Test

The intelligence test devised by Lewis Terman and based on the original by Alfred Binet measured a child's mental age based on the tasks he or she was able to complete correctly. The modern Stanford-Binet draws heavily on the original version. Below are a few of the standards and tasks used today to measure mental age.

Aged 3	Child should be able to name pictures of objects such as chair and repeat lists of two words or digits.
Aged 4	Child should be able to define words such as ball and bat; repeat 10-word sentences.
Aged 6	Child should be able to state differences between similar items (e.g., bird and dog); solve analogies (e.g., "An inch is short; a mile is ____.").
Aged 9	Child should be able to solve verbal problems (e.g., "Think of a number that rhymes with tree."); repeat four digits in reverse order.
Aged 12	Child should be able to define several words and repeat five digits in reverse order.

skills rather than the speed of reasoning measured by Galton.

During World War I (1914–1918) a group of U.S. psychologists led by Robert M. Yerkes offered to help the army select recruits using intelligence tests. Yerkes and his colleagues developed two intelligence tests: the Army Alpha exam for literate recruits and the Army Beta exam for non-English speakers and illiterates. Until then tests had required an examiner to interact with each test-taker individually, but these tests could be administered to large groups of people simultaneously.

The Alpha exam included arithmetic problems, tests of practical judgment, tests of general knowledge, synonym-antonym comparisons, number series problems, and analogies. The Beta exam required recruits to complete mazes, fill in missing elements in pictures, and recognize patterns in a series. The army considered the highest-scoring recruits as candidates for officer training and rejected the lowest-scoring recruits from military service. By the end of World War I psychologists had given intelligence tests to approximately 1.7 million people.

The use of intelligence tests by the U.S. military enhanced the credibility of group mental tests. Following World War I, these tests grew in popularity. Most were short-answer tests modeled on the army tests or the Stanford-Binet. Yerkes and Terman developed the National Intelligence Test, a group test for schoolchildren, around 1920. The Scholastic Aptitude Test, or SAT, was introduced in 1926 as a multiple-choice

CASE STUDY

ARMY EXAMINATION ALPHA

During World War I (1914–1918) educational psychologists developed an intelligence test for recruits into the U.S. Army. The test, known as Examination Alpha, consisted of a variety of short-answer tests to measure general intelligence. Critics objected that the test was only of general knowledge. The following are typical sample questions.

Instructions

In each of the sentences below you have four choices for the last word. Only one of them is correct. Select the answer that makes the truest sentence.

1. America was discovered by
   (A) Drake (B) Hudson (C) Columbus (D) Cabot
2. Pinochle is played with
   (A) rackets (B) cards (C) pins (D) dice
3. The most prominent industry of Detroit is
   (A) automobiles (B) brewing (C) flour (D) packing
4. The Wyandotte is a kind of
   (A) horse (B) fowl (C) cattle (D) granite
5. The U.S. School for Army Officers is at
   (A) Annapolis (B) West Point (C) New Haven (D) Ithaca
6. Salsify is a kind of
   (A) snake (B) fish (C) lizard (D) vegetable
7. Coral is obtained from
   (A) mines (B) elephants (C) oysters (D) reefs
8. Rosa Bonheur is famous as a
   (A) poet (B) painter (C) composer (D) sculptor
9. Maize is a kind of
   (A) corn (B) hay (C) oats (D) rice
10. Velvet Joe appears in advertisements for
   (A) tooth powder (B) dry goods (C) tobacco (D) soap

Answers

1. C 2. B 3. A 4. B 5. B 6. D 7. D 8. B 9. A 10. C

American soldiers in World War I were recruited partly on their performance in a specially devised intelligence test. Critics objected that the exam was so culture-specific that it was more a test of Americanness than of intelligence.

exam to aid colleges and universities in their selection of students.

Most of these tests measured intelligence as a single number. Unfortunately, most multiple intelligences are difficult to measure through standardized testing. In a rare exception psychologists Robert Sternberg and Robert Wagner developed in 1990 a test of "managerial intelligence" and showed that effective executives tend to score highly on this test, but not necessarily on tests of general intelligence.

IQ tests

The method of scoring intelligence tests has changed over the years. The measure of "mental age" used originally by Binet identified individual children in need of extra help. But as intelligence testing became more widespread, scientists wanted to find a way of comparing one person's performance with that of others. The first intelligence quotient (IQ) test was developed in 1912 by German psychologist William Stern (1871–1938). The way in which this quotient was expressed was refined by Lewis Terman, who divided the subject's mental age (which was determined by performance on the test) by his or her chronological age and then multiplied by 100 to get rid of the decimal point. For example, if a five-year-old girl had a mental age of 10 (in other words, if she scored as well as a 10-year-old would have been expected to perform), she would be assigned an IQ of 200 (10/5 x 100). If a 12-year-old boy scored a mental age of nine, he would be given an IQ of 75 (9/12 x 100). Although this formula works well for comparing children, it does not work for adults because intelligence levels are generally agreed to level off during adulthood. Thus a 40-year-old who scored the same as an average 20-year-old would not be given an IQ of only 50 (20/40 x 100).

Even though most people still use the term IQ to refer to intelligence test scores, modern intelligence tests no longer compute scores using the IQ formula. Instead, they give a score that reflects how far the person's performance deviates from the average performance of other people of the same age. The farther above average a person's score is, the higher his or her intelligence should be.

How is this done? IQ scores, like many other biological and psychological characteristics, are spread along a normal distribution, which forms a normal curve,

> ***"If the Aborigine drafted an IQ test, all of Western civilization would presumably flunk it."***
> ***—Stanley Garn, 1962***

or bell curve, when plotted on a graph (*see* diagram below). In a normal distribution most values fall near the average. Normal distribution is defined by its mean (average score) and its standard deviation (a measure of how much scores are spread out around the mean). On most IQ tests the mean is arbitrarily set at 100 with a standard deviation of 15. That is, a score

The normal curve. IQ scores fit a normal distribution, meaning that most people's scores are clustered around the mean.

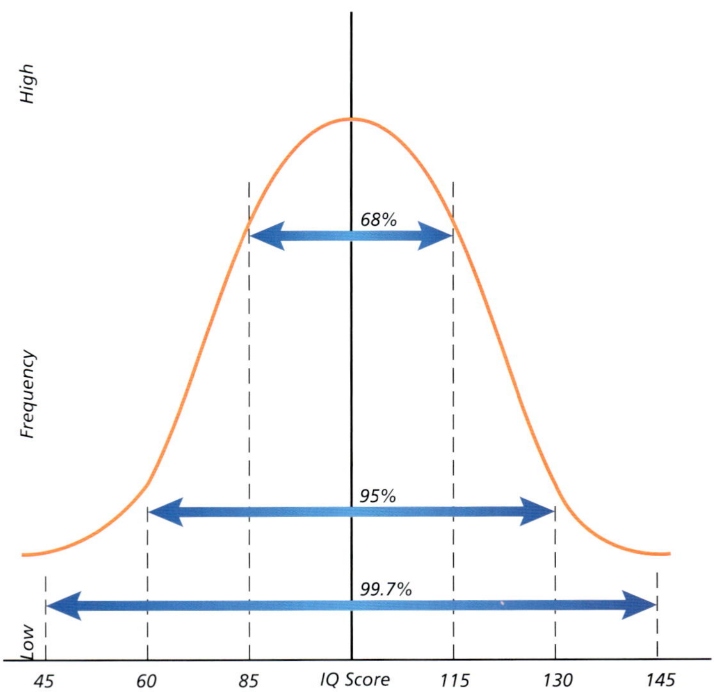

must be lower than 85 (100 minus 15) or higher than 115 (100 plus 15) for it to be considered below or above average.

Because IQs are distributed along a normal curve, a fixed percentage of scores falls between the mean and any standard deviation value. For example, 34 percent of IQ scores fall between the mean and one standard deviation. For a standard IQ distribution with a mean of 100 and a standard deviation of 15, 34 percent of the cases would fall between 100 and 115. Since the curve is the same on both sides of the mean, 34 percent of the scores would also fall between 85 and 100, which represents one standard deviation below the mean. If a person obtains a score of 115 on an IQ test, approximately 16 percent of the population will score higher and 84 percent will score lower. In other words, IQ is now a measure of a person's intelligence relative to that of others in the population.

Before an intelligence test can be scored in this manner, it must be standardized, standardization being the process of determining the average scores on a test. The test designers give the test to a sample of the population similar to the people for whom the test is designed. This selection of people is known as a normative sample because it is used to establish norms (standards) for the average performance on the test. The test scores of people in the sample are used to determine the test norms. When the test is put into general use, these norms are used to determine a score for each person who takes the test.

The most widely used tests

Today three intelligence tests are used most often: the Stanford-Binet, the Wechsler Intelligence Scale for Children (WISC), and the Wechsler Adult Intelligence Scale (WAIS). The Stanford-Binet measures intelligence in four areas: verbal reasoning, quantitative reasoning, abstract/visual reasoning, and short-term memory. The WAIS relies less on verbal processing and contains both a verbal and a performance component. Each of these tests consists of a series of 10 or more subtests. Each item has scoring criteria that can be used by the examiner to determine if the answer given is correct.

Items on each subtest are given in order of difficulty until the person being tested misses a certain number of items. The test-taker is assigned a score on each of the subtests. The subtest scores are then added together to obtain a total raw score; it is then converted into an IQ score based on how a person does relative to others in the population. Some tests, such as the Wechsler tests, give separate verbal and performance (nonverbal) scores as well as an overall score.

> ***"Intelligence is the global capacity to act purposefully, to think rationally, and to deal effectively with the environment."***
> ***—David Wechsler, 1955***

Other tests include only one type of item. In Raven's Progressive Matrices, devised in the 1940s by the British psychologist J. C. Raven, the test-taker is shown a set of patterns, one of which is missing. The person must learn the rules for the patterns and then use those rules to pick the item that best fills in the gap. Raven's test was designed to minimize the influence of culture by relying on nonverbal problems that require abstract reasoning rather than knowledge of a particular civilization and its conventions.

Achievement tests and aptitude tests are often designed like intelligence tests, but they measure different things. An achievement test measures what a person has already learned, either in school or in everyday life. An aptitude test measures a person's potential for future achievement or performance. There is currently debate over whether tests such as the Scholastic Aptitude Test (SAT) reflect academic achievement or general intelligence. The SAT was developed originally to identify students with a good deal of innate ability who performed poorly on traditional achievement tests because they attended low-quality high schools. Labeling the SAT as an aptitude test, however, implied that people scoring higher on it would also perform better in college. This was not always the case. Eventually, the Educational Testing Service (ETS) changed the name in response to public criticism. The SAT is now called the Scholastic Assessment Test to convey the idea that it measures more than innate ability.

Reliability and validity

As with any psychological measure, intelligence tests have to meet certain criteria of reliability and validity. Reliability refers to the consistency or dependability of a measure. If a test is reliable, anyone should have the same scores if he or she retakes the test under similar conditions. Different forms of the test (for example, when the questions are asked in a different order) should produce the same results. This is known as test-retest reliability. Individual items on the same subtest should show similar scores. This is known as interitem reliability. By these standards intelligence tests are highly reliable.

Validity is the extent to which a test measures what it claims to measure. For an intelligence test to be valid, it must provide a real measure of intelligence. If a test instead measures school learning or

PSYCHOLOGY & SOCIETY

Test Bias

Intelligence tests are often criticized for being biased against certain groups. From a testing perspective bias refers to systematic differences in scores that are unrelated to what the test measures. For example, in an essay on Roman history a candidate with good writing skills but a limited knowledge of the period might outperform a highly knowledgeable candidate who wrote badly. If the test is only about Roman history, writing skills should not be relevant. Because certain ethnic groups tend to score lower on intelligence tests, many critics have argued that the tests are culturally biased in favor of white people. This has led researchers to be very precise in the way they talk about test bias.

In the 1990s Harvard sociologist Christopher Jencks argued that tests may be biased in three different ways:

Labeling bias refers to a mismatch between what the test claims to measure and what it really measures. The SAT debate described in the main text reflects this type of bias. Labeling bias occurs when construct validity is low—for example, it would probably be no good asking children in a remote African village the difference between a freeway and a turnpike.

Content bias occurs when questions favor one group over another, such as when American and Hispanic children both take a vocabulary test written in English. If American children perform better on this test, it does not necessarily reflect their superior intelligence or even their superior vocabulary.

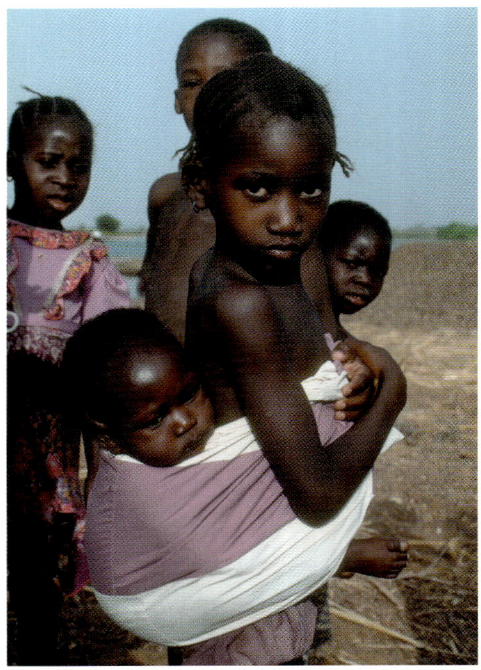

Intelligence tests must be culturally neutral—for example, African children cannot fairly be expected to display familiarity with western culture.

Methodological bias refers to problems with the test administration that may lead to an underestimation of the knowledge and skills of a particular group.

motivation, then it is not a valid test of intelligence. There are two main types of validity. Predictive validity refers to how well a test predicts what it should predict. Intelligence tests were designed to predict school achievement, and they do so rather well, at least if those who take them are from the same cultural background.

As we have seen, intelligence is difficult to define, partly because it is an abstract quality, or construct. The second type of validity, construct validity, refers to the extent to which a test captures the abstract quality it is trying to measure. The more an intelligence test taps into intelligence, the higher its construct validity. However, it is difficult to create a test that everyone will agree is high in construct validity. To avoid this problem, test-makers usually rely on predictive validity to evaluate the test's overall effectiveness.

> ***Many highly intelligent people are poor thinkers. Many people of average intelligence are skilled thinkers. The power of a car is separate from the way the car is driven."***
> ***—Edward de Bono, 1994***

Lewis Terman (1877–1956), the cognitive psychologist who in 1906, while at Stanford University, published a revised version of Alfred Binet's intelligence test. This new form of examination became known as the Stanford-Binet Test.

HEREDITY AND ENVIRONMENT

One of the hottest topics in intelligence research is the source of differences in intelligence test scores. Because test scores are used to make important decisions about education and employment, the source of the differences matters greatly. If the differences are the result of inherited biological capacities, then efforts to increase intelligence may be ineffective. On the other hand, if they are the result of environmental influences, then it may be possible to reduce them.

The first category of theories links differences in test scores with differences in general intelligence, which is thought to have a strong genetic component. That means a child's intelligence is determined in large part by his or her parents' genes and in a smaller part by the environment.

It is important to distinguish between the terms inheritance and heritability as geneticists use them (*see* pp. 142–163). Inheritance is defined in this context as genes passed from parents to a child, and is unconstrained by the environment. Heritability is a statistical term used to explain the proportion of differences in a trait in a specific population that can be linked to genetics. The genes that may influence IQ are 100 percent inherited, but IQ itself is not. IQ is only partially heritable, and so, by definition, variations are partly due to environmental factors. Heritability refers to a population, not to individuals. It is impossible to determine what percentage of an individual's intelligence is due to genetic factors.

Most of the data on the heritability of intelligence come from extensive studies of identical twins. Typically, researchers compare the intelligence test scores of

PSYCHOLOGY & SOCIETY

RISING IQ SCORES

Many researchers have noted a steady worldwide increase in IQ scores, but New Zealand political scientist James Flynn was the first to document it systematically. Flynn has argued that the increase in IQ suggests a reinterpretation of IQ scores. Worldwide the average gain is about three IQ points per decade, or about 15 points between the 1940s and the turn of the millennium. In some countries the increase is amazing: Norway, for example, showed a gain of 20 points between 1952 and 1982.

James Flynn of the University of Otago, New Zealand, whose research in the 1980s concluded that our IQs are increasing. Why might that be the case? Many theories have been proposed but there are few certainties.

It seems unlikely that these rises in IQ scores reflect real increases in intelligence in the population. Flynn points out that if that were the case, countries such as Norway should be experiencing a "cultural renaissance too great to be overlooked." However, there is no evidence that any such renaissance has occurred. According to Flynn, this indicates that IQ tests are related only weakly to intelligence.

Several hypotheses have been proposed to explain what has become popularly known as the "Flynn Effect." One of the most persuasive theories is that of British psychologist Richard Lynn, who in the 1990s linked the increase to improvements in nutrition. He notes that during the same period as the IQ gains there have been large increases in height—they are linked to improved diet. It is at least possible that there have been corresponding increases in brain size or processing speed that are also attributable to the same cause.

The most intriguing explanation links the increase in IQ scores to changes in the environment. Fifty years ago urban children had IQs that were, on average, six points higher than those of rural children, but the gap narrowed to about two points in a 25-year period as the differences between town and country decreased (for example, less rural isolation, improved rural schools, more technology used on farms). Similar enhancements in the environment have occurred worldwide since the 1940s. We are exposed to more information and experiences through the mass media; schools are better, and children stay in them longer; working conditions and the quality of life have improved dramatically over the past 50 years. It is certainly plausible that these social improvements might have led to improved performance on tests of intelligence.

identical twins raised apart, identical twins raised together, and fraternal twins raised apart and together. Identical twins are especially informative when it comes to studying genetic influences. Identical twins develop from a single fertilized egg and are thus genetically identical. Fraternal twins develop from separate eggs and share only about half their genes in common. Researchers have discovered that the IQ scores of identical twins are much more similar than those of fraternal twins or nontwin siblings. Although there is some consensus that genes account for between 40 and 80 percent of differences in intelligence, it is impossible to correlate exact causes and effects—all that we know is that intelligence is always a combination of both nature and nurture.

Some of the strongest evidence for genetic influences in intelligence comes from studies of identical twins adopted into different homes early in life. Any differences in the IQ scores of identical twins must be due entirely to the environment; some similarities may be due to genetics. The results of these studies indicate that the IQ scores of identical twins raised apart are highly similar—nearly as similar as those of identical twins raised together.

Another way of studying the genetic contribution to intelligence is through adoption studies in which researchers compare adopted children with their biological and adoptive families. Adopted children have no genetic relationship to their adoptive parents or to their adoptive parents' biological children. Thus any similarity in IQ between the adopted children and their adoptive parents or the parents' biological children is probably due to the similarity of the environment they all live in and not to genetics.

> ***"Our biology has made us into creatures whose individual lives are the outcomes of an extraordinary multiplicity of intersecting causal pathways. Thus, it is our biology that makes us free."***
> ***—Richard Lewontin, 1995***

There are two interesting findings from studies of adopted children. First, the IQs of adopted children are weakly related to the IQs of their adoptive parents and the parents' biological children. Second, after the adopted child leaves home, this small relationship becomes even smaller. In general, the IQs of adopted children are always more similar to those of their biological parents than to those of their adoptive parents. Furthermore once they leave the influence of their adoptive home, they become even more similar to their biological parents. Both these findings suggest the importance of hereditary factors in intelligence.

People sometimes assume that if a characteristic is highly heritable, then it cannot be changed or improved through environmental factors. This is not true. For example, nearsightedness is highly heritable, but almost 100 percent correctable with eyeglasses. Similarly, performance on IQ tests has increased with each generation (*see* box p. 132), but few scientists attribute this to genetic changes. Many experts believe that environmental improvements can increase a person's intelligence.

In The Triple Helix, *Richard Lewontin demonstrates that no matter how much our DNA may tell us about particular diseases, it provides a false and simplified picture of the interaction between genes and the environment that creates uniquely individual organisms.*

Genetic codes

DNA (deoxyribonucleic acid) carries the genetic code. Its shape is often likened to that of a twisted ladder (double helix). The sides are composed of phosphates and sugar; the rungs are paired nucleotide bases. The ladder splits through the rungs to make proteins; each triplet of unpaired bases contains the code for a particular amino acid. So genes contain "instructions" for making the proteins necessary to create and develop the physiological structures of the body and determine how those structures will respond in a given environment. When scientists speak of "a gene" for intelligence, they are speaking of genes that lead people to process information more quickly and efficiently in such a way that improves performance on IQ tests and facilitates adaptation to the environment. The exact genes involved in intelligence—or any complex behavior—are not yet understood.

A growing body of evidence suggests that our genes provide a threshold, or a "norm of reaction," for intelligence. U.S. evolutionary biologist Richard Lewontin (born 1929) has argued that our genetic makeup sets the limits for what we can do in a particular environment. Two groups of people with identical inheritance will not have the same heritability unless their respective environments are equal. For example, humans will never sprout wings no matter what their environment, but two people with identical inheritance for height will grow up differently if one is well nourished and the other is not.

Environmental influences

There is evidence that genetic factors contribute to intelligence within groups, but there is still plenty of room for environmental influence. If genetic influences account for 50 percent of the differences in intelligence test scores, then the other 50 percent should be caused by environmental influences. The "environment" covers everything people encounter in the outside world, including their socioeconomic status (SES), family environment, years of schooling completed, job status, and exposure to toxic substances such as lead.

SES combines several measures of the home environment in what is known as a summary variable. One of these measures, occupational level (job status), correlates with IQ scores. This could mean that intelligent people obtain higher-status jobs more often than less intelligent people. Higher-status jobs may be more complex, and that may increase the "intellectual flexibility" of those who do them. In the 1990s Harvard sociologist Christopher Jencks showed that parental SES accounts for about 20 percent of the differences in children's future income and about 30 percent of the differences in children's social status when they grow up.

If parental job status predicts children's job status and IQ scores, and if IQ scores are correlated with occupational level, then the odds are doubly stacked against a low-SES child obtaining a high-status job. In the 1990s American psychologist Ulrich Neisser argued that some of the inevitable aspects of poverty, such as poor nutrition, inadequate prenatal care, and a lack of intellectual resources in the home (for example, computers, reference books), may influence children's developing intelligence. Also, poor parents may have less time to spend on the intellectual development of their children.

> ***"Look at all the technological advances. We couldn't have done this with the intellectual skills people had in the 19th century."***
> ***—Ulrich Neisser, 1998***

IQ scores are also highly correlated with years of schooling completed. But school attendance might be either the outcome or the cause. Genetic theorists argue that students with higher IQ scores will stay in school longer because they are more likely to be promoted to later grades and more likely to understand the material. On the other hand, many researchers have argued that IQ scores reflect school learning and are therefore influenced by school attendance.

An American child taking part in Head Start, an educational development program that has served low-income children and families since 1965.

A recent review of the evidence suggests quantity of schooling has a significant effect on IQ scores. To separate the effects of attendance on IQ from the effects of IQ on attendance, in the 1990s Stephen Ceci of Cornell University focused on situations in which school attendance is influenced by factors beyond students' control. For example, there is a small decrease in IQ over the summer vacation, especially among low-income children, who may not have exposure to learning or access to intellectual resources during the long summer break. Additionally, when children are unable to start school on time for reasons having to do with war, a shortage of teachers, or refusal to integrate schools, IQ scores appear to drop dramatically due to missed schooling.

If schools do increase IQ scores, how does this occur? Schools provide children with basic information (for example, "12 x 12 = 144" and "The Declaration of Independence was signed in 1776") that sometimes shows up on tests of intelligence and achievement. Schools also provide the opportunity to practice the intellectual skills—such as abstract thinking, categorization, problem solving, acquisition of concepts, and use of perceptual skills—that are necessary for performance on these tests. Western-style schooling is also associated with improved memory and recall.

Except in extreme cases, quality of schooling seems to have less effect on IQ scores than quantity of schooling. This suggests that the opportunity to practice the intellectual skills necessary for IQ tests may be sufficient to improve performances on them. However, this conclusion is limited to the effects on IQ scores and does not mean that better schools do not make a difference.

Head Start

Several researchers have investigated the effects of educational intervention programs. In the United States Head Start is a federally funded preschool program for children from families whose income is below the poverty level. Head Start and similar programs in other countries attempt to provide children with activities that might enhance their cognitive development, including reading books, learning the alphabet and numbers, learning the names of colors, drawing, and other related activities.

Most of those who participate in the program show a 15-point increase in IQ while the program is in progress, but by the end of elementary school there are no significant differences in IQ or achievement test performance between participants and nonparticipants. It is easy to see how these data could be critical of Head Start, but this conclusion ignores two important facts. First, children who enroll in Head Start do so because they are at risk of dropping out or have fallen behind their peers in school. If these children are performing at the same level as nonparticipants by the end of elementary school, then Head Start is successful after all. Second, success in school depends on more than IQ, and Head Start appears to teach social and motivational skills that may improve children's later school performance.

Other, similar intervention programs have been even more successful than Head Start in reducing teen pregnancy and welfare use and increasing employment. What appears to separate successful programs from unsuccessful ones is that the former are more extensive and focused on teaching specific skills rather than on raising IQ. More research is needed into how specific skills are learned, and there should be further investigation into different program designs.

The environment consists of a number of biological variables that have been linked to changes in IQ scores. One such variable is nutrition (*see* box below). Exposure to the poisonous metal lead has been associated with a drop in intelligence test scores over the course of childhood. Prenatal exposure to excessive levels of alcohol produces fetal alcohol syndrome, a condition associated with mental retardation, behavioral problems, and physical deformities. Smaller doses of alcohol may also have adverse effects on intelligence. However, at present it is unknown how much alcohol a pregnant woman can ingest without damaging her unborn child.

Accounting for differences in IQ scores

The "nature versus nurture" debate is one of the oldest arguments in the intelligence field. The latest evidence suggests that both heredity and environment influence test scores. The mechanisms by which this happens remain unknown, however, and the search for them is one of the most important challenges facing psychologists.

The debate is controversial because researchers have observed differences in intelligence test scores between men and women and between certain ethnic groups. Are these differences genetic, cultural, or situational? The answers to this question have wide-ranging implications.

Psychologists have long studied sex differences in intelligence. While there appears to be no substantial difference between men and women in IQ scores, men tend to be more heavily represented at the extremes of the distribution curve. Men are affected by mental retardation more frequently than women, and they

CASE STUDY

The Effects of Nutrition

The effects of nutrition on intelligence test scores are complicated. Only one extensive study of prenatal malnutrition has been conducted in which children born just after a famine were tested 19 years later as part of a large sample. No effects of the famine were found, but these subjects received normal nutrition after birth. Prolonged malnutrition during childhood has been associated with long-term impairments in IQ. Small variations in nutrients received appear to have significant effects on intelligence, but long-term follow-up studies are needed to confirm this suspicion.

Some genetic disorders, such as phenylketonuria (PKU) and Down's syndrome, may result in mental retardation and low IQ. In PKU a rare combination of genes leads to a number of biochemical interactions that ultimately result in low IQ. However, these interactions occur only in the presence of the amino acid phenylalanine. If the disorder is detected early in life, and phenylalanine is withheld from the infant's diet, then large IQ deficits do not appear to develop (see box p. 155).

The prenatal environment is the subject of some debate. Low-birthweight babies tend to have lower test scores in later childhood, but the correlations are small. American educational psychologist Arthur Jensen (born 1923) has argued that the tendency for twins to have slightly lower IQs than nontwin siblings reflects the influence of a shared prenatal environment (that is, fewer resources for each twin). However, twins raised together may face other difficulties, such as trying to form a separate identity or competing for attention.

PSYCHOLOGY & SOCIETY

The Meaning of Sex Differences

Are differences in abilities between men and women biologically based, or are they due to cultural influences? There is some evidence on both sides. On the biological side researchers have studied androgynized females who are genetically female but were exposed to high levels of testosterone (a male hormone that is also present to some extent in females) from their mothers while in the womb. As these individuals grow up, they are culturally identified as female, but they tend to play with "boys' toys," such as blocks and trucks, and have higher levels of spatial ability than females who were not so exposed.

On the cultural side many social scientists take the view that differences in abilities between men and women arise from society's different expectations of them and from their different experiences. Girls do not participate as extensively as boys in various cultural activities that are thought to increase spatial and mathematical ability. As children, girls are expected to play with dolls and other toys that develop verbal and social skills, while boys play with blocks, video games, and other toys that encourage spatial visualization. Later during adolescence girls take fewer math and science courses than boys. This may be due to stereotypes of math and science as "masculine" subjects and less encouragement from teachers, peers, and parents. Many social scientists believe cultural influences account for the relatively low representation of women in the fields of mathematics, engineering, and the physical sciences.

outnumber women at very high levels of measured intelligence. Women's scores are more closely clustered around the mean.

Although there are no overall differences between men and women in IQ test performance, there do seem to be differences in specific abilities. Men on average perform better than women in tests of spatial ability. The reason for this is unknown. Some psychologists speculate that spatial ability evolved to a higher level in men because men were hunters who needed this ability to track prey and find their way home. Others believe that the differences result from parents' different expectations of boys' and girls' abilities.

A 1995 study of more than 100,000 American adolescents on various mental tests found that on averages females performed slightly better than males on reading comprehension, writing, perceptual speed, and certain memory tasks. Males performed slightly better on tests of math, science, and social studies. But all the average sex differences were small.

Researchers have long been aware that men outperform women on standardized math tests. Girls start to fall behind boys in math at around the start of junior high. This gap continues to widen through high school and college. By the postgraduate level women are grossly underrepresented in math and science programs. Male high-school seniors average about 50 points higher on the math portion of the SAT than females. Yet other research indicates that the average girl's grades in math equal or exceed those of the average boy. Such anomalies have not been fully explained.

> ***"If we want to measure intelligence, we should measure it broadly rather than in the narrow ways that have failed to give a true picture of human capacities."***
>
> ***—Robert Sternberg, 1985***

One problem with studying sex differences on intelligence tests is that testers tend to avoid questions that show differences between males and females to eliminate bias. Intelligence tests therefore may not show such differences even if they exist. Even when gender differences have been explicitly studied, they are hard to detect because they tend to be small.

It is also important to remember that sex differences, where they exist at all,

represent only average differences between men and women in general, not individuals. Knowing whether someone is female or male reveals little about that person's intellectual abilities.

Ethnic differences

Differences in test performance between black people and white people in the U.S. are well documented. On tests that are thought to reflect general intelligence black people tend to score an average of one standard deviation below white people. Black children start school with school test scores approximately equal to those of white children, but the gap widens to as much as two grade levels by grade six and persists through junior high. Among students enrolled in four-year college courses 70 percent of black students drop out, compared to only 45 percent of white students. Of those who remain in college black students tend to underperform relative to their academic preparation. Therefore, on average, black students have lower college grades than white students with the same SAT scores. Although these differences are substantial, there are much larger differences between people within each group than between the means of the groups. This large variability within groups means that a person's ethnic origin cannot be used to extrapolate his or her intelligence.

Little girls pretend to cook with toy utensils; little boys play with power tools. Despite the changing roles of adult men and women in society, childhood stereotypes remain firmly entrenched.

Something is causing a reliable gap in intelligence test scores between black people and white people. As with sex differences, the debate is not about whether these differences exist but about what causes them. Many explanations have been proposed, ranging from genetic differences between the two groups to cultural differences. Some research has suggested that the two groups experience the testing environment differently.

In 1969 U.S. psychologist Arthur Jensen rekindled the modern debate by suggesting that differences in IQ scores between black people and white people reflected genetic differences between these groups. This argument was not new. Some of the first efforts to measure intelligence in the 1820s assumed that northern European whites would have bigger brains than other groups. Bigger brains would certainly be determined by genetic differences. In 1994 psychologist Richard Herrnstein and social analyst Charles

Murray repeated this argument in their book *The Bell Curve* (*see* box below).

The idea that genetics contributes to IQ score differences between black people and white people is based on two suppositions: first, that differences in intelligence must have a genetic basis; and second, that if intelligence has a genetic basis, then differences between groups must also have a genetic basis.

> ***"Scientific positions on the IQ controversy often become highly supercharged with ethical, philosophical, or religious feelings."***
> ***—Raymond E. Fancher, 1985***

Yet the claim that there is a genetic basis to group differences is not supported by adequate evidence. In 1970 Herrnstein and Murray were largely discredited by Richard Lewontin, whose comparison between ethnic groups and fields of corn undermined the assumption that high within-group heritability somehow implies that differences between groups must be genetic in origin. His analogy went like this: Imagine a random mix of corn grown on two different plots of land, one of which is rich in nutrients, and the other of which is poor. The corn grows taller, on average, on the first plot than on the second for purely environmental reasons, while within-group differences must be entirely genetic because of the internal uniformity assumption. For IQ variation between groups to be primarily genetic, the respective environments of both would have to be equivalent in every meaningful respect. Different environments would contribute to environmental variation. A large body of evidence suggests that differences exist between the average environments of black people and white people, and that they influence the development of intellectual skills.

The expectations that teachers have of a particular student's abilities can affect his or her performance. The key question, then, is whether teachers have different expectations for black children and white children. In the 1990s Pamela Rubovits of Rhode Island College and Martin Maehr of the University of Michigan assigned 66 white female undergraduates enrolled in a teaching course to interact with a group of black and white "gifted" and "nongifted" students who had been randomly selected from a range of ability groups. Rubovits

PSYCHOLOGY & SOCIETY

THE BELL CURVE

In 1994 American psychologist Richard Herrnstein and U.S. social analyst Charles Murray caused great controversy with their book *The Bell Curve*, part of which repeated the old argument that certain ethnic groups score lower on intelligence tests because intelligence was assumed to be determined by genetics.

The book's defenders said it was wrong to condemn an argument because it was unpopular. Those who condemned it said its arguments in favor of genetic differences ignored the evidence about environmental differences between black people and white people, and that many of the statistics used were based on experiments that had been conducted incorrectly or the results of which had been misinterpreted.

The U.S. civil rights movement in the 1960s coincided with—and may have been at least partly responsible for—a rise in the measurable intelligence of ethnic minorities.

and Maehr found that black students were given less attention, ignored more, praised less, and criticized more than their white counterparts.

John Ogbu, professor of anthropology at the University of California, Berkeley, has observed that minority group membership is associated with poorer achievement and IQ scores relative to the dominant group even when the minority is of the same race as the dominant group. For example, the Burakumin of Japan are genetically the same as the Japanese, but the Burakumin are an oppressed minority. Perhaps because of this status the Burakumin consistently score lower on IQ tests. Ogbu argues that something inherent in minority status leads to lower test scores.

Stereotype threat

Research by Stanford psychologist Claude Steele and his colleagues in the 1990s suggested that the underperformance of women and minorities is not related to stable differences in personalities, genetic makeup, or cultures. Rather, women and minorities find themselves in a unique situation in academic domains. Steele has termed this situation "stereotype threat." Stereotype threat is an apprehension felt by targets of stereotyping whenever they are in a situation in which a negative stereotype could be used to explain their poor performance. Because there are negative stereotypes about black people's performance on standardized tests, those taking a test face the possibility of confirming this stereotype if they perform poorly. This is a distraction that makes it harder for them to concentrate on the task and leads to poor performance.

Steele and Joshua Aronson of the University of Texas at Austin found that changing the description of the verbal SAT had an effect on performance. When they described the test as diagnostic of intellectual ability, the stereotypes about black people's intellectual ability became relevant. In this case black people scored lower than white people. When they described the test as a problem-solving task, the stereotypes were no longer relevant. In that case black people scored the same as white people. It is possible that simply changing the way a test is presented could reduce ethnic differences on IQ scores. At present researchers have not yet investigated this with any of the standard intelligence tests.

Narrowing the gap

There is some evidence that the performance gap, as measured by school tests and achievement tests, between black people and white people is diminishing. There is a consensus that this gap has narrowed since 1965, with the most substantial reduction happening between

1965 and 1972. A 1995 study by Larry Hedges of the University of Chicago and his research assistant Amy Nowell found it significant that this improvement occurred during the civil rights' era. It is possible that African Americans during this time saw more opportunities for academic achievement. Increased parental education and decreased family size may also have contributed to the narrowing of the gap.

> ***"Everyone experiences stereotype threat. We are all members of some group about which negative stereotypes exist."***
>
> ***—Claude Steele, 1999***

Other ethnic groups have not received as much attention in psychological studies. Hispanic students tend to score somewhere between African Americans and Anglo Americans on intelligence tests. Asian Americans reliably score the highest of all. Asian American students get better grades on average, score higher on math achievement and aptitude tests, and are more likely to graduate from high school and college. Yet the exact reasons for their high academic performance are unknown. One explanation points to Asian cultural values that place central importance on academic achievement and link success in school with later occupational success.

Summary

Although there is little consensus about what intelligence is, what if anything it predicts, or how to measure it, almost everyone agrees that it is important. It is inextricably linked with society's notions of what is "valuable" in a person. Thus intelligence testing is likely to remain with us even if its future direction remains unclear. Meanwhile, it seems inevitable that tests will from time to time be accused—and in many cases be guilty—of cultural bias. What, for example, if a test contains a question that requires familiarity with baseball—why should non-Americans be expected to answer it correctly? But if they get it wrong, they will lose points and thus be at an unfair disadvantage in competition with Mets' fans. On the other hand, we may reasonably doubt the possibility of devising a test that is completely culturally neutral—even pattern recognition, a standard component of nonverbal reasoning tests, is thought to favor urban children because they are more familiar with angular shapes through their greater experience of buildings than their country cousins. Further, it is often objected that since the formats of these tests are widely known, children can be coached in the required techniques, with the result that the test tells us nothing about their intelligence, merely their ability to do the test.

As a reaction to several legal cases about the fairness of making educational decisions on the basis of IQ many public schools have now become reluctant to give such tests, which are today taken almost exclusively by pupils with special educational needs such as a learning disability or a particular gift. Nevertheless, the tests are still around, albeit in thinly disguised form—the Scholastic Aptitude Test may have become known as the Scholastic Assessment Test, but it remains a partly veiled measure of intelligence. Even if someone comes up with an intelligence test that is culturally neutral, that still takes us back to the original question—what does it tell us?

CONNECTIONS

- Nature and Nurture: Volume 1, pp. 22–29
- Cognitive Psychology: Volume 1, pp. 104–117
- Cross-cultural Psychology: Volume 1, pp. 152–161
- The Mind: Volume 2, pp. 40–61
- Problem Solving: Volume 3, pp. 136–163
- Nature and Nurture: pp. 142–163

Nature and Nurture

"Half of the . . . variance in personality traits is due to genetic causes."

Eysenck & Eysenck

One of the most long-standing debates in psychology concerns a fundamental question about the human mind: Is it shaped by biology or by experience? In other words, is human nature innate (inborn), or it is learned? Following the example of geneticists studying physical features, behavioral geneticists try to explore the influence of genes on behavior—an area made more complicated by the difficulties of accurately defining and measuring behavioral traits.

From the fourth century B.C. most philosophers believed that experience shaped the mind (*see* Vol. 1, pp. 22–29), a view that persisted through the Middle Ages. English teacher Richard Mulcaster introduced the terms nature and nurture in the 16th century A.D., but it wasn't until Charles Darwin published *On the Origin of Species* in 1859 that the role of biology began to be properly considered (*see* Vol. 1, pp. 134–143). Darwin's ideas were developed by the English scientist Francis Galton (*see* box p. 143), who focused on the differences between individuals. Although he knew little about the mechanism of inheritance and nothing about genes, he is considered to be the founder of behavior genetics. Behavior geneticists still debate the roles played by biology and culture in defining human nature, but they have come to realize that there are two key aspects at issue. By clarifying the differences between these two aspects, they have gone a long way toward resolving the debate.

The development of individual traits

The first aspect of the nature–nurture debate focuses on how specific people come to be the way they are. It considers the causes of an individual's physical and behavioral traits by asking questions such as: "Why does Betty have poor eyesight?" and "Why does Johnny hit other boys on

Genes are determined by the structure of DNA —a complex molecule found in the cells of living organisms (see diagram p. 159). Geneticists can study DNA using a method called agarose gel electophoresis, which produces different separation patterns on a slab of gel (see left) according to the structure of the DNA fragment studied.

the playground?" People used to think that questions like these had answers such as "It is 40 percent genetic and 60 percent cultural." But scientists now know that this kind of answer cannot be correct. Development occurs as a result of genes interacting with the environment in extremely complex ways. There is no feature of any organism, including any individual person, that is not the result of a gene–environment interaction. So, the answer to any question like the ones above should always be "Because of interaction between genes and the environment." Separating the effects of one or the other for an individual is just not possible.

Consider a rectangle. Its area can be determined by multiplying its length by its width. It is not possible to say that either its length or its width is responsible for its area—they both are. The influence of one cannot be separated from the other. The same is true for any biological trait. If the relevant genes change, the trait will change; and if the environment that influences the trait changes, the trait will change. Genes and environment jointly produce traits, even those that seem to be "cultural." So while it may seem reasonable to say, "James loves his mother because of culture, not biology," you should not forget that James' brain was formed by genes that caused it to develop in a certain way in concert with the environment.

It is also important to remember that environment has a broad meaning when it is used to discuss genes. The environment of a particular gene might include other genes, internal factors such as the uterus, the physical exterior environment, and the social environment (the individuals or groups of people who influence a person). Some part of this environment is critical for the development of any trait.

BIOGRAPHY

Francis Galton

Sir Francis Galton believed that intelligence was largely determined by genetic factors.

Sir Francis Galton (1822–1911) was born in England, and his early career was varied: He attended medical school for a short time, went exploring in Africa, and conducted meteorological research. It was only later that he focused on research into intelligence.

Galton was heavily influenced by Darwin's *Origin of Species,* and in 1869 he published *Hereditary Genius*, in which he argued that intelligence was determined largely by heredity rather than environment. He also used data from his research on the physical and mental characteristics of twins to investigate the effects of "nature" and "nurture" long before behavior genetics became established as a field of study.

Although Galton made important contributions to many areas of science, he was also an early proponent of eugenics: the science of improving the physical and mental makeup of the human species by selective parenthood. Eugenics quickly became a controversial issue (*see* Vol. 1, pp. 22–29), and that has adversely affected Galton's reputation in recent times.

KEY FACTS

- Both physical and behavioral traits are the result of genes interacting in complex ways with the environment.
- People can differ either because they have different genes that interact in different ways with similar environments, or because they have similar genes that are exposed to different environments.
- Researchers use heritability—a measure of the amount of variation in a trait that is caused by genes within a population—to try to estimate the influence of genes.
- However, the heritability of a particular trait can vary according to the population studied and the environment in which the trait is measured.
- Behavioral traits such as personality or intelligence are particularly difficult to define and measure, and the interactions with the environment are more complex.

The nature-versus-nurture debate has often been framed in terms of what is genetic, or innate, as opposed to what is learned. We now know that all traits result from gene–environment interactions, which means that what is innate is, in essence, a set of instructions written in the language of DNA about how to interact with the environment to construct an organism. So, on the one hand, no trait can be innate in the sense that there is no environmental influence on it. On the other hand, every trait is innate in that genes play a role in producing that trait. For this reason genetic is not the opposite of learned. Genes, together with the environment, create the ability to learn. Genes, again acting in concert with the

PSYCHOLOGY & SOCIETY

CLONING

During cloning, genetic material from one individual is used to make a new individual. Thus a clone has exactly the same genes as the organism from which cells were taken to make the clone. Organisms that can reproduce without mating, such as bacteria and many plants, generate clones whenever they reproduce.

In the 1950s scientists tried to clone frogs but with limited success. In these experiments DNA from frog embryos was put into a frog's egg cell and allowed to develop. Finally, in 1996 British researchers working in Scotland successfully used cells from an adult sheep to make a clone, which they named Dolly. This was an important breakthrough because it was the first time that cells from an adult organism, rather than an embryo, had been used to make a clone.

The cloning of an adult sheep raised serious ethical issues in many people's minds. One fear was that cloning techniques might lead scientists to try to improve the human race genetically: a process called eugenics. Other concerns were also raised, such as whether individuals would be psychologically damaged by knowing about their origins. Defenders have pointed out that a cloned person would essentially be no different from an identical twin, except that twins are born at virtually the same time. They have also emphasized how the effects of the environment on development would create a clone different from the individual who provided the DNA.

As early as February 1997 in the United States some legislators drafted a bill that would make cloning a person a federal crime. In 1998 the Food and Drug Administration stated that human cloning could be carried out only with their approval. More generally, the rapid pace of progress in fields such as molecular genetics has forced politicians and other influential people to grapple with the moral implications of such major advances in technology.

Dolly the sheep (left) was the first example of a successful cloning from an adult animal. The breakthrough raised serious ethical questions about the cloning of people but also inspired films such as Multiplicity, *in which Michael Keaton (right) plays a man whose lifestyle is so hectic that he asks a geneticist for help and ends up with three clones of himself.*

environment, produce the human brain, which gathers and processes information from the surrounding world.

A new addition to this area of debate is the concept of "reliably developing traits": physical or mental traits that seem to be present in all, or virtually all, members of a given species. This means that across a wide range of environments these traits will almost always emerge. The concept of reliable development helps explain the differences between individuals.

The origin of differences

The second aspect of the debate focuses on the differences that occur between individuals, asking why and what causes them. Researchers have also wondered how they might limit these differences.

If two organisms differ from each other, there can be only two possible reasons. First, the organisms might have different genes that interact with the environment in different ways. Second, the organisms might have identical genes but be exposed to different environmental circumstances. Tracing the origins of these differences is an important goal for contemporary researchers in biology and psychology, but it is far from a simple exercise.

> ***"Our brains are separate and independent enough from our genes to rebel against them."***
> ***—Richard Dawkins, 1989***

If the environment is held constant for a group of individuals, any differences that are observed must be due to genes. Unfortunately, it is virtually impossible to keep the environment exactly the same for an entire group of people, which makes it difficult to separate environmental and genetic sources of difference. In a similar fashion, if a large number of people with identical genes were placed in different environments, any differences observed would be due to the environment. In real life, however, the only people who share exactly the same genes are identical twins. One theoretical solution to this problem would be to study clones (*see* box p. 144).

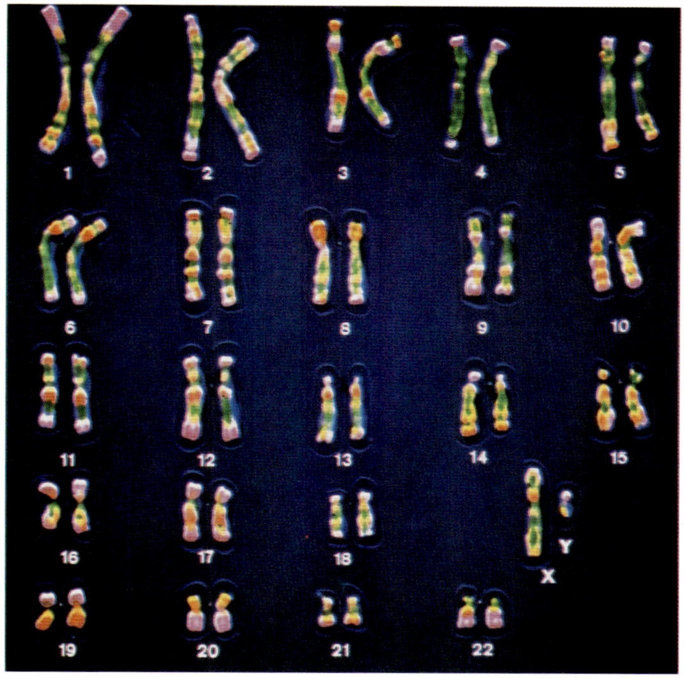

The nucleus of each human cell contains 46 chromosomes, 23 from the mother and 23 from the father. The chromosomes shown above are placed in maternal–paternal pairs, and from the XY pairing (near the bottom right-hand corner) we can deduce that they are from a male. An XX pairing would produce a female.

GENES AND HERITABLE TRAITS

An individual's genetic makeup may be compared to two sets of encyclopedias. Most people (apart from a few exceptions with chromosomal aberrations) have 23 pairs of chromosomes—half of each pair coming from the mother, the other half from the father. Each chromosome is made of DNA, which carries genes. So a chromosome is like a volume in one of the two encyclopedia sets, and the genes are similar to the entries in each volume.

Similar genes occur at corresponding points on each chromosome of a pair, rather like having the same alphabetical entries in the equivalent volumes of each encyclopedia set. Thus the genes for eye color, for example, would be in the same place on equivalent chromosomes. What might differ are the instructions in each gene: One of the genes might be for blue eyes, and one might be for brown eyes, and the individual's eye color depends on which gene is dominant (masks the other). Some of the variations are so slight that they have no substantial effect on a person, but other genes may differ in ways that are equivalent to major discrepancies in the text. They might lead to differences in a person's appearance, personality, or in his or her susceptibility to disease, and so on.

The genes that occupy corresponding positions on two chromosomes in a pair are called alleles, and most people have similar chromosome pairs with similar alleles, although the precise instructions vary. Some genes have many different alleles, and some have only one; the combinations differ to varying degrees from person to person. It is the different combinations that make each individual unique. Unique combinations arise because people inherit half of their genes from their father and half from their mother, each parent passing on only one of each pair of chromosomes. Which ones they pass on is essentially random, and there are so many different genes that every child inherits a new combination of alleles that has never existed before. Although each person has a different combination of alleles, every person is a member of the human species.

KEY TERMS

Chromosome: a linear DNA-containing structure that holds part of the genetic material of a cell.

Genotype: the complete genetic makeup of an organism.

Hereditary trait: a trait that can be passed genetically from parent to offspring.

Heredity: the sum of the qualities derived from ancestors.

Heritability: the proportion of observed variation for a trait in a specific population that can be attributed to genetic factors rather than environmental ones. It is expressed as a ratio of genetically caused variation to total variation.

Heritable trait: trait for which differences in a population appear to bear some relation to differences in genes. It is *not* the same as a hereditary trait.

Phenotype: the observable characteristics of an organism.

Genotypes and phenotypes

Genetic research is always based on the relationship between two things: genotype and phenotype. An organism's genotype is its genetic makeup; its phenotype consists of observable characteristics, such as how tall or short it is. Geneticists have studied many organisms in their attempts to understand heredity—including plants and insects—and have made considerable progress. People pose more of a problem, however, since researchers are not ethically allowed to control either people's genes or their environments. They have made some progress in determining the role of genes in producing certain traits, especially physical traits that are easily observable and that involve only a few alleles. Behavioral traits are harder to investigate, however, since they are more difficult to measure and involve complex interactions between genes and the environment.

Heritability

Researchers often approach the problem by trying to figure out how differences in genes relate to specific trait differences in

A father and his daughter might look alike because she has inherited half of her father's genes, which help determine physical features such as eye color and facial shape. But shared environmental factors also play a part.

a population. To try to quantify the extent to which variations between individuals result from genetic differences rather than differences in the environment, they use a measure called broad-sense heritability. They express their results as a proportion of the genetically based variation to total variation on a scale from zero and one. A heritability of one suggests that all the variance among a population is genetically based; a heritability of zero suggests that all the variance is environmentally based.

Heritability does not measure the extent to which a given trait can be passed on genetically: It is a variable measure of difference that can be applied only to a population of individuals. By contrast, genetic determination is an intuitive notion that lacks quantitative definition: A trait could be said to be genetically determined if it was caused by genes and was certain to develop in a "normal" environment (whatever that might be).

> ***"We are, in sum, incomplete or unfinished animals who complete or finish ourselves through culture."***
> ***—Clifford Geertz, 1962***

High and low-scoring traits

So what kinds of traits might have a high heritability? Consider hair. Differences in people's natural hair color are closely related to the genetic differences between individuals, so natural hair color is a highly heritable trait with a value close to one. Compare this with the number of fingers on people's hands. Most people with fewer than five fingers per hand lost fingers as the result of an accident. So, with a few rare exceptions, differences in the number of fingers per hand between individuals are due to environmental factors. Finger number, therefore, has low heritability with a value close to zero.

One complication in the concept of heritability is that the heritability of a trait can vary depending on the population studied and on the environment in which it is measured. In some environments a trait might have high heritability, while in others heritability might be much lower. Consider height, for example. In many populations (especially those in which everyone receives an adequate diet) height is highly heritable because most of the differences are caused by differences in genes. In developing countries, however, food is not always readily available, so at least some of the variation in height is caused by environmental factors such as diet. In these populations the heritability of height would be much lower.

These examples also help explain the concept of reliable development. A trait that is reliably developing is one that has either very low or zero heritability in many environments. Finger number, for example, has low heritability around the world in every environment. Variations are not caused by gene differences or by gene–environment interactions, so almost every person will have five fingers unless an environmental action changes this.

A second complication is that traits can show heritability even when they are not genetically determined. Consider IQ, for

FOCUS ON

Evolution and Heritability

Evolutionary theory tells us a certain amount about which traits we might expect to be highly heritable. According to this theory, evolution occurs through natural selection (*see* Vol. 1, pp. 134–143), which can only work if certain genes result in some organisms having a greater ability to survive and reproduce than others.

If a particular variation of an inherited trait helps an organism perform a task more efficiently than its competitors (such as finding food, avoiding predators, or attracting mates), then more of the organisms with that variation will survive. Ultimately the genes that produce less useful variations of this trait will vanish, and the only genes left in a population will be those that produce the useful trait. At this point heritability for that trait will be zero because any variation will be caused by environmental factors.

For this reason we would expect traits that are unimportant for survival and reproduction to have high heritability and traits that are critical for survival and reproduction to have low heritability.

These fraternal twins are no more or less genetically related than if they had been sisters. They are the result of two different eggs being fertilized by two different sperm. Studies of fraternal and identical twins provide scientists with useful information when they are trying to estimate the heritability of traits.

example. If a culture decreed that only men should learn how to read and women should learn how to sew, women would score badly on an IQ test that measured reading ability. Consequently, reading ability would have a high heritability

> ***"We know nothing about the hereditability of human . . . intellectual traits."***
> ***—Richard Lewontin, 1993***

because it would be affected by genetic differences (whether you were a man or a woman), even though it was culturally rather than genetically determined. In behavior genetics much of the confusion and criticism stems from the mistaken tendency to equate heritability (being heritable) with genetic determination, when, in fact, it can only be used as an indication of whether genes are involved.

Another related problem is that if a certain trait has high heritability in some environments, that does not necessarily tell us anything about how difficult it will be to eliminate the differences between individuals. Some scientists have shown that traits such as intelligence have high heritability in some environments, but that does not mean it is impossible or even difficult to eliminate these differences. Changing the environment can change the heritability of a trait and alter the amount of variance due to genes (*see* box p. 155).

RESEARCH METHODS

To research the origins of differences between people, behavior geneticists rely on a critical idea about the relationship between genotype and phenotype. For any heritable trait people who have similar genotypes should be more alike. In other words, if some of the differences between people are caused by differences in genes, then people with the same genes for a trait should be more similar to each other than those with different genes. Of course, if a trait shows no heritability—if differences between individuals are due to nongenetic factors—then for this trait it does not matter if the individuals share genes in common. Genes are not the only reason people have similar traits; it is entirely possible for two people to have similar traits and different genes.

For this reason behavior geneticists need to know something about the genetic similarity of the people they are studying to draw any conclusions about the sources of difference between them. Similarly, they also need to know about the environment, so people's history is important, too.

Twin studies

Since it is vital for behavior geneticists to know how similar or different people are genetically to draw any conclusions about the role of genes in creating different behaviors, the most convenient subjects for research are twins. Twins are of two basic types. Monozygotic (MZ) twins develop from a single fertilized egg (a zygote). They have identical genes because they come from the same original cell. They are also called identical twins because of the high degree of physical resemblance between them. Dizygotic (DZ) twins develop in the same uterus but are the result of two different eggs fertilized by two different sperm cells. They are called fraternal twins because they share no more or no less genes in common than they would if they were brothers or sisters.

Comparisons of the two types of twins can provide a rich source of data about heritability. For any given trait, if the differences between individuals are not due to differences in genes, then identical twins should resemble one another in that particular trait no more than fraternal twins. In contrast, if a trait has high heritability, then identical twins should resemble each other more than fraternal twins because they share more of their genes in common. By comparing how similar identical twins are to one another with how similar fraternal twins are to one another, researchers can attempt to calculate heritability for a particular trait (*see* box below).

Family studies

Individuals do not need to be genetically identical for behavior geneticists to make estimates about heritability. Relatives share genes in common, too, so it can also

FOCUS ON

CORRELATION

Behavior genetics requires many complex statistical tools, but one relatively simple method is correlation: a statistical measure of how similar pairs of individuals are for a given characteristic. Positive correlations range from 0.0 to 1.0 —a correlation of 1.0 meaning that both members of any pair in a chosen study group will share exactly the same trait. (Negative correlations ranging from -1.0 to 0.0 are possible but unlikely to occur in behavior genetics.)

The example of height illustrates the concept of correlation and shows how useful it is in behavior genetics. Identical twins tend to be almost exactly the same height: If you know the height of one, you can be pretty certain about the height of the other. This means their heights are highly correlated (studies of identical twins have shown that height has an overall correlation of 0.9). In contrast, the heights of fraternal twins are more variable (studies have shown that height in fraternal twins has a correlation value of only 0.45). This big difference in the amount of variation leads us to assume that genes are the main cause of the height similarities found in identical twins. So, if people were selected randomly from the population, the overall correlation for height would probably have a value of 0.0. Using figures like these, researchers can then estimate the heritability of height.

be useful to investigate the extent to which family members resemble one another for any particular trait. If close relatives are more similar than unrelated individuals, it suggests genes are partly responsible for causing the variations. Galton based some of his early work on this idea and found that genius tended to run in families.

Children in adoptive families such as the one above are not genetically related to their parents. Studies of adoptive families can therefore help researchers investigate the effects of the environment on traits.

Adoption

One problem that applies both to studies of identical and fraternal twins and to studies of close relatives is that people who are closely related often share the same environment. Thus it is difficult to determine whether any similarities found are caused by common genes or common environments. One way around this problem is to study identical twins who were raised in different environments, since any similarities between them would have to be due to the genes they shared. Unfortunately for researchers, few identical twins are reared separately. They are rarely given up for separate adoption; and when they are, records of their whereabouts are not always easy to obtain. When separated twins have been studied, however, they have provided surprising results in terms of the traits they share (*see* box p. 151).

Adoption studies are not restricted to twins. Researchers can also investigate the similarities between children and their adoptive parents. Because adopted children and their parents are genetically unrelated, any similarities observed can be attributed to environmental rather than genetic causes. Adoption studies can also compare adopted and biological siblings. The best way to approach such a study would be to compare one pair of genetically unrelated siblings who were reared together with a second set of genetically similar siblings who were reared in different family environments. For any given trait, if the siblings who are biologically related resemble one another more than the unrelated siblings who shared the same environment, this provides evidence for heritability of the trait in question (in other words, genes cause at least some of the variance for that trait).

BEHAVIORAL RESEARCH

The founder of behavior genetics, Francis Galton(*see* box p. 143), focused much of his research on the origin of differences in intelligence. Intelligence remains a major area of interest for modern researchers, and a wealth of data have been gathered. But the subject also has strong political implications and remains fiercely debated. One problem is that there is no general agreement on what intelligence is or how to measure it (*see* pp. 118–141). That is frustrating for researchers, and some would heartily agree with the sentiments of psychologist E. G. Boring (1886–1968), who said that "intelligence is what the intelligence test measures." Historically, intelligence research has used the IQ test, although other testing technologies have emerged in recent times. Twin studies, family studies, and adoption studies have all been used, and the number of subjects that have been investigated over the years is well into the millions.

CASE STUDY

Separated Identical Twins

In the case of identical twins separated at or near birth and raised in different places it is much more difficult to attribute similarities to shared environments.

David Lykken, Thomas Bouchard, Nancy Segal, and colleagues at the University of Minnesota studied twins, and their reunions of identical twins reared apart revealed surprising similarities. In 1979 the "Jim twins," Jim Lewis and Jim Spring, who had been adopted at birth, were reunited after 39 years. They both weighed 180 pounds (81.6kg) and were 6 feet (1.8m) tall. Both had married a woman named Linda, divorced, and married a second woman named Betty. Both had a son named James Allan (with slightly different spellings); and when they were young, both had a dog named Toy. The Jims also seemed to share personality traits and tastes. They had both liked mathematics and hated spelling in school, both trained in law enforcement and worked as deputy sheriffs, both liked mechanical drawing and carpentry, and they both went on vacations to the same Florida beach, smoked the same brand of cigarettes, and drank the same brand of beer.

Other pairs of twins reared apart have also revealed surprising similarities. One pair of twins both used a rare toothpaste imported from Sweden and wrapped rubber bands around their wrists, while another pair of twins used the same hair tonic. A particularly striking case concerned a pair of twins who were raised in dramatically different circumstances. One had been brought up as a Catholic in Czechoslovakia and had planned to join the Hitler Youth before World War II (1939–1945); the other was brought up as a Jew in Trinidad and had spent time in Israel on a kibbutz. They shared some unusual traits such as flushing the toilet both before and after using it and reading books from back to front. Both also reported enjoying sneezing loudly in crowded elevators.

Different methods have yielded slightly different results, but researchers have still been able to draw some broad conclusions. The IQ scores of identical twins have been correlated in the range of 0.8 to 0.9, which is remarkably strong, and drops to roughly 0.7 for identical twins reared apart. The correlation is still higher than that for fraternal twins, however, which is around 0.5. These studies have enabled researchers to generate heritability estimates using various methods of calculation. The lowest of these estimates is about 0.3. The highest estimate is about 0.7.

Psychologist and historian E. G. Boring was recruited by the U.S. Army during World War I (1914–1918) to devise intelligence tests for conscripts. He once commented that intelligence is "what the intelligence test measures."

Although people disagree about the precise value of the heritability of IQ, they broadly agree that intelligence is, at least to some degree, heritable: Differences in IQ in the populations studied can be partly attributed to differences in genes. But that does not mean that differences in IQ are inevitable or unchangeable, as the box on phenylketonuria illustrates (*see* p. 155). Some researchers have tried to study environmental variables that might cause differences in IQ and have found that the economic status of the family in which a child is raised can affect IQ scores.

Other developments in the field of intelligence research have suggested there might be different types of intelligence, so behavior geneticists have also tried to investigate the possibility that some aspects of intelligence are more heritable than others. The Hawaii Family Study of Cognition was a large experimental

THE CYRIL BURT SCANDAL

BIOGRAPHY

The heated debate surrounding issues of nature and nurture is illustrated vividly by the case of British psychologist Sir Cyril Burt (1883–1971). Burt achieved great renown during his lifetime: He was head of the psychology department at University College London and he was knighted in 1946. He was a strong believer in the importance of heredity in determining intelligence, and he was also one of the first people to research twins, publishing studies showing extremely high correlations in the IQ of identical twins.

After his death Burt was accused of scientific fraud. His biographer, Leslie Hearnshaw, alleged that he made up data to support the theory he favored. Burt had reported on the correlation of intelligence for identical twins in several studies, and his correlations were exactly the same in multiple experiments, out to three decimal places. Statistically this is extremely unlikely, and it seemed to point strongly toward falsified data. It was also thought to be suspicious when no one could trace the two research assistants who were supposed to have helped him with his studies. In 1980 the Council of the British Psychological Society declared that Burt was guilty of fraud.

Later two books were published by Robert Joynson and Ronald Fletcher, who looked into the evidence against Burt and revealed important errors. They claimed Burt had given his research assistants pseudonyms—eccentric, but not fraudulent behavior—and that while there was evidence of dishonesty and sloppy procedures, the charges were not proven. Their attempted defense has since been undermined by Nicholas Mackintosh in *Cyril Burt: Fraud or Framed* (1985), illustrating the heated controversy that has been generated by the nature–versus–nurture debate.

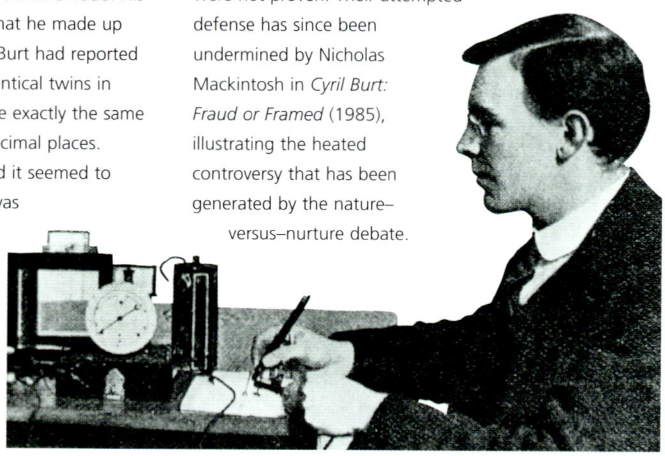

During his lifetime Cyril Burt was a respected psychologist. His research supported the theory that IQ variability is the result of genetic rather than environmental influences, but doubt has since been cast on the integrity and validity of his research methods and findings.

program set up in 1983 to investigate specific cognitive abilities. The results of this research indicated that all of the abilities under investigation showed some heritability, including reasoning, verbal comprehension, memory, and spatial skills. Although these abilities all showed heritable differences, some had higher heritability than others. Verbal and spatial abilities, for example, seemed to have a slightly higher heritability than other skills, whereas memory seemed to have a slightly lower rating. Research into the heritability of different aspects of intelligence continues, helping behavior geneticists clarify exactly what intelligence is. But since different intellectual abilities have different heritabilities, it seems likely that intelligence is a trait with many parts.

The large amount of data gathered on intelligence has also enabled behavior geneticists to ask another question: How does the heritability of an ability change with age? This question lies at the heart of a research area called developmental behavior genetics. The answer surprised many researchers: It seems the heritability of IQ does change with time and that it tends to be greater in adulthood than in infancy or childhood.

This increase in the heritability of IQ is surprising because you might expect the cumulative effects of the environment to have a greater impact on people as they age, causing more variation between them. But that is not what has been observed. The increase in heritability might be due to several factors. For instance, it is possible that certain genes are activated, or "turned on," during a person's lifetime and that they generate some of the observed differences. In other words, it is impossible to observe variations caused by differences in these genes until they are active. As with many areas of IQ research, more study is needed to clarify this issue.

IQ controversy

Research on intelligence has been the source of great controversy (*see* box p. 152), and the debate intensified in 1994 with the publication of *The Bell Curve* by Richard J. Herrnstein and Charles Murray. The authors set out to show that IQ was heritable and suggested that differences in IQ led to very real differences in economic outcomes: More intelligent individuals got better jobs, earned more money, and so forth. They backed up their arguments with a large collection of data and analyses, and suggested that these facts pointed to certain policies in education and welfare.

> ***"The Bell Curve is bad science. It trades on the hard factual image of statistical data and peddles conclusions which threaten to exacerbate . . . social divisions."***
>
> ***—Drew et al., 1995***

FOCUS ON

Bell Curves

The Bell Curve took its name from the shape of a normal distribution graph, which looks similar to a bell viewed from the side (tall and rounded with tapering edges). A bell curve is produced when researchers plot the results for any experiment or study in which most of the results cluster around an average.

This type of graph appears regularly when psychologists plot the results for a given trait in a population, with most people clustering around the average, and fewer and fewer people displaying extreme values of the trait. Most men in the United States, for example, are within a couple of inches of the average height for the population—about 5 feet 10 inches (1.7m). The number of men who are 6 feet 4 inches (1.9m) is smaller than the number who are 6 feet 2 inches (1.8m), and so on. Almost no adult males are taller than 7 feet (2.1m) or shorter than 5 feet (1.5m). Behavioral traits such as intelligence also tend to produce a bell curve when they are measured and plotted on a graph.

The most controversial part of the book was a section entitled "Ethnic Differences in Cognitive Ability." In it Herrnstein and Murray used bell curves (*see* box right) to demonstrate how the average IQ for certain ethnic or racial groups differed in tests. They argued that these differences, combined with the finding that IQ was heritable, suggested that these variations in IQ might be due entirely to differences in genes. Consequently, they expressed pessimism about the possibility of raising IQ through different kinds of government education and social welfare programs.

Debate over *The Bell Curve* has raged in scientific and popular media. Opponents have criticized the authors for many reasons, arguing that they defined IQ using western standards, that they only measured certain aspects of intelligence, and that people's scores could have been affected by variables such as distrust or a lack of familiarity. They also argued that there is no way to exclude the influence of environmental factors: IQ tests measure the way innate intelligence develops in interaction with the environment. As a result, heritability cannot be used to draw reliable conclusions about the precise cause of differences between populations. If different genes generate differences in individuals within a population, it does not mean that genes account for variations between populations (*see* box p. 163).

Another complication that researchers should take into account when calculating heritability is that the heritability of a trait can depend on which part of a population is investigated. The heritability of human intelligence has been calculated at about 0.5 for many populations, but this could reflect IQ heritability for people with average intelligence. In a group with above- or below-average intelligence heritability might be significantly higher or lower.

Research with unusual groups

That is one of the reasons why behavior geneticists have carried out considerable research on special populations—groups of people who are extreme in some way. This includes investigations of the possible genetic influences on certain cognitive disorders. For example, some evidence suggests reading disabilities are heritable. Studies of twins with reading disabilities have shown that when one twin is reading disabled, the other twin is likely to be, too. Estimates of heritability for this problem are roughly 0.3, a relatively small figure.

Mental retardation has been defined as an IQ below 70 (*see* pp. 118–141), and it has many different causes. One of them is a disorder called PKU, which is known to be heritable (*see* box p. 155). Another genetic cause of mental retardation is a condition known as fragile X syndrome, which is caused by a defect on the X chromosome (one of the sex chromosomes, *see* image p. 145). Mental retardation caused by this defect is highly heritable, but the environment is also important: People who have inherited fragile X syndrome can be more or less severely retarded depending on the environment.

Three generations of a family. Research suggests a surprising number of personality traits are influenced by hereditary factors, including neuroticism and extroversion.

Genetic differences also account for some of the variability in retardation. If one parent is retarded, for example, it is more likely that a child will be. If both parents are retarded, the likelihood is even greater.

Personality differences

Personality researchers also attempt to understand the ways in which individual people differ from one another (*see* pp. 94–117), usually by asking them to answer a questionnaire focusing on the personality trait in question. Many different tests have been designed, but researchers disagree about how best to organize personality differences. As a result, behavior geneticists often have the difficult task of assessing the heritability of traits before personality psychologists have agreed how to measure them. Another problem is that personality researchers often ask subjects to report on their own self-assessments—a method that has led some researchers to question the validity of personality surveys.

Some of the best available data on the heritability of personality traits comes from studies of twins, especially those who have grown up in different environments (*see* pp. 150–151). Findings from twin studies such as the Minnesota Study of Twins Reared Apart, published in 1990 in the journal *Nature*, indicated levels of heritability that came as a

FOCUS ON

PKU (Phenylketonuria)

Research into a disorder called PKU (phenylketonuria) demonstrates that a trait with high heritability is not necessarily unchangeable. Patients with PKU lack a certain enzyme that makes it impossible for them to break down an amino acid called phenylalanine, which is found in many foods. As a result, this amino acid builds up in the body. During early childhood large amounts of phenylalanine can disrupt development of the brain, causing mental retardation, so children with PKU rarely develop beyond the mental age of about two.

The only people who develop PKU are those who inherit a particular gene from both parents. Consequently, it is highly heritable—all the variation in the incidence of PKU is due to differences in genes.

Once scientists understood how PKU was caused, however, they could develop a treatment. In this case the solution was easy: They simply changed patients' diets to exclude foods with phenylalanine—a treatment that has proven to be very effective. So, although the disease is highly heritable, changing the outcome is relatively easy.

surprise to many. For many personality traits heritability estimates were roughly 0.5—that is, about half of the differences were caused by differences in genes. In fact, it was surprising how many aspects of personality seemed to show heritability. Some questionnaires in the Minnesota study asked about aspects of peoples' lives that you might think would depend on the family environment, but the results did not support this. For the questionnaire that assessed the importance of religion to an individual, for example, there was a heritability of about 0.5. For another that asked about people's beliefs in discipline, rules, and obeying authority, heritability was also around 0.5. This score is relatively high for traits that were expected to differ because of different family environments.

> ***"To ask whether heredity or environment is more important to life is like asking whether fuel or oxygen is more necessary for making a fire."***
> ***—Robert Woodworth, 1941***

Literature on the heritability of personality traits has focused on those elements of personality that psychologists most agree on. For example, there has been extensive research on extroversion and neuroticism. Extroversion measures how sociable or outgoing people are, and neuroticism measures how emotionally stable they are. Tens of thousands of pairs of twins have been surveyed for these two traits across many countries, and the results indicate that these personality dimensions have a heritability of about 0.5. Other methods of assessing heritability for these personality traits have yielded different results, however. For example, family resemblance studies investigating how similar parents and offspring are or how similar brothers and sisters are have suggested lower heritability. The same is also true of adoption studies. Findings such as these suggest it is important for researchers to use multiple methods when trying to reach a broad understanding of the influence of genes on personality traits.

Another surprising result emerging from this research program is that for some traits there is as much resemblance between twins reared apart as between twins reared together. Traditionally, psychologists have stressed the importance of upbringing for children, but these findings imply that sharing an environment does not make twins significantly more like one another.

DISEASE AND DISORDER

Disease is another key area of study for researchers. Several diseases are now known to be highly heritable, including PKU (*see* box above). Another well-studied disorder is Tay-Sachs disease, which is caused by a defective gene. People with this disease are unable to produce an important chemical in the body and often die after a few years of life. The genetic transmission of Tay-Sachs disease is well understood: It only occurs when a child receives two copies of the defective gene, one from each parent. What is particularly interesting for behavior geneticists is that members of certain ethnic groups are more likely to have a copy of this defective gene, especially Ashkenazi Jews. Because Tay-Sachs disease only appears in people who have two copies of the defective gene, heritability for this disorder is essentially one: All of the differences between people are due to differences in genes.

Sickle-cell anemia is a disease that leads to serious blood problems and possibly an early death. It is also caused by inheriting two copies of a mutated gene—one from each parent. As with Tay-Sachs disease, the mutated gene occurs more frequently in certain populations, such as those of African descent. Having one copy of the mutated gene carries a benefit in countries where malaria occurs, however, because it makes the carrier resistant to malaria, a disease spread by mosquitoes. So in regions where malaria is common, such as parts of Africa, the mutated gene remains in the population for longer than in other places. This unusual circumstance has helped geneticists understand why potentially harmful genes remain in populations instead of being eliminated by natural selection.

Psychological disorders

Schizophrenia is a serious mental illness that affects almost one out of every one hundred people (*see* Vol. 6, pp. 142–163). Symptoms include withdrawal from society, delusions (believing things that are not true), and hallucinations (hearing or seeing things that are not there). The relatives of thousands of schizophrenia victims have been studied in an attempt to assess the heritability of this disorder. If the rate of schizophrenia for these family members were greater than one in a hundred, it

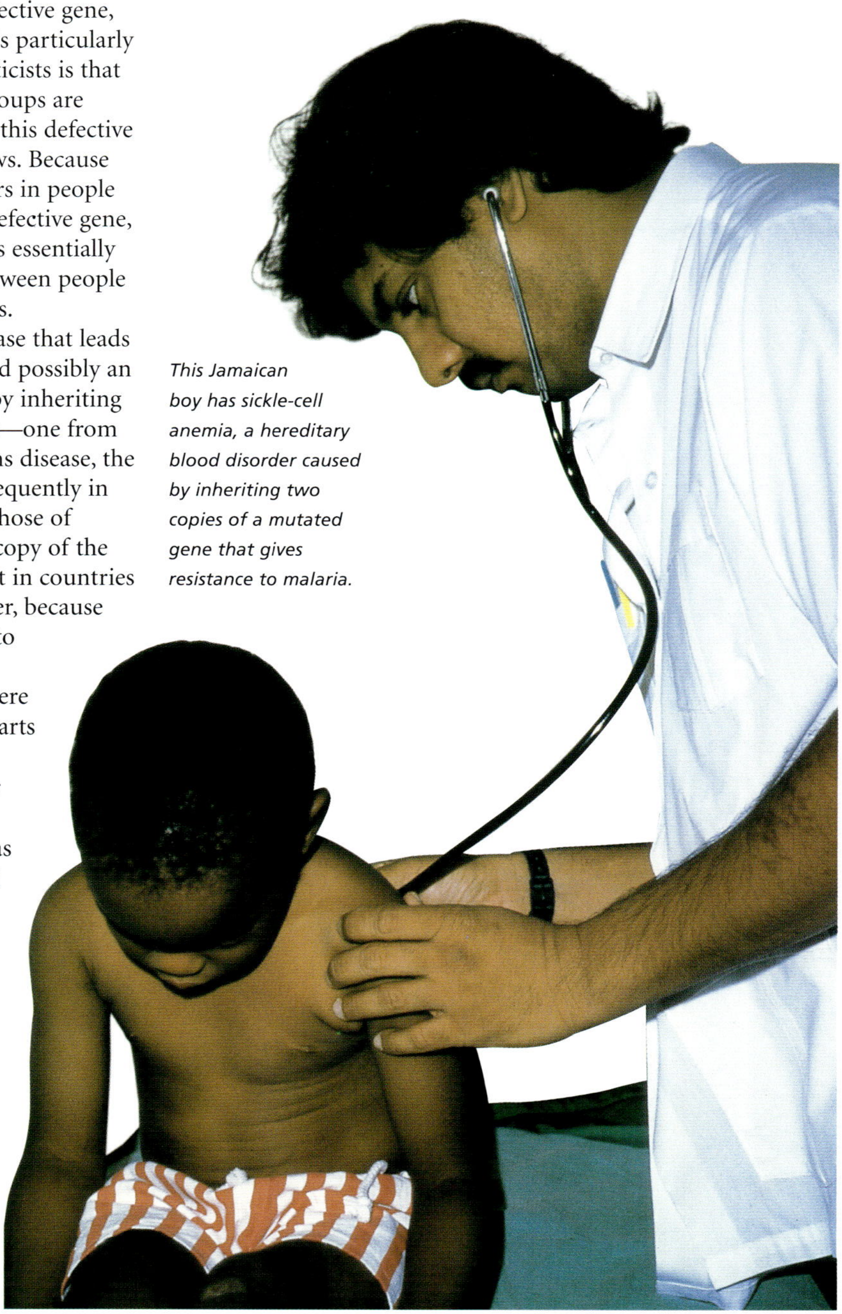

This Jamaican boy has sickle-cell anemia, a hereditary blood disorder caused by inheriting two copies of a mutated gene that gives resistance to malaria.

would suggest a heritable component for schizophrenia. And researchers have found that rates are well above this level. For brothers and sisters of people with schizophrenia the probability that they will also suffer from this mental disorder is roughly one in ten. Research involving twins has also shown that schizophrenia can be traced to differences in genes. Studies with identical twins and fraternal twins indicate that identical twins are more likely than fraternal twins to share the disease. Taken together, all this research suggests schizophrenia is a highly heritable disorder. Estimates of its heritability are in the range of 0.7 or 0.8, indicating that people with schizophrenia have genes that differ from the rest of the population.

The high heritability of schizophrenia prompted researchers to try to identify the specific gene or genes that increase the chances of having the illness. A team carrying out a study in Iceland in 2000 announced it had identified a gene for schizophrenia, but subsequent research has cast doubt on these findings. Given the high distribution of schizophrenia, it is unlikely that a single gene is responsible, and it is now thought that there are many genes implicated in increasing the chances of developing the disorder.

Depression has also been studied extensively, and a great deal is now known about the inheritance patterns for this disorder. Depression comes in two basic forms. The first, unipolar depression, is characterized by extreme sadness, a sense of worthlessness, and thoughts of suicide. Bipolar 1 disorder, or manic depression, may involve symptoms of depression, but during the manic phase symptoms are almost the opposite. Afflicted individuals display extremely high levels of happiness, optimism, and activity interspersed with bouts of depression. Estimates of the occurrence rates for these disorders run between two in one hundred and seven in one hundred in the general population.

> ***"Schizophrenia, manic depression, Alzheimer's disease, even alcoholism—all are giving up their genetic secrets."***
> ***—Robin McKie, 1989***

As with schizophrenia, close relatives of a sufferer are more likely to develop the disorder than would be expected to occur purely by chance. In a study of twins researchers found that if one identical twin was diagnosed with depression, the other twin would also be diagnosed in 65 percent of cases. For fraternal twins the figure was only 14 percent. This suggested that common genes were responsible for

FOCUS ON

ALCOHOLISM

Until recently it was assumed that environmental factors were solely responsible for alcoholism, but research in behavior genetics has indicated that differences in genes account for at least some of the variability in alcohol abuse.

It has been known for some time that alcohol problems run in families, and that people with a parent or sibling with an alcohol problem are more likely to develop one themselves. Studies of identical and fraternal twins have indicated that alcoholism has a modest heritability in the range of 0.2 to 0.4—a figure that is slightly higher when alcoholism occurs early in life. Adoption studies have also indicated some heritability for alcohol-related difficulties, while heritability has also been shown to be higher for males than for females.

More recently, experiments with laboratory rats have shown that differences in genes in strains of mice account for differences in these animals' tendency to drink alcohol and to recover from its effects. Despite this, it is generally agreed that more than one gene is involved in humans and that environmental aspects are important. For instance, alcoholism decreases if access to alcohol is restricted, if alcohol is more expensive, and if bars close earlier.

both identical twins having the condition. This conclusion was reinforced by a study that investigated the children of identical twins when only one twin suffered from a bipolar 1 disorder. For these twins the chance that their children would suffer from depression was the same for each twin—roughly one in ten—suggesting they both inherited and could pass on a susceptibility to the disease even if they did not develop it themselves.

There is no general consensus on the precise heritability of depression, and the rate differs for the unipolar and bipolar varieties. Estimates are generally high, however, ranging from 0.6 to 0.9. Because of the high heritability some researchers have tried to identify the genes involved in causing the disorder. Initially they claimed to have made some progress when a study with the Amish (a religious group living in Pennsylvania) suggested that a specific gene on chromosome 11 was involved. Subsequent research, however, has cast serious doubt on this finding.

Behavior geneticists have also studied a number of other mental disorders. One of them, Alzheimer's disease, is of particular interest because significant progress has been made in identifying a gene that is strongly implicated in causing the disease. Alzheimer's can affect people at any time between their 30s and their 80s, causing disorientation, confusion, and a general inability to function. In the early 1990s researchers discovered a gene called APP that played a vital role in Alzheimer's, the likelihood of individuals getting the disease depending on which versions of the APP gene they inherited from their parents. Since then, however, researchers have realized that multiple genes are involved in causing the disease, so the research continues in this area.

> ***"All psychological traits . . . possess a significant genetic component."***
> ***—M. van Court & S. Saetz, 1985***

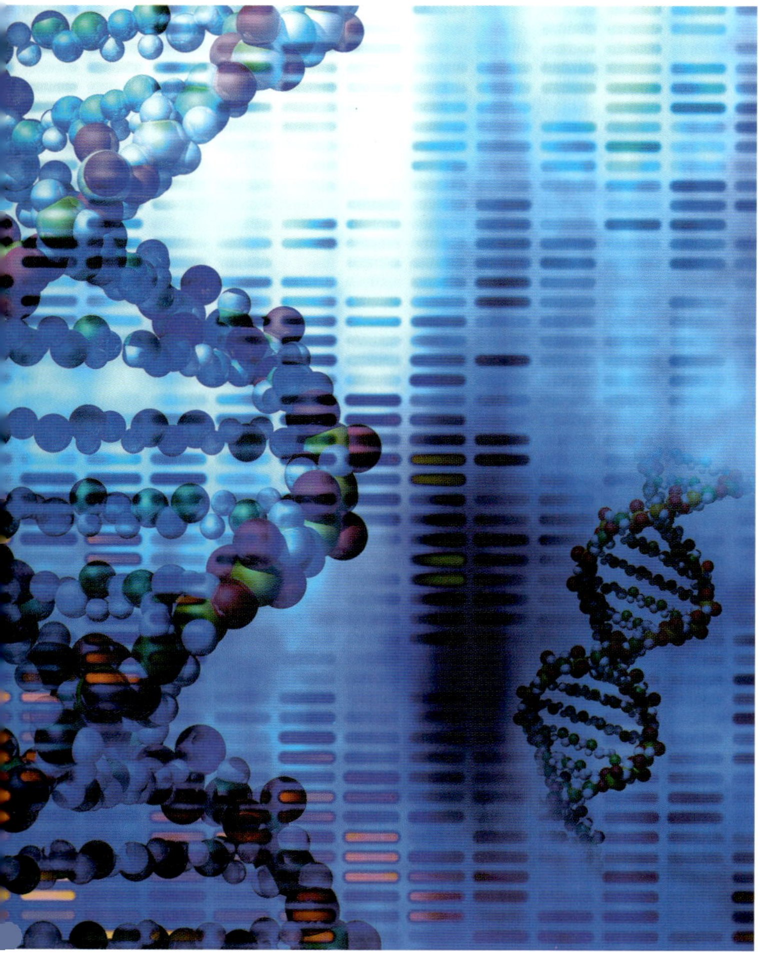

A molecular model of DNA. Different genes are contained within the chemical structure of a DNA strand, and each one plays a crucial role in the mechanism of genetic inheritance. Scientists have tried unsuccessfully to isolate single genes for mental disorders and now believe that a number of different genes combine to cause mental illness.

The role of genes

It is important to bear in mind what behavior genetics does and does not tell us about disease. Reports about behavior genetics research often discuss a gene "for" a disease or disorder, but the concept of heritability is critical for understanding what this means. A gene "for" Alzheimer's disease, for example, would indicate that this gene played a role in causing the disease. In other words, people who had different versions of this gene would be more or less likely, in a given environment, to have the condition. It would not mean that eliminating all versions of the gene would eliminate the disease. Heritability of a condition means that one or more genes are not functioning normally and that people with the disease have inherited a version of the gene that is different from the one that is normally inherited.

Genes also tend to have multiple effects. For example, the version of the gene "for" Alzheimer's that causes the disease could also have other effects in the same way that the gene responsible for sickle-cell anemia gives resistance to malaria (*see* p. 156). This second effect does not make the gene any less likely to cause the first effect. A gene for a particular trait simply means that differences in the gene translate into differences in that trait.

If a disease shows low heritability, it does not mean that genes are not involved. Remember the earlier example of finger number (*see* p. 147). This trait has very low heritability, but genes play a critical role in determining it. Like any other trait, diseases result from a complex interaction of genes and environment, and a disease with low heritability simply indicates that the differences between individuals (those with and without the disease) are not due to genetic differences.

OTHER AREAS OF RESEARCH

Behavior geneticists have investigated many other areas, including the role of genes in influencing violence and criminal behavior—a highly controversial topic. Generally, people are reluctant to accept explanations for violence that involve genes, possibly because they believe that biology is inalterable, which contradicts the idea that violent people can change their behavior. This view is encapsulated in the 1986 Seville Statement on Violence, which has been adopted by UNESCO, an agency of the United Nations. Part of the statement declares, "It is scientifically incorrect to say that war or any other violent behavior is genetically programmed into our human nature." Current views in biology do not support this statement, however, since most researchers believe that all behaviors are influenced by both genes and the environment. Evidence from behavior genetics also suggests that variations in violent and criminal behavior can be linked to differences in genes.

Twin research on criminality is one source of evidence. Identical twins tend to be more alike than fraternal twins in terms of criminal behavior, suggesting a genetic influence. Indeed, one twin study, which used data gathered between 1881 and 1910, was published in 1977—well before the Seville Statement was drafted. Evidence from adoption studies indicates that criminality is slightly less heritable than twin studies suggest. Nevertheless,

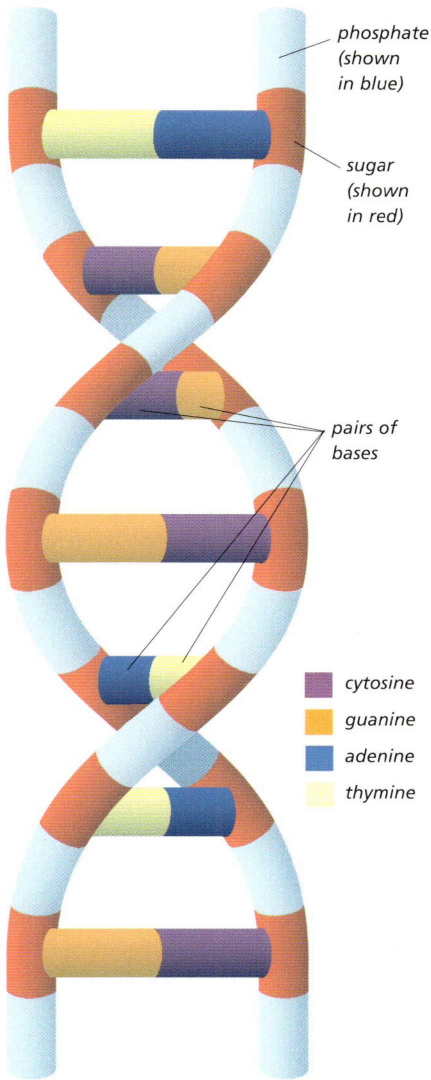

The twisted structure of a DNA molecule is called a double helix. It is composed of two chains of alternating phosphate and sugar molecules that are held together by substances called bases. There are four base types—adenine, thymine, cytosine, and guanine—that occur in pairings linking adenine and thymine and cytosine and guanine. These base pairings can be compared to the rungs of a ladder. The coding for different genes is determined by the precise sequence of bases along each side of the ladder.

it appears that children with law-abiding adoptive parents but whose biological parents have at least one conviction for criminal behavior are more likely to end up becoming criminals than children with law-abiding biological parents but whose adoptive parents have at least one criminal conviction. This suggests that criminal behavior is heritable.

Despite these findings, there is no doubt that criminality also depends heavily on the environment. In 1982 a study of Swedish children found that the rate of criminality in adopted children was 6.7% if their adoptive parents had committed a crime, 12.1% if their biological parents were criminals, and 40% if both sets of parents had indulged in criminal behavior. Together, genes and environment seemed to be several times more compelling than either force acting alone.

> ***"There is not one jot or tittle of evidence of any genetic basis for any behavioral trait, except schizophrenia—whether it be intelligence or nastiness or aggressiveness."***
>
> ***—R. C. Lewontin, 1976***

The search for the specific genetic causes of differences in violent behavior has a long history. An early theory focused on the chromosomes that determine sex in humans. Men generally inherit a Y chromosome from their fathers and an X from their mothers, while women inherit two X chromosomes—one from each parent. Occasionally, however, a sperm cell carries two Y chromosomes; and if it fertilizes an egg, the resulting individual has three sex chromosomes. XYY males are uncommon, but they were once thought to be present in greater numbers in prison populations than in the general population. This link between violence and the XYY chromosome is currently uncertain and remains a subject of debate.

Although the specific genes involved in violent behavior remain largely unknown, most evolutionarily informed researchers consider it likely that natural selection would, at some time in the past, have favored genes that caused violent behavior under certain circumstances. Of course, many environmental factors play a part in determining whether people are likely to resort to violence. For instance, cultural values, the availability of alcohol, or even overcrowding are all likely to influence the prevalence of violence in a society.

Sexual preference

Another controversial area of research involves sexual preference. Remember that the sex of a child is determined by which chromosome, an X or a Y, is inherited from the father. Men have an X and a Y chromosome, while women have two X chromosomes. Heterosexual men, by definition, prefer female sexual partners, while female heterosexuals prefer male sexual partners. So if discussion is limited to heterosexuals, sexual preference would have a heritability of one, since it is entirely determined by genes.

But what about the heritability of sexual preference among those who have homosexual tendencies? This question has been addressed using standard methods in behavior genetics. One twin study found that male identical twins were more likely to share the same sexual orientation than two male fraternal twins. The same study also looked at adoptive brothers, finding that the percentage of homosexual men who had homosexual adoptive brothers was no greater than the percentage of homosexual men in the population as a whole. Both these findings suggest that sexual preference for men is heritable, and the estimate of heritability for this study was about 0.5. Other studies investigating the way in which both male and female homosexuality runs in families have also suggested the trait is heritable. Estimates of its heritability using different methods vary, however, ranging from as low as 0.25 to as high as 0.75.

Studies with twin pairs and adoptive children have indicated that homosexuality is a heritable trait, which suggests variations in genes might cause variations in our choice of sexual partners.

Some progress has been made in finding the genes that contribute to differences in sexual orientation. Research investigating the genetic makeup of biological brothers, for example, has shown that a certain piece of the X chromosome is identical for many pairs of homosexual brothers. Other scientists have been skeptical about this finding, however, and laboratories have been unable to duplicate this result. In any event, sexual preference is believed to be a complex phenomenon, so researchers continue to look for genes that might be important in influencing this trait.

The homosexuality debate reached a peak in 1991, when neurobiologist Simon LeVay published a paper reporting on his research into the differences between the brains of heterosexual and homosexual men. He reported finding a certain brain structure that was larger in heterosexual than in homosexual men. LeVay's findings were widely publicized and generated a great deal of debate. His research was criticized because all of the homosexuals in his study had HIV, and some argued that this could explain the difference.

As with diseases, much of the debate surrounding homosexuality research relates to the existence of a gene or genes "for" homosexuality. The heritability estimates for homosexuality suggest that such genes exist—that is, differences in genes account for at least some of the differences between individuals for this trait. But since researchers already know that chromosomes determine sexuality, the debate focuses on which, rather than whether, genes influence sexual preference.

THE ENVIRONMENTAL ROLE

Advances in biology and genetics have strongly influenced the development of social psychology, but the role of the environment should never be forgotten. We are a product of our own, unique evolutionary history, and every person has genes that have been preserved over the course of countless generations. But these genes do not determine behavior on their own; they only exert their influence in a certain environment. Without the right genes no environment can determine how a person will develop; but without an appropriate environment the instructions contained in genes have no effects.

A major part of the environment in which individuals develop is determined by their interactions with other people. The evolutionary history of humans has produced an exceedingly social animal. Unlike many organisms, a developing human depends on family members for survival. Dependency on family is not a unique characteristic, but it is a universal characteristic—we carry genes that make us dependent during early life.

> ***"Genes and glands are obviously important, but social learning also has a dramatic role."***
>
> ***—Walter Mischel, 1981***

We remain social creatures even after early development. We carry genes that lead us to desire contact with others and that cause us to be lonely when deprived of this contact. Unlike many species, we seek others not just for mating, but for all

A typical family group. Being dependent on family members is a universal human trait, which means there must be genetic influences for this behavior that have stayed in the human makeup through the process of evolution.

kinds of interactions. The environment in which we evolved was clearly a social one, and the genes that helped create a social animal persisted in our species.

Our social nature leads us to create a complex social world: We form alliances for mutual gain, compete for status and resources, and arrange ourselves into hierarchies. Competition both within and between groups is a part of human life; and while some of this competition can be positive and healthy, it can be a serious problem. Our social nature also means that communication plays a large role in our lives. We use language and other forms of communication to convey information from one person to another, performing many social functions.

Social groups

Though we share an evolutionary history, there are many ways in which we differ. These variations include differences in skin color, language, dress, attitudes, beliefs, and many others. Some of these variations are caused by differences in genes, while others are influenced by the environment. Behavior genetics has made great strides since the time of Francis Galton, and researchers are beginning to understand how heredity and environment interact.

One big surprise is the number of ways in which genes appear to play a role in making individuals different from one another. For many behavioral traits the variations between individuals in many populations have been shown to be partly due to genes. As we have seen, there is now general agreement that intelligence is heritable, although there is no consensus about how to interpret this result and what, if anything, should be done with it.

But while it is clear that a great many variations emerge as a result of genetic differences, it is also clear that many others emerge as a result of development in different environments. For example, many linguists now believe that people share essentially the same mechanisms for learning language, but that the specific language a person learns comes from the social world (*see* Vol. 1, pp. 118–125). In a similar manner fashions, attitudes, and beliefs are transmitted from one person to the next. In this way people in one social group come to differ from people in

FOCUS ON

Misconceptions about Heritability

The intense emotion surrounding the nature–nurture debate is compounded by racial issues, and these issues have been exacerbated by misunderstandings about the difference between calculating heritability within groups as opposed to between groups. This difference is extremely important, and confusion about the relevance of heritability to between-group studies has led to various instances in which results have been misinterpreted.

Imagine a bucket of peas and two uniform plots of land. The peas are genetically different from one another, and the two plots of land are different from one another. Now the peas are divided, and half are planted on one plot and half on the other. When they have grown, we measure the height of each plant.

First, consider the heritability within a plot. Each plot provides a uniform environment, so any differences in pea plant height *within* a plot will be largely due to genes. So the heritability of pea plant height within a plot will be close to one. This is similar to the way that heritability for human traits is calculated.

Now consider the differences between the pea plants in the two different plots, which we calculate by averaging the height of the pea plants in each plot and comparing the two. Because all the peas originally came from the same bucket, this average difference must be due to the different environments rather than to genetic differences. Heritability *between* plots is therefore roughly zero.

The application of this idea to people is simple. We can calculate the heritability of a trait for a particular group, and in many cases we will find that heritability is high (as for IQ, for example). However, this does not mean that differences in the average scores of people from two different groups are due to differences in genes. So even if we find that IQ is heritable, and that IQ differences between racial groups exist, this does not mean these differences are genetic; environment is also important.

another group. Genes might interact with the environment to build in the human ability to learn, but the things people learn depend on the social environment.

Behavior genetics has made a great deal of progress in understanding the origins of differences between individuals, but researchers still struggle to understand the origins of differences between groups (*see* box above). Between-group differences are often referred to as cultural differences (*see* Vol. 1, pp. 152–161), and they are an important research area for psychologists, sociologists, and anthropologists.

What is clear is that these differences between individuals and between groups are quite compatible with the idea that we evolved as social beings. Individuals with the same genes can develop differently, and identical twins raised in separate countries will learn different languages. In the same way universal human nature expresses itself according to time and place.

The modern understanding of the ways in which genes work makes it clear that the traditional view of "genetic determinism" is wrong. It is true that genes are what make us human: They make us different from every other species on the planet. But the fact that genes also play a role in making people different from one another does not mean that the differences are inevitable or unchangeable. What is clear is that as researchers develop a better understanding of the ways that people's genes interact with the environment, it becomes easier to change people's environments and experiences to help them achieve their social goals. Behavior geneticists will never be able to tell us what goals we should set as a society, but they will help us understand which things will help society reach the goals it sets.

CONNECTIONS

- Nature and Nurture: Volume 1, pp. 22–29
- Evolutionary Psychology: Volume 1, pp. 134–143
- Social Development: Volume 4, pp. 130–149
- Applications and Future Challenges: Volume 4, pp. 150–163
- Relating to Society: pp. 50–71
- Intelligence: pp. 118–141

Set Glossary

abnormality Within abnormal psychology abnormality is the deviation from normal or expected behavior, generally involving maladaptive responses and personal distress both to the individuals with abnormal behavior and to those around them.

abnormal psychology The study and treatment of mental disorders.

acquisition The process by which something, such as a skill, habit, or language, is learned.

adaptation A change in behavior or structure that increases the survival chances of a species. Adjective: adaptive

addiction A state of dependence on a drug or a particular pattern of behavior.

adjustment disorder A mental disorder in which a patient is unable to adjust properly to a stressful life change.

affect A mood, emotion, or feeling. An affect is generally a shorter-lived and less-pronounced emotion than mood.

affective disorder A group of mental disorders, such as depression and bipolar 1 disorder, that are characterized by pronounced and often prolonged changes of mood.

agnosia A group of brain disorders involving impaired ability to recognize or interpret sensory information.

Alzheimer's disease A progressive and irreversible dementia in which the gradual destruction of brain tissue results in memory loss, impaired cognitive function, and personality change.

amnesia A partial or complete loss of memory.

amygdala An almond-shaped structure located in the front of the brain's temporal lobe that is part of the limbic system. Sometimes called the amygdaloid complex or the amygdaloid nucleus, the amygdala plays an important role in emotional behavior and motivation.

anorexia nervosa An eating disorder in which patients (usually young females) become obsessed with the idea that they are overweight and experience dramatic weight loss by not eating enough.

antidepressants A type of medication used to treat depression.

antianxiety drugs A type of medication used to treat anxiety disorders.

antipsychotic drugs A type of medication used to treat psychotic disorders such as schizophrenia. Sometimes known as neuroleptics.

anxiety disorder A group of mental disorders involving worry or distress.

anxiolytics *See* antianxiety drugs

aphasia A group of brain disorders that involve a partial or complete loss of language ability.

arousal A heightened state of awareness, behavior, or physiological function.

artificial intelligence (AI) A field of study that combines elements of cognitive psychology and computer science in an attempt to develop intelligent machines.

attachment theory A theory that describes how infants form emotional bonds with the adults they are close to.

attention The process by which someone can focus on particular sensory information by excluding other, less immediately relevant information.

attention deficit disorder (ADD) A mental disorder in which the patient (usually a child) is hyperactive, impulsive, and unable to concentrate properly.

autism A mental disorder, first apparent in childhood, in which patients are self-absorbed, socially withdrawn, and engage in repetitive patterns of behavior.

automatization The process by which complex behavior eventually becomes automatic. Such a process may be described as having automaticity or being automatized.

autonomic nervous system A part of the nervous system that controls many of the body's self-regulating (involuntary or automatic) functions.

aversion therapy A method of treating patients, especially those suffering from drink or drug addiction, by subjecting them to painful or unpleasant experiences.

axon Extension of the cell body of a neuron that transmits impulses away from the body of the neuron.

behavioral therapy A method of treating mental disorders that concentrates on modifying abnormal behavior rather than on the underlying causes of that behavior.

behaviorism A school of psychology in which easily observable and measurable behavior is considered to be the only proper subject of scientific study. Noun: behaviorist

bipolar I disorder A mental (affective) disorder involving periods of depression (depressed mood) and periods of mania (elevated mood).

body image The way in which a person perceives their own body or imagines it is perceived by other people.

body language The signals people send out to other people (usually unconsciously) through their gestures, posture, and other types of nonverbal communication.

Broca's area A region of the brain (usually located in the left hemisphere) that is involved with processing language.

bulimia nervosa An eating disorder in which patients consume large amounts of food in binges, then use laxatives or self-induced vomiting to prevent themselves putting on weight.

CAT scan *See* CT

causality The study of the causes of events or the connection between causes and effects.

central nervous system The part of the body's nervous system comprising the brain and spinal cord.

cerebellum A cauliflower-shaped structure at the back of the brain underneath the cerebral hemispheres that coordinates body movements.

cerebral cortex The highly convoluted outer surface of the brain's cerebrum.

cerebrum The largest part of the brain, consisting of the two cerebral hemispheres and their associated structures.

classical conditioning A method of associating a stimulus and a response that do not normally accompany one another. In Pavlov's well-known classical conditioning experiment dogs were trained so that they salivated (the conditioned response or CR) when Pavlov rang a bell (the conditioned stimulus or CS). Normally, dogs salivate (an unconditioned response or UR) only when food is presented to them (an unconditioned stimulus or US).

clinical psychology An area of psychology concerned with the study and treatment of abnormal behavior.

cognition A mental process that involves thinking, reasoning, or some other type of mental information processing. Adjective: cognitive

cognitive behavioral therapy (CBT) An extension of behavioral therapy that involves treating patients by modifying their abnormal thought patterns as well as their behavior.

cognitive psychology An area of psychology that seeks to understand how the brain processes information.

competency In psycholinguistics the representation of the abstract rules of a language, such as its grammar.

conditioned stimulus/response (CS/CR) *See* classical conditioning

conditioning *See* classical conditioning; instrumental conditioning

connectionism A computer model of cognitive processes such as learning and memory. Connectionist models are based on a large network of "nodes" and the connections between them. Adjective: connectionist

consciousness A high-level mental process responsible for the state of self-awareness that people feel. Consciousness is thought by some researchers to direct human behavior and by others simply to be a byproduct of that behavior.

cortex *See* cerebral cortex

cross-cultural psychology The comparison of behavior, such as language acquisition or nonverbal communication, between different peoples or cultures.

cross-sectional study An experimental method in which a large number of subjects are studied at a particular moment or period in time. Compare longitudinal study

CT (computed tomography) A method of producing an image of the brain's tissue using X-ray scanning, which is commonly used to detect brain damage. Also called CAT (computerized axial tomography).

culture-specific A behavior found only in certain cultures and not observed universally in all humankind.

declarative knowledge A collection of facts about the world and other things that people have learned. Compare procedural knowledge

declarative memory *See* explicit memory

defense mechanism A type of thinking or behavior that a person employs unconsciously to protect themselves from anxiety or unwelcome feelings.

deficit A missing cognitive function whose loss is caused by a brain disorder.

delusion A false belief that a person holds about themselves or the world around them. Delusions are characteristic features of psychotic mental illnesses such as schizophrenia.

dementia A general loss of cognitive functions usually caused by brain damage. Dementia is often, but not always, progressive (it becomes worse with time).

Dementia of the Alzheimer's type (DAT) See Alzheimer's disease

dendrite A treelike projection of a neuron's cell body that conducts nerve impulses toward the cell body.

dependency An excessive reliance on an addictive substance, such as a drug, or on the support of another person.

depression An affective mental disorder characterized by sadness, low self-esteem, inadequacy, and related symptoms.

desensitization A gradual reduction in the response to a stimulus when it is presented repeatedly over a period of time.

developmental psychology An area of psychology concerned with how people develop throughout their lives, but usually concentrating on how behavior and cognition develop during childhood.

discrimination In perception the ability to distinguish between two or more stimuli. In social psychology and sociology unequal treatment of people based on prejudice.

dysgraphia A brain disorder involving an ability to write properly.

dyslexia Brain disorders that disrupt a person's ability to read.

eating disorders A group of mental disorders that involve disturbed eating patterns or appetite.

echoic memory See sensory memory

ego The central part of a person's self. In Freudian psychology the ego manages the balance between a person's primitive, instinctive needs and the often conflicting demands of the world around them.

egocentric A person who is excessively preoccupied with themselves at the expense of the people and the world around them.

eidetic An accurate and persistent form of visual memory that is generally uncommon in adults (often misnamed "photographic memory").

electroconvulsive therapy (ECT) A treatment for severe depression that involves passing a brief and usually relatively weak electric shock through the front of a patient's skull.

electroencephalogram (EEG) A graph that records the changing electrical activity in a person's brain from electrodes attached to the scalp.

emotion A strong mood or feeling. Also a reaction to a stimulus that prepares the body for action.

episodic memory A type of memory that records well-defined events or episodes in a person's life. Compare semantic memory

ethnocentricity The use of a particular ethnic group to draw conclusions about wider society or humankind as a whole.

event-related potential (ERP) A pattern of electrical activity (the potential) produced by a particular stimulus (the event). EVPs are often recorded from the skull using electrodes.

evoked potential See event-related potential (ERP)

evolution A theory suggesting that existing organisms have developed from earlier ones by processes that include natural selection (dubbed "survival of the fittest") and genetic mutation.

evolutionary psychology An approach to psychology that uses the theory of evolution to explain the mind and human behavior.

explicit memory A type of memory containing information that is available to conscious recognition and recall.

flashbulb memory A very clear and evocative memory of a particular moment or event.

fMRI (functional magnetic resonance imaging) An MRI-based scanning technique that can produce images of the brain while it is engaged in cognitive activities.

functionalism An approach to psychology that concentrates on the functions played by parts of the mind and human behavior.

generalized anxiety disorder (GAD) A type of nonspecific anxiety disorder with symptoms that include worry, irritability, and tension.

genes A functional unit of the chromosome that determines how traits are passed on and expressed from generation to generation. Adjective: genetic

Gestalt psychology A psychology school that emphasizes the importance of appreciating phenomena as structured wholes in areas such as perception and learning, as opposed to breaking them down into their components. Most influential in the mid-1900s.

gray matter The parts of the nervous system that contain mainly nerve cell bodies.

habituation *See* desensitization

hallucination A vivid but imaginary perceptual experience that occurs purely in the mind, not in reality.

heritability The proportion of observed variation for a trait in a specific population that can be attributed to genetic factors rather than environmental ones. Generally expressed as a ratio of genetically caused variation to total variation.

hippocamus A part of the limbic system in the temporal lobe that is thought to play an important role in the formation of memories.

Humanism A philosophy that stresses the importance of human interests and values.

hypothalamus A small structure at the base of the brain that controls the autonomic nervous system.

hysteria A type of mental disturbance that may include symptoms such as hallucinations and emotional outbursts.

implicit memory A type of memory not normally available to conscious awareness. Sometimes also known as procedural or nondeclarative memory. Compare explicit memory

imprinting A type of learning that occurs in a critical period shortly after birth, such as when chicks learn to accept a human in place of their real mother.

individual psychology An approach to psychology that focuses on the differences between individuals. Also a theory advanced by Alfred Adler based on the idea of overcoming inferiority.

information processing In cognitive psychology the theory that the mind operates something like a computer, with sensory information processed either in a series of discrete stages or in parallel by something like a connectionist network.

ingroup A group whose members feel a strong sense of collective identity and act to exclude other people (the outgroup).

innate A genetically determined trait that is present at birth, as opposed to something that is acquired by learning.

instinct An innate and automatic response to a particular stimulus that usually involves no rational thought.

instrumental conditioning A type of conditioning in which reinforcement occurs only when an organism makes a certain, desired response. Instrumental conditioning occurs, for example, when a pigeon is trained to peck a lever to receive a pellet of food.

internalize To make internal, personal, or subjective; to take in and make an integral part of one's attitudes or beliefs:

introspection A behaviorist technique of studying the mind by observing one's own thought processes.

language acquisition device (LAD) According to linguist Noam Chomsky, a part of the brain that is preprogrammed with a universal set of grammatical rules that can construct the rules of a specific language according to the environment it is exposed to.

libido The sexual drive.

limbic system A set of structures in the brain stem, including the hippocampus and the amygdala, that lie below the corpus callosum. It is involved in emotion, motivation, behavior, and various functions of the autonomic nervous system.

long-term memory A type of memory in which information is retained for long periods after being deeply processed. Generally used to store events and information from the past. Compare short-term memory

longitudinal study An experimental method that follows a small group of subjects over a long period of time. Compare cross-sectional study

maladaptive Behavior is considered maladapative or dysfunctional if it has a negative effect on society or on a person's ability to function in society.

medical model A theory that mental disorders, like diseases, have specific underlying medical causes, which must be addressed if treatment is to be effective.

mental disorder A psychiatric illness such as schizophrenia, anxiety, or depression.

metacognition The study by an individual of their own thought processes. *See also* introspection

mnemonic A technique that can be used to remember information or improve memory.

modeling The technique by which a person observes some ideal form of behavior (a role model) and then attempts to copy it. In artificial intelligence (AI) people attempt to build computers that model human cognition.

modularity A theory that the brain is composed of a number of modules that occupy relatively specific areas and that carry out relatively specific tasks.

morpheme The smallest unit of a language that carries meaning.

motor neuron *See* neuron.

MRI (magnetic resonance imaging) A noninvasive scanning technique that uses magnetic fields to produce detailed images of body tissue.

nature–nurture A long-running debate over whether genetic factors (nature) or environmental factors (nurture) are most important in different aspects of behavior.

neuron A nerve cell, consisting of a cell body (soma), an axon, and one or more dendrites. Motor (efferent) neurons produce movement when they fire by carrying information *from* the central nervous system *to* the muscles and glands; sensory (afferent) neurons carry information *from* the senses *to* the central nervous system.

neuropsychology An area of psychology that studies the connections between parts of the brain and neural processes, on one hand, and different cognitive processes and types of behavior, on the other.

neurotransmitter A substance that carries chemical "messages" across the synaptic gaps between the neurons of the brain.

nonverbal communication The way in which animals communicate without language (verbal communication), using such things as posture, tone of voice, and facial expressions.

operant conditioning *See* instrumental conditioning

outgroup The people who do not belong to an ingroup.

parallel processing A type of cognition in which information is processed in several different ways at once. In serial processing information passes through one stage of processing at a time.

peripheral nervous system All the nerves and nerve processes that connect the central nervous system with receptors, muscles, and glands.

personality The collection of character traits that makes one person different from another.

personality disorder A group of mental disorders in which aspects of someone's personality make it difficult for them to function properly in society.

PET (positron emission tomography) A noninvasive scanning technique that makes images of the brain according to levels of metabolic activity inside it.

phenomenology A philosophy based on the study of immediate experiences.

phobia A strong fear of a particular object (such as snakes) or social situation.

phoneme A basic unit of spoken language.

phrenology An early approach to psychology that studied the relationship between areas of the brain (based on skull shape) and mental functions. Phrenology has since been discredited.

physiology A type of biology concerned with the workings of cells, organs, and tissues.

positive punishment A type of conditioning in which incorrect responses are punished.

positive reinforcement A type of conditioning in which correct responses are rewarded.

primary memory *See* short-term memory

probability The likelihood of something happening.

procedural knowledge The practical knowledge of how to do things ("know-how"). Compare declarative knowledge

prosody A type of nonverbal communication in which language is altered by such things as the pitch of someone's voice and their intonation.

psyche The soul or mind of a person or a driving force behind their personality.

psychiatry The study, classification, and treatment of mental disorders.

psychoanalysis A theory of behavior and an approach to treating mental disorders pioneered by Austrian neurologist Sigmund Freud. Adjective: psychoanalytic

psychogenic A mental disorder that is psychological (as opposed to physical) in origin.

psycholinguistics The study of language-related behavior, including how the brain acquires and processes language.

psychosurgery A type of brain surgery designed to treat mental disorders.

psychotherapy A broad range of treatments for mental disorders based on different kinds of interaction between a patient and a therapist.

psychosis A mental state characterized by disordered personality and loss of contact with reality that affects normal social functioning. Psychosis is a feature of psychotic disorders, such as schizophrenia. Adjective: psychotic

reaction time The time taken for the subject in an experiment to respond to a stimulus.

recall The process by which items are recovered from memory. Compare recognition

recognition The process by which a person realizes they have previously encountered a particular object or event. Compare recall

reductionism A philosophy based on breaking complex things into their individual components. Also, an attempt to explain high-level sciences (such as psychology) in terms of lower-level sciences (such as chemistry or physics).

reflex An automatic response to a stimulus (a "knee-jerk" reaction).

reflex arc The neural circuit thought to be responsible for the control of a reflex.

rehearsing The process by which a person repeats information to improve its chances of being stored in memory.

representation A mental model based on perceptions of the world.

repression In psychoanalysis an unconscious mental process that keeps thoughts out of conscious awareness.

response The reaction to a stimulus.

reuptake The reabsorption of a neurotransmitter from the place where it was produced.

risk aversion A tendency not to take risks even when they may have beneficial results.

schema An abstract mental plan that serves as a guide to action or a more general mental representation.

schizophrenia A mental disorder characterized by hallucinations and disordered thought patterns in which a patient becomes divorced from reality. It is a type of psychotic disorder.

secondary memory *See* long-term memory

selective attention *See* attention

self-concept The ideas and feelings that people hold about themselves.

semantic memory A type of long-term memory that stores information based on its content or meaning. Compare episodic memory

senses The means by which people perceive things. The five senses are vision, hearing, smell, touch, and taste.

sensory memory An information store that records sensory impressions for a short period of time before they are processed more thoroughly.

sensory neuron *See* neuron

serotonin A neurotransmitter in the central nervous system that plays a key role in affective (mood) disorders, sleep, and the perception of pain. Serotonin is also known as 5-hydroxytryptamine (5-HT).

shaping A type of conditioning in which behavior is gradually refined toward some ideal form by successive approximations.

short-term memory A memory of very limited capacity in which sensory inputs are held before being processed more deeply and passing into long-term memory. Compare long-term memory

social cognition An area of psychology that combines elements of social and cognitive psychology in an attempt to understand how people think about themselves in relation to the other people around them.

social Darwinism A theory that society behaves according to Darwinian principles, with the most successful members thriving at the expense of the least successful ones.

social psychology An area of psychology that explores how individuals behave in relation to other people and to society as a whole.

sociobiology A theory that seeks to explain social behavior through biological approaches, notably the theory of evolution. *See also* evolutionary psychology

somatic Something that relates to the body as opposed to the mind; something physical as opposed to something mental.

stereopsis The process by which the brain assembles one 3-D image by combining a pair of 2-D images from the eyes.

stimulus A type of sensory input that provokes a response.

subject The person studied in a psychological experiment.

synapse The region across which nerve impulses are transmitted from one neuron to another. It includes the synaptic cleft (a gap) and the sections of the cell membranes on either side of the cleft. They are called the presynaptic and postsynaptic membranes.

synesthesia A process by which the stimulation of one sense (such as hearing a sound) produces a different kind of sensory impression (such as seeing a color).

thalamus A structure in the forebrain that passes sensory information on to the cerebral cortex.

theory of mind The realization by an individual (such as a growing child, for example) that other people have thoughts and mental processes of their own. It is universally accepted that humans have a theory of mind, and research has shown that some other animals, such as chimpanzees and dolphins, might also have a theory of mind, but this is still debated. Theory of mind is of interest to developmental psychologists since it is not something people are born with, but something that develops in infancy.

tranquilizers A type of medication with sedative, muscle-relaxant, or similar properties. Minor tranquilizers are also known as antianxiety or anxiolytic drugs; major tranquilizers are also known as antipsychotic drugs.

unconditioned stimulus/response (US/UR) *See* classical conditioning

unconscious In psychoanalytic and related theories the area of the mind that is outside conscious awareness and recall but that informs the contents of such things as dreams. In general usage *unconscious* simply refers to automatic cognitive processes that we are not aware of or the lack of consciousness (that is, "awareness") at times such as during sleep.

working memory *See* short-term memory

Resources

Further Reading

Altmann, G. T. M. *The Ascent of Babel: An Exploration of Language, Mind, and Understanding.* Cambridge, MA: Oxford University Press, 1999.

American Psychiatric Association. *Diagnostic and Statistical Manual of Mental Disorders, 4th edition, Text Revision.* Washington, DC: American Psychiatric Press, 2000.

Argyle, M. *The Psychology of Interpersonal Behaviour (5th edition).* London, UK: Penguin, 1994.

Asher, S. R. and Coie, J. D. (eds.). *Peer Rejection in Childhood.* Cambridge, UK: Cambridge University Press, 1990.

Atkinson, R. L. *et al. Hilgard's Introduction to Psychology (13th edition).* London, UK: International Thomson Publishing, 1999.

Barnouw, V. *Culture and Personality.* Chicago, IL: Dorsey Press, 1985.

Baron, J. *Thinking and Deciding.* Cambridge, UK: Cambridge University Press, 1994.

Barry, M. A. S. *Visual Intelligence: Perception, Image, and Manipulation in Visual Communication.* Albany, NY: State University of New York Press, 1997.

Beck, J. *Cognitive Therapy: Basics and Beyond.* London, UK: The Guildford Press, 1995.

Bickerton, D. *Language and Species.* Chicago, IL: The University of Chicago Press, 1990.

Blackburn, I. M. and Davison, K. *Cognitive Therapy for Depression and Anxiety: A Practitioner's Guide.* Oxford, UK: Blackwell, 1995.

Boden, M. A. *Piaget (2nd edition).* London, UK: Fontana Press, 1994.

Brehm, S. S., Kassin, S. M., and Fein, S. *Social Psychology (4th edition).* Boston, MA: Houghton Mifflin, 1999.

Brody, N. *Intelligence (2nd edition).* San Diego, CA: Academic Press, 1997.

Brown, D. S. *Learning a Living: A Guide to Planning Your Career and Finding a Job for People with Learning Disabilities, Attention Deficit Disorder, and Dyslexia.* Bethesda, MD: Woodbine House, 2000.

Bruhn, A. R. *Earliest Childhood Memories.* New York: Praeger, 1990.

Buunk, B. P. "Affiliation, Attraction and Close Relationships." *In* M. Hewstone and W. Stroebe (eds.), *Introduction to Social Psychology: A European Perspective.* Oxford, UK: Blackwell, 2001.

Cacioppo, J. T., Tassinary, L. G., and Berntson, G. G. (eds.). *Handbook of Psychophysiology (2nd edition).* New York: Cambridge University Press, 2000.

Cardwell, M. *Dictionary of Psychology.* Chicago, IL: Fitzroy Dearborn Publishers, 1999

Carson, R. C. and Butcher, J. N. *Abnormal Psychology and Modern Life (9th edition).* New York: HarperCollins Publishers, 1992.

Carter, R. *Mapping the Mind.* Berkeley, CA: University of California Press, 1998.

Cavan, S. *Recovery from Drug Addiction.* New York: Rosen Publishing Group, 2000.

Clarke-Stewart, A. *Daycare.* Cambridge, MA: Harvard University Press, 1993.

Cohen, G. *The Psychology of Cognition (2nd edition).* San Diego, CA: Academic Press, 1983.

Cramer, D. *Close Relationships: The Study of Love and Friendship.* New York: Arnold, 1998.

Daly, M. and Wilson, M. *Homicide.* New York: Aldine de Gruyter, 1988.

Davis, R. D., Braun, E. M., and Smith, J. M. *The Gift of Dyslexia: Why Some of the Smartest People Can't Read and How They Can Learn.* New York: Perigee, 1997.

Davison, G. C. and Neal, J. M. *Abnormal Psychology.* New York: John Wiley and Sons, Inc., 1994.

Dawkins, R. *The Selfish Gene.* New York: Oxford Universty Press, 1976.

Dennett, D. C. *Darwin's Dangerous Idea: Evolution and the Meanings of Life.* Carmichael, CA: Touchstone Books, 1996.

Dobson, C. *et al. Understanding Psychology.* London, UK: Weidenfeld and Nicolson, 1982.

Duck, S. *Meaningful Relationships: Talking, Sense, and Relating.* Thousand Oaks, CA: Sage Publications, 1994.

Durie, M. H. "Maori Psychiatric Admissions: Patterns, Explanations and Policy Implications." *In* J. Spicer, A. Trlin, and J. A. Walton (eds.), *Social Dimensions of Health and Disease: New Zealand Perspectives.* Palmerston North, NZ: Dunmore Press, 1994.

Eliot, L. *What's Going on in There? How the Brain and Mind Develop in the First Five Years of Life.* New York: Bantam Books, 1999.

Eysenck, M. (ed.). *The Blackwell Dictionary of Cognitive Psychology.* Cambridge, MA: Blackwell, 1991.

Faherty, C. and Mesibov, G. B. *Asperger's: What Does It Mean to Me?* Arlington, TX: Future Horizons, 2000.

Fernando, S. *Mental Health in a Multi-Ethnic Society: A Multi-Disciplinary Handbook.* New York: Routledge, 1995.

Fiske, S. T. and Taylor, S. E. *Social Cognition (2nd Edition).* New York: Mcgraw-Hill, 1991.

Franken, R. E. *Human Motivation (5th edition).* Belmont, CA: Wadsworth Thomson Learning, 2002.

Freud, S. and Brill, A. A. *The Basic Writings of Sigmund Freud.* New York: Modern Library, 1995.

Gardner, H. *The Mind's New Science: A History of the Cognitive Revolution.* New York: Basic Books, 1985.

Garnham, A. and Oakhill, J. *Thinking and Reasoning.* Cambridge, MA: Blackwell, 1994.

Gaw, A. C. *Culture, Ethnicity, and Mental Illness.* Washington, DC: American Psychiatric Press, 1992.

Giacobello, J. *Everything You Need to Know about Anxiety and Panic Attacks.* New York: Rosen Publishing Group, 2000.

Gazzaniga, M. S. *The Mind's Past.* Berkeley, CA: University of California Press, 1998.

Gazzaniga, M. S. (ed.). *The New Cognitive Neurosciences (2nd edition).* Cambridge, MA: MIT Press, 2000.

Gazzaniga, M. S., Ivry, R. B., and Mangun, G. R. *Cognitive Neuroscience: The Biology of the Mind (2nd edition).* New York: Norton, 2002.

Gernsbacher, M. A. (ed.). *Handbook of Psycholinguistics.* San Diego, CA: Academic Press, 1994.

Gigerenzer, G. *Adaptive Thinking: Rationality in the Real World.* New York: Oxford University Press, 2000.

Goodglass, H. *Understanding Aphasia.* San Diego, CA: Academic Press, 1993.

Gordon, M. *Jumpin' Johnny Get Back to Work! A Child's Guide to ADHD/Hyperactivity.* DeWitt, NY: GSI Publications Inc., 1991.

Gordon, M. A *I Would if I Could: A Teenager's Guide to ADHD/Hyperactivity.* DeWitt, NY: GSI Publications Inc., 1992.

Goswami, U. *Cognition in Children.* London, UK: Psychology Press, 1998.

Graham, H. *The Human Face of Psychology: Humanistic Psychology in Its Historical, Social, and Cultural Context.* Milton Keynes, UK: Open University Press, 1986.

Grandin, T. *Thinking in Pictures: And Other Reports from my Life with Autism.* New York: Vintage Books, 1996.

Greenberger, D. and Padesky, C. *Mind over Mood.* New York: Guilford Publications, 1995.

Groeger, J. A. *Memory and Remembering: Everyday Memory in Context.* New York: Longman, 1997.

Gross, R. and Humphreys, P. *Psychology: The Science of Mind and Behaviour.* London, UK: Hodder Arnold, 1993.

Halford, G. S. *Children's Understanding: The Development of Mental Models.* Hillsdale, NJ: Lawrence Erlbaum Associates, 1993.

Harley, T. A. *The Psychology of Language: From Data to Theory (2nd edition).* Hove, UK: Psychology Press, 2001.

Harris, G. G. *Casting out Anger: Religion among the Taita of Kenya.* New York: Cambridge University Press, 1978.

Hayes, N. *Psychology in Perspective (2nd edition).* New York: Palgrave, 2002.

Hearst, E. *The First Century of Experimental Psychology.* Hillsdale, NJ: Lawrence Erlbaum Associates, 1979.

Hecht, T. *At Home in the Street: Street Children of Northeast Brazil.* New York: Cambridge University Press, 1998.

Hetherington, E. M. *Coping with Divorce, Single Parenting, and Remarriage: A Risk and Resiliency Perspective.* Mawah, NJ: Lawrence Erlbaum Associates, 1999.

Higbee, K. L. *Your Memory: How It Works and How to Improve It (2nd edition).* New York: Paragon 1993.

Hinde, R. A. *Individuals, Relationships and Culture: Links between Ethology and the Social Sciences.* Cambridge, UK: Cambridge University Press, 1987.

Hogdon, L. A. *Solving Behavior Problems in Autism.* Troy, MI: Quirkroberts Publishing, 1999.

Hogg, M. A. (ed.). *Social Psychology.* Thousand Oaks, CA: Sage Publications, 2002.

Holden, G. W. *Parents and the Dynamics of Child Rearing*. Boulder, CO: Westview Press, 1997.

Holmes, J. *John Bowlby and Attachment Theory.* New York: Routledge, 1993.

Hughes, H. C. *Sensory Exotica: A World Beyond Human Experience.* Cambridge, MA: MIT Press, 1999.

Hyde, M. O. and Setano, J. F. *When the Brain Dies First*. New York: Franlin Watts Inc., 2000.

Ingersoll, B. D. *Distant Drums, Different Drummers: A Guide for Young People with ADHD.* Plantation, FL: A.D.D. WareHouse, 1995.

Jencks, C. and Phillips, M. *The Black-White Test Score Gap*. Washington, DC: Brookings Institution Press, 1998.

Johnson, M. J. *Developmental Cognitive Neuroscience.* Cambridge, MA: Blackwell, 1997.

Johnson, M. H. and Morton, J. *Biology and Cognitive Development. The Case of Face Recognition.* Cambridge, MA: Blackwell, 1991.

Johnson-Laird, P. N. *The Computer and the Mind: An Introduction to Cognitive Science*. Cambridge, MA: Harvard University Press, 1988.

Jusczyk, P. W. *The Discovery of Spoken Language.* Cambridge, MA: MIT Press, 1997.

Kalat, J. W. *Biological Psychology (7th edition).* Belmont, CA: Wadsworth Thomson Learning, 2001.

Kaplan, H. I. and Sadock, B. J. *Synopsis of Psychiatry: Behavioral Sciences, Clinical Psychiatry*. Philadelphia, PA: Lippincott, Williams and Wilkins, 1994.

Karen, R. *Becoming Attached: First Relationships and How They Shape Our Capacity to Love*. New York: Oxford University Press, 1998.

Kirk, S. A. and Kutchins, H. *The Selling of DSM: The Rhetoric of Science in Psychiatry*. New York: Aldine de Gruyter, 1992.

Kinney, J. *Clinical Manual of Substance Abuse.* St. Louis, MO: Mosby, 1995.

Kleinman, A. *Rethinking Psychiatry: From Cultural Category to Personal Experience*. New York: Free Press, 1988.

Kosslyn, S. M. and Koenig, O. *Wet Mind: The New Cognitive Neuroscience*. New York: Free Press, 1992.

Kutchins, H. and Kirk, S. A. *Making Us Crazy: DSM: The Psychiatric Bible and the Creation of Mental Disorders*. New York: Free Press, 1997.

LaBruzza, A. L. *Using DSM-IV; A Clinician's Guide to Psychiatric Diagnosis*. St. Northvale, NJ: Jason Aronson Inc., 1994.

Leahey, T. A. *A History of Psychology: Main Currents in Psychological Thought (5th edition)*. Upper Saddle River, NJ: Prentice Hall, 2000.

LeDoux, J. *The Emotional Brain.* New York: Simon and Schuster, 1996.

Levelt, W. J. M. *Speaking: From Intention to Articulation.* Cambridge, MA: MIT Press, 1989.

Lewis, M. and Haviland-Jones, J. M. (eds.). *Handbook of Emotions (2nd edition)*. New York: Guilford Press, 2000.

Lowisohn, J. H. *et al. Substance Abuse: A Comprehensive Textbook (3rd edition).* Baltimore, MD: Williams & Wilkins, 1997.

McCabe, D. *To Teach a Dyslexic*. Clio, MI: AVKO Educational Research, 1997.

McCorduck, P. *Machines Who Think: A Personal Inquiry into the History and Prospects of Artificial Intelligence.* San Francisco: W. H. Freeman, 1979.

McIlveen, R. and Gross, R. *Biopsychology (5th edition)*. Boston, MA: Allyn and Bacon, 2002.

McLachlan, J. *Medical Embryology*. Reading, MA: Addison-Wesley Publishing Co., 1994.

Manstead, A. S. R. and Hewstone M. (eds.). *The Blackwell Encyclopaedia of Social Psychology.* Oxford, UK: Blackwell, 1996.

Marsella, A. J., DeVos, G., and Hsu, F. L. K. (eds.). *Culture and Self: Asian and Western Perspectives.* New York: Routledge, 1988.

Matlin, M. W. *The Psychology of Women*. New York: Harcourt College Publishers, 2000.

Matsumoto, D. R. *People: Psychology from a Cultural Perspective*. Pacific Grove, CA: Brooks/Cole Publishing, 1994.

Matsumoto, D. R. *Culture and Modern Life*. Pacific

Grove, CA: Brooks/Cole Publishing, 1997.

Mazziotta, J .C., Toga, A. W., and Frackowiak, R. S. J. (eds.). *Brain Mapping: The Disorders.* San Diego, CA: Academic Press, 2000.

Nadeau, K. G., Littman, E., and Quinn, P. O. *Understanding Girls with ADHD.* Niagara Falls, NY: Advantage Books, 2000.

Nadel, J. and Camioni, L. (eds.). *New Perspectives in Early Communicative Development.* New York: Routledge, 1993.

Nobus, D. *Jacques Lacan and the Freudian Practice of Psychoanalysis.* Philadelphia, PA: Routledge, 2000.

Oakley, D. A. "The Plurality of Consciousness." *In* D. A. Oakley (ed.), *Brain and Mind*, New York: Methuen, 1985.

Obler, L. K. and Gjerlow, K. *Language and the Brain.* New York: Cambridge University Press, 1999.

Ogden, J. A. *Fractured Minds: A Case-study Approach to Clinical Neuropsychology.* New York: Oxford University Press, 1996.

Owusu-Bempah, K. and Howitt, D. *Psychology beyond Western Perspectives.* Leicester, UK: British Psychological Society Books, 2000.

Paranjpe, A. C. and Bhatt, G. S. "Emotion: A Perspective from the Indian Tradition." *In* H. S. R. Kao and D. Sinha (eds.), *Asian Perspectives on Psychology*. New Delhi, India: Sage Publications, 1997.

Peacock, J. *Depression*. New York: Lifematters Press, 2000.

Pfeiffer, W. M. "Culture-Bound Syndromes." *In* I. Al-Issa (ed.), *Culture and Psychopathology*. Baltimore, MD: University Park Press, 1982.

Pillemer, D. B. *Momentous Events, Vivid Memories.* Cambridge, MA: Harvard University Press, 1998.

Pinel, J. P. J. *Biopsychology (5th edition)*. Boston, MA: Allyn and Bacon, 2002.

Pinker, S. *The Language Instinct.* New York: HarperPerennial, 1995.

Pinker, S. *How the Mind Works*. New York: Norton, 1997.

Porter, R. *Medicine: A History of Healing: Ancient Traditions to Modern Practices.* New York: Barnes and Noble, 1997.

Ramachandran, V. S. and Blakeslee, S. *Phantoms in the Brain: Probing the Mysteries of the Human Mind.* New York: William Morrow, 1998.

Ridley, M. *Genome: The Autobiography of a Species in 23 Chapters.* New York: HarperCollins, 1999.

Robins, L. N. and Regier, D. A. *Psychiatric Disorders in America*. New York: Free Press, 1991.

Robinson, D. N. *Toward a Science of Human Nature: Essays on the Psychologies of Mill, Hegel, Wundt, and James*. New York: Columbia University Press, 1982.

Rugg, M. D. and Coles, M. G. H. (eds.). *Electrophysiology of the Mind: Event-Related Brain Potentials and Cognition.* Oxford, UK: Oxford University Press, 1995.

Rutter, M. "The Interplay of Nature and Nurture: Redirecting the Inquiry." *In* R. Plomin and G. E. McClearn (eds.), *Nature, Nurture, and Psychology*. Washington, DC: American Psychological Association, 1993.

Sarason, I. G. and Sarason B. R. *Abnormal Psychology: The Problem of Maladaptive Behavior (9th edition)*. Upper Saddle River, NJ: Prentice Hall, 1998.

Savage-Rumbaugh, S., Shanker, S. G., and Taylor, T. J. *Apes, Language, and the Human Mind.* New York: Oxford University Press, 1998.

Schab, F. R., & Crowder, R. G. (eds.). *Memory for Odors.* Mahwah, NJ: Lawrence Erlbaum Associates, 1995.

Segal, N. L. *Entwined Lives: Twins and What They Tell Us about Human Behavior.* New York: Plume, 2000.

Seeman, M. V. *Gender and Psychopathology.* Washington, DC: American Psychiatric Press, 1995.

Seligman, M. E. P. *Helplessness: On Depression, Development, and Death.* San Francisco, CA: W. H. Freeman and Co., 1992.

Shorter, E. *A History of Psychiatry: From the Era of Asylum to the Age of Prozac*. New York: John Wiley and Sons, Inc., 1997.

Siegler, R. S. *Children's Thinking (3rd edition).* Englewood Cliffs, NJ: Prentice Hall, 1998.

Simpson, E. M. *Reversals: A Personal Account of Victory over Dyslexia*. New York: Noonday Press, 1992.

Singer, D. G. and Singer, J. L. (eds.). *Handbook of Children and the Media*. Thousand Oaks, CA: Sage Publications, 2001.

Skinner, B. F. *Science and Human Behavior*. New York: Free Press, 1965.

Slavney, P. R. *Psychiatric Dimensions of Medical Practice: What Primary-Care Physicians Should Know about Delirium, Demoralization, Suicidal Thinking, and Competence to Refuse Medical Advice.* Baltimore, MD: The Johns Hopkins University Press, 1998.

Smith McLaughlin, M., Peyser Hazouri, S., and Peyser Hazouri, S. *Addiction: The "High" That Brings You Down*. Springfield, NJ: Enslow publishers, 1997.

Sommers, M. A. *Everything You Need to Know about Bipolar Disorder and Depressive Illness*. New York: Rosen Publishing Group, 2000.

Stanovich, K. E. *Who Is Rational? Studies of Individual Differences in Reasoning*. Mahwah, NJ: Lawrence Erlbaum Associates, 1999.

Symons, D. *The Evolution of Human Sexuality*. New York: Oxford University Press, 1979.

Symons, D. "Beauty is in the Adaptations of the Beholder: The Evolutionary Psychology of Human Female Sexual Attractiveness." *In* P. R. Abramson and S. D. Pinkerton (eds.), *Sexual Nature, Sexual Culture.* Chicago, IL: University of Chicago Press, 1995.

Tavris, C. *The Mismeasure of Women*. New York: Simon and Schuster, 1992.

Triandis, H. C. *Culture and Social Behavior.* New York: McGraw-Hill, 1994.

Tulving, E and Craik, F. I. M. *The Oxford Handbook of Memory*. Oxford, UK: Oxford University Press, 2000.

Vygotsky, L. S. *Mind in Society: The Development of Higher Psychological Processes.* Cambridge, MA: Harvard University Press, 1978.

Weiten, W. *Psychology: Themes and Variations.* Monterey, CA: Brooks/Cole Publishing, 1998.

Werner, E. E. and Smith, R. S. *Overcoming the Odds: High-Risk Children from Birth to Adulthood*. Ithaca, NY: Cornell University Press, 1992.

White, R. W. and Watt, N. F. *The Abnormal Personality (5th edition)*. Chichester, UK: John Wiley and Sons, Inc., 1981.

Wickens, A. *Foundations of Biopsychology*. Harlow, UK: Prentice Hall, 2000.

Wilson, E. O. *Sociobiology: A New Synthesis.* Cambridge, MA: Harvard University Press, 1975.

Winkler, K. *Teens, Depression, and the Blues: A Hot Issue.* Springfield, NJ: Enslow publishers, 2000.

Wolman, B. (ed.). *Historical Roots of Contemporary Psychology*. New York: Harper and Row, 1968.

Wrightsman, L. S. and Sanford, F. H. *Psychology: A Scientific Study of Human Behavior.* Monterey, CA: Brooks/Cole Publishing, 1975.

Yap, P. M. *Comparative Psychiatry: A Theoretical Framework*. Toronto, Canada: University of Toronto Press, 1974.

Zarit, S. H. and Knight, B. G. *A Guide to Psychotherapy and Aging.* Washington, DC: American Psychological Association, 1997.

Useful Websites

Amazing Optical Illusions
http://www.optillusions.com
See your favorite optical illusions at this fun site.

Bedlam
http://www.museum-london.org.uk/MOLsite/exhibits/bedlam/f_bed.htm
The Museum of London's online exhibition about Bedlam, the notorious mental institution.

Bipolar Disorders Information Center
http://www.mhsource.com/bipolar
Articles and information about bipolar 1 disorder.

Brain and Mind
http://www.epub.org.br/cm/home_i.htm
An online magazine with articles devoted to neuroscience, linguisitics, imprinting, and a variety of related topics.

Exploratorium
http://www.exploratorium.edu/exhibits/nf_exhibits.html
Click on "seeing" or "hearing" to check out visual and auditory illusions and other secrets of the mind.

Freud and Culture
http://www.loc.gov/exhibits/freud
An online Library of Congress exhibition that examines Sigmund Freud's life and key ideas and his effect on 20th-century thinking.

Great Ideas in Personality
http://www.personalityresearch.org
This website looks at scientific research programs in personality psychology. Pages on attachment theory, basic emotions, behavior genetics, behaviorism, cognitive social theories, and more give concise definitions of terms as well as links to further research on the web.

Jigsaw Classroom
http://www.jigsaw.org
The official web site of the Jigsaw Classroom, a

cooperative learning technique that reduces racial conflict between schoolchildren. Learn about its history and how to implement the techniques.

Kidspsych
http://www.kidspsych.org/index1.html
American Psychological Association's childrens' site, with games and exercises for kids. Also useful for students of developmental psychology. Follow the "about this activity" links to find out the theories behind the fun and games.

Kismet
http://www.ai.mit.edu/projects/humanoid-robotics-group/kismet/kismet.html
Kismet is the MIT's expressive robot, which has perceptual and motor functions tailored to natural human communication channels.

Neuroscience for Kids
http://faculty.washington.edu/chudler/neurok.html
A useful website for students and teachers who want to learn about the nervous system. Enjoy activities and experiments on your way to learning all about the brain and spinal cord.

Neuroscience Tutorial
http://thalamus.wustl.edu/course
The Washington University School of Medicine's online tutorial offers an illustrated guide to the basics of clinical neuroscience, with useful artworks and user-friendly text.

Psychology Central
http://emerson.thomsonlearning.com/psych
Links to many useful articles grouped by subject as well as cool, animated figures that improve your understanding of psychological principles.

Schizophrenia.com
http://www.schizophrenia.com
Information and resources on this mental disorder provided by a charitable organization.

Seeing, Hearing, and Smelling the World
http://www.hhmi.org/senses
A downloadable illustrated book dealing with perception from the Howard Hughes Medical Institute.

Sigmund Freud Museum
http://freud.t0.or.at/freud
The online Sigmund Freud Museum has videos and audio recordings of the famous psychoanalyst—there are even images of Freud's famous couch.

Social Psychology Network
http://www.socialpsychology.org
The largest social psychology database on the Internet. Within these pages you will find more than 5,000 links to psychology-related resources and research groups, and there is also a useful section on general psychology.

Stanford Prison Experiment
http://www.prisonexp.org
A fascinating look at the Stanford Prison Experiment, which saw subjects placed in a prison to see what happens to "good people in a bad environment." Learn why the experiment had to be abandoned after six days due to the unforeseen severity of the effects on participants.

Stroop effect
http://www.dcity.org/braingames/stroop/index.htm
Take part in an online psychological experiment to see the Stroop effect in action.

Quote Attributions

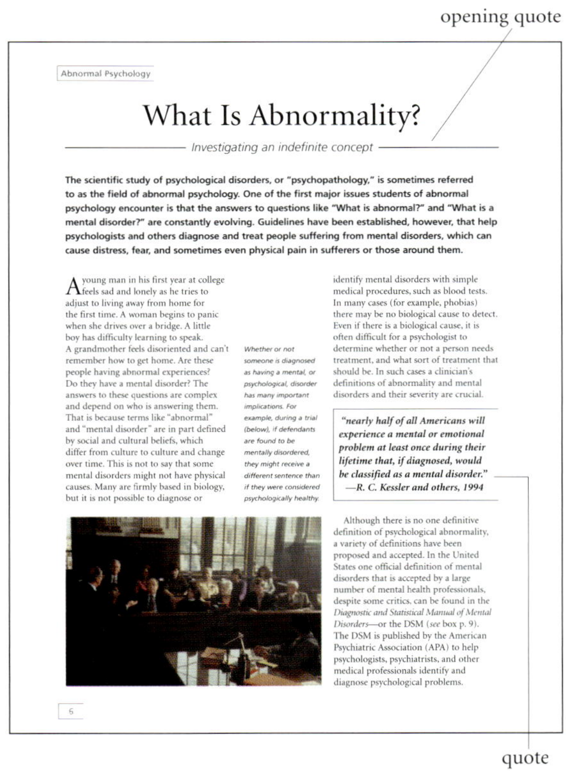

Abnormal Psychology

What Is Abnormality?

Investigating an indefinite concept

The scientific study of psychological disorders, or "psychopathology," is sometimes referred to as the field of abnormal psychology. One of the first major issues students of abnormal psychology encounter is that the answers to questions like "What is abnormal?" and "What is a mental disorder?" are constantly evolving. Guidelines have been established, however, that help psychologists and others diagnose and treat people suffering from mental disorders, which can cause distress, fear, and sometimes even physical pain in sufferers or those around them.

A young man in his first year at college feels sad and lonely as he tries to adjust to living away from home for the first time. A woman begins to panic when she drives over a bridge. A little boy has difficulty learning to speak. A grandmother feels disoriented and can't remember how to get home. Are these people having abnormal experiences? Do they have a mental disorder? The answers to these questions are complex and depend on who is answering them. That is because terms like "abnormal" and "mental disorder" are in part defined by social and cultural beliefs, which differ from culture to culture and change over time. This is not to say that some mental disorders might not have physical causes. Many are firmly based in biology, but it is not possible to diagnose or identify mental disorders with simple medical procedures, such as blood tests. In many cases (for example, phobias) there may be no biological cause to detect. Even if there is a biological cause, it is often difficult for a psychologist to determine whether or not a person needs treatment, and what sort of treatment that should be. In such cases a clinician's definitions of abnormality and mental disorders and their severity are crucial.

Whether or not someone is diagnosed as having a mental, or psychological, disorder has many important implications. For example, during a trial (below), if defendants are found to be mentally disordered, they might receive a different sentence than if they were considered psychologically healthy.

"nearly half of all Americans will experience a mental or emotional problem at least once during their lifetime that, if diagnosed, would be classified as a mental disorder."
—R. C. Kessler and others, 1994

Although there is no one definitive definition of psychological abnormality, a variety of definitions have been proposed and accepted. In the United States one official definition of mental disorders that is accepted by a large number of mental health professionals, despite some critics, can be found in the *Diagnostic and Statistical Manual of Mental Disorders*—or the DSM (*see* box p. 9). The DSM is published by the American Psychiatric Association (APA) to help psychologists, psychiatrists, and other medical professionals identify and diagnose psychological problems.

6

Each chapter in *Psychology* contains quotes that relate to the topics covered. These quotes appear both within the main text and at the start of the chapters, and their attributions are detailed here. Quotes are listed in the order that they appear in the chapter, and the page numbers at the end of each attribution refer to the pages in this volume where the quote appears.

People as Social Animals

Baron, R. and Bryne, D. *Social Psychology*. Boston, MA: Allyn and Bacon, 1974, p. 7.

Heider, F. *The Psychology of Interpersonal Relations*. New York: John Wiley and Sons, 1958, p. 9.

Goddard, H. "Mental Tests and the Immigrant." *Journal of Delinquency*. **2**, 1917, p. 12.

Tolman, E. C. "Cognitive Maps in Rats and Men." *The Psychological Review*, 55, 1948, p. 13.

Kohonen, V. *In* D. Nunan, *Second Language Teaching and Learning*. Boston: Heinle & Heinle, 1992, p. 15, p. 16.

Branden, N. *The Art of Living Consciously*. New York: Simon and Schuster, 1997, p. 17.

Mortimore, P. *In* J. MacBeath and P. Mortimore (eds.), *Improving School Effectiveness*. Buckingham, UK: Open University Press, 2001, p. 20.

Mbiti, J. S. *African Religions and Philosophy*. Portsmouth, NH: Heinemann, 1969, p. 22.

Relating to Others

Plutarch. *Demetrius*. *c*. 100 A.D. p. 29.

Asch, S. "Forming Impressions of Personality." *Journal of Abnormal and Social Psychology*, **41**, 1946, p. 30.

Schiller, J. *Essays, Aesthetical and Philosophical, Including the Dissertation on the Connexions between the Animal and the Spiritual in Man*. London, UK: Bell, 1882, p. 33.

Fiske, S. and Taylor, S. *Social Cognition*. New York: McGraw-Hill, 1991, p. 37.

Radley, A. "Relationships in Detail: The Study of Social Interaction." *In* D. Miell and R. Dallos (eds.), *Social Interaction and Personal Relationships*. London, UK: Sage Publications, 1996, p. 40.

Argyle, M. *The Psychology of Interpersonal Behaviour*. London, UK: Penguin, 1994, p. 41, p. 49.

Duck, S. *Meaningful Relationships: Talking, Sense, and Relating*. Thousand Oaks, CA: Sage Publications, 1994, p. 43.

Trevarthen, C. "The Function of Emotions in Early Infant Communication and Development." *In* J. Nadel and L. Camioni (eds.), *New Perspectives in Early Communicative Development*. London: Routledge, 1992, p. 46.

Dallos, R., "Creating Relationships: Patterns of Actions and Beliefs." *In* D. Miell and R. Dallos (eds.), *Social Interaction and Personal Relationships*. London: Sage Publications, 1996, p. 48.

Relating to Society

Bacon, F. *The Advancement of Learning*. 1605, p. 50.

Franklin, B. Signing the Declaration of Independence, July 4, 1776, p. 51.

Cialdini, R. *Influence, Science, and Practice*. Boston, MA: Allyn and Bacon, 2001, p. 52, p. 67.

Duke of Windsor (formerly King Edward VIII), March 5, 1957, p. 54.

Milgram, S. *Obedience to Authority: An Experimental View*. New York: Harper & Row, 1974, p. 55.

Kotter, J. *Leading Change*. Boston: Harvard Business School Press, 1996, p. 56.

Wallas, G. *The Art of Thought*. New York: Harcourt, 1926, p. 58.

de Montaigne, M. *Essais*. 1588, p. 59.

Fields, W. C. (1880–1946). Unpublished quote, p. 61.

James, W. *The Principles of Psychology*. 1890, p. 63.

Swami Sivananda, S. "God as Mother" lectures. Rishikesh, India: Divine Life Society, 1953, p. 68.

Bushman, B., Baumeister, R., and Stack, A. "Catharsis, Aggression, and Persuasive Influence: Self-Fulfilling or Self-Defeating Prophecies?" *Journal of Personality and Social Psychology*. **76**, 1999, p. 70.

Communication

Shakespeare, W. *Troilus and Cressida*. *c*. 1602, p. 72.

Shannon, C. "A Mathematical Theory of Communication." *Bell System Technical Journal*, **27**, 1948, p. 73.

Marx, K. and Engels, F. *The German Ideology*. 1846, p. 75.

Gleitman, L. R. and Gleitman, H. *Phrase and Paraphrase: Some Innovative Uses of Language*. New York: Norton, 1970, p. 77.

Darwin, C. R. *The Expression of the Emotions in Man and Animals*. Oxford: Oxford University Press, 1872, p. 80.

Fast, J. *Body Language*. New York: Evans and Co., 1970, p. 85.

Argyle, M. *Person to Person: Ways of Communicating*. New York: Harper & Row, 1979, p. 87.

Austen, J. *Persuasion*. 1818, p. 89.

Wallace, P. *The Psychology of the Internet*. New York: Cambridge University Press, 1999, p. 89.

Johnson-Laird, P. *In* D. H. Mellor (ed.), *Ways of Communicating*. New York: Cambridge University Press, 1990, p. 93.

Leacock, S. *The Garden of Folly*. New York: Dodd, Mead, and Company, 1924, p. 93.

Personality

Prince, M. *The Dissociation of a Personality*. 1906, p. 94.

Freud, S. *Five Lectures on Psychoanalysis*. New York: Norton, 1923, p. 95.

Freud, S. *The Ego and the Id*. London: Hogarth Press, 1923, p. 97.
Winnicott, D. *The Family and Individual Development*. London, UK: Routledge, 1965, p. 101.
Goldberg, S. *In Attachment Theory: Social, Developmental, and Clinical Perspectives*. Hillsdale, NJ: Analytic Press, 2000, p. 103.
Van Ijzendoorn, M. H. "Attachment across the Life-span." Keynote address to the 10th International Congress of the European Society for Child and Adolescent Psychiatry, Utrecht, Netherlands, 1995, p. 105.
Bandura, A. and Ribes-Inesta, E. *Analysis of Delinquency and Aggession*. Hillsdale, NJ: Lawrence Erlbaum Associates, 1976, p. 107, p. 108.
Adler, A. *The Neurotic Constitution*. 1912, p. 112.
Jerome, J. K. *The Idle Thoughts of An Idle Fellow*. 1886, p. 116.

Intelligence

Robinson, J. H. (1863–1936). Unpublished quote, p. 118
Pascal, B. *Pensées*. 1670, p.120.
Hildebrand, J. *Science in the Making*. Westport, CN: Greenwood Press, 1985, p. 121.
Gardner, H. "Rethinking the Value of Intelligence Tests." *New York Times Education Supplement*, November 3, 1986, p. 123.
Fancher, R. *The Intelligence Men: Makers of the IQ Controversy*. New York: Norton, 1985, p. 124.
Binet, A. Cited in S. J. Gould, *The Mismeasure of Man*. New York, Norton, 1981, p. 126.
Garn, S. *Culture and the Direction of Human Evolution*. Toronto, Canada: Ambassador Books, 1962, p. 128.
Wechsler, D. *The Measurement of Adult Intelligence*. Baltimore, MD: The Williams and Wilkins Company, 1941, p. 129.
de Bono, E. *Thinking Course*. New York: Facts On File, 1994, p. 131.
Lewontin, R. *Human Diversity*. San Francisco: W. H. Freeman and Co., 1982, p. 133.
Neisser, U. "Stories, Selves and Schemata: A Review of Ecological Findings." *In* M. A. Conway, S. E. Gathercole and C. Cornoldi (eds.), *Theories of Memory (Vol. 2)*. Hove, UK: Psychology Press, 1988, p. 134.
Sternberg, R. *Beyond IQ: A Triarchic Theory of Human Intelligence*. New York: Cambridge University Press, 1985, p. 137.
Steele, C. "Thin Ice: 'Stereotype threat' and Black College Students." *The Atlantic Monthly*, August 1999, p. 140.

Nature and Nurture

Eysenck, H. J. and Eysenck, M. W. *Personality and Individual Differences*. New York: Plenum, 1985, p. 142.
Dawkins, R. *The Selfish Gene*. New York: Oxford Universty Press, 1976, p. 145.
Geertz, C. Cited in I. M. Scher, *Theories of the Mind*. New York: Free Press, 1962, p. 147.
Rose, S., Kamin, L., and Lewontin, R. *Not in Our Genes*. New York: Pantheon Books, 1984, p. 148.
Drew, C. J., Hardman, M. J., and Hart, A. W. *Designing and Conducting Research: Inquiry in Education and Social Science (2nd edition)*. Needham Heights, MA: Allyn and Bacon, 1995, p. 153.
Woodworth, R. *Heredity and Environment: A Critical Survey of Recently Published Material on Twins and Foster Children*. New York: Social Science Research Council, 1941, p. 155.
McKie, R. *The Observer*, June 4 1989, p. 157.
van Court, M. and Saetz, S. B. "Comment on Caldwell." *Politics and the Life Sciences*, **4**, 1985, p. 158.
Lewontin R. Cited in R. Travis Osborne, *Twins: Black and White*. Athens, GA: Foundation for Human Understanding, 1980, p. 160.
Mischel, W. *Introduction to Personality*. New York: Holt, Rinehart, and Winston, 1981, p. 161.

Every effort has been made to attribute the quotes throughout *Psychology* correctly. Any errors or omissions brought to the attention of the publisher are regretted and will be credited in subsequent editions.

Set Index

Page numbers in *italics* refer to picture captions. Page numbers in **bold** refer to main articles and particular books in the *Introducing Psychology* set:
1. History of Psychology
2. The Brain and the Mind
3. Thinking and Knowing
4. Developmental Psychology
5. Social Psychology
6. Abnormal Psychology